socialist alternative

This work was published by Red Flag books, an imprint of Socialist Alternative, Australia's largest revolutionary socialist group.

Find out more about Socialist Alternative, read our fortnightly newspaper, and browse our bookstore at *redflag.org.au*

The Crisis of German Social Democracy first published 1915
Militarism and Anti-Militarism first published 1907
Translations by Dave Hollis

This edition published by Red Flag Books
Melbourne, April 2025

Red Flag Books is an imprint of Socialist Alternative
redflag.org.au

Edited by Mick Armstrong and Tess Lee Ack
Proofread by Tess Lee Ack
Cover design by Jeremy Laycock
Interior Layout by Luka Kiernan

Printed by IngramSpark

Capitalism and War:
German revolutionaries speak against WWI

ROSA LUXEMBURG & KARL LIEBKNECHT

RED FLAG BOOKS

The Crisis of German Social Democracy
(The Junius Pamphlet)

2025 Introduction – Mick Armstrong	9
Chapter 1	17
Chapter 2	25
Chapter 3	35
Chapter 4	41
Chapter 5	59
Chapter 6	67
Chapter 7	75
Chapter 8	91

Militarism and Anti-Militarism

2025 Introduction – Mick Armstrong	103
Preface	107

Part I – Militarism

Chapter 1. General	113
Chapter 2. Capitalist militarism	121
Chapter 3. Methods and effects of militarism	135
Chapter 4. Particulars of some of the main sins of militarism	149

Part II – Anti-Militarism

Chapter 1. Anti-militarism of the Old and the New International	183
Chapter 2. Anti-militarism abroad, with special regard to the young socialist organisations	187
Chapter 3. Threats to anti-militarism	215
Chapter 4. Anti-militarist tactics	219
Chapter 5. The need for special anti-militarist propaganda	231
Chapter 6. Anti-militarism in Germany and German Social Democracy	235
Chapter 7. The anti-militarist tasks of German Social Democracy	241

Appendices

Appendix 1: Theses on the Tasks of International Social Democracy (1915)
    Rosa Luxemburg   245

Appendix 2: The War and Russian Social Democracy (1914)
    VI Lenin   249

Appendix 3: The Tasks of Revolutionary Social Democracy in the European War
    VI Lenin   253

Appendix 4: Manifesto of the International Socialist Conference at Zimmerwald   257

Glossary   264

The Crisis of German Social Democracy (The Junius Pamphlet)

ROSA LUXEMBURG

Introduction

> At last there has appeared in Germany, illegally, without any adaption to the despicable Junker censorship, a Social-Democratic pamphlet dealing with the questions of the war!... Written in a very lively style, Junius's pamphlet has undoubtedly played and will continue to play an important role in the struggle against the ex-Social-Democratic Party of Germany, which has deserted to the bourgeoisie and the Junkers, and we extend our hearty greetings to the author.
>
> – Lenin, July 1916[1]

Rosa Luxemburg finished writing *The Junius Pamphlet* (actual title: *The Crisis of German Social Democracy*) in her prison cell in April 1915, at the darkest time for the revolutionary movement in Germany. On 4 August 1914 the Social Democratic Party (SPD), the leading party of the Second Socialist International, had irrevocably crossed the class line and abandoned the working class. By voting for war credits in the Reichstag (German parliament) the SPD leaders had backed the ruling class in what was to be the greatest slaughter in human history to that point. This set a terrible precedent for the working-class movement internationally, with the leaders of the French, English, Belgian, Austrian, Australian and other Socialist and Labor parties also rallying to back their ruling classes in the imperialist war.

It was to get even worse. Having crossed the Rubicon by voting for war credits, the SPD leaders, in the name of national unity, placed themselves entirely at the service of the military dictatorship imposed by the German capitalists. Party and trade union leaders came, in Luxemburg's words, to "play the role of the gendarme over the working class", enforcing immense sacrifices, both in lives and living standards, opposing strikes and all forms of opposition to the war. This ensured that the Krupps and the Stinnes and the other leading German capitalists made record profits from war contracts. It was workers and the poor who had to carry the enormous burden of war time "national unity".

---

1. Lenin 1964, p.305.

The SPD's once powerful radical wing was thrown into disarray by the outbreak of war and the vote for war credits. A number of one-time leftists capitulated to pro-war chauvinism. Those who stood by their socialist principles were isolated, often demoralised and had not cohered as a significant organised force by April 1915. To compound this terrible situation for committed revolutionaries like Luxemburg, the German army seemed to be in a commanding position and working-class revolt against the war was yet to erupt. This discouraging picture is reflected in the pamphlet's rather bleak tone, something unusual for the inspiring Rosa Luxemburg, presumably compounded by her isolation in prison.

Nonetheless she had lost nothing of her sharpness and fire, both against the horrors of capitalism and the SPD leaders who had betrayed the workers' cause:

> Business is flourishing upon the ruins. Cities are turned into shambles, whole countries into deserts, villages into cemeteries, whole nations into beggars…
>
> Shamed, dishonoured, wading in blood and dripping with filth, thus capitalist society stands…as a roaring beast, as an orgy of anarchy, as a pestilential breath, devastating culture and humanity…
>
> And in the midst of this orgy a world tragedy has occurred: the capitulation of the social democracy.
>
> *This world war* means a reversion to barbarism… Thus we stand today, as Friedrich Engels prophesied more than a generation ago, before the awful proposition: either the triumph of imperialism and the destruction of all culture, and, as in ancient Rome, depopulation, desolation, degeneration, a vast cemetery; or, the victory of socialism, that is, the conscious struggle of the international proletariat against imperialism…against war. This is the dilemma of world history, its inevitable choice, whose scales are trembling in the balance awaiting the decision of the proletariat. Upon it depends the future of culture and humanity.

Luxemburg went on to make a strident argument for anti-war socialists to stand against the stream. They might now be an isolated minority, but they had to stand their ground and prepare for the future, when workers began to raise their heads once again. She argued that if the SPD had opposed the war from the start:

> At first we would perhaps have accomplished nothing but to save the honour of the proletariat. And thousands upon thousands of proletarians who are dying in the trenches in mental darkness would not have died in spiritual confusion but with one certainty that that which has been everything in their lives, the international, liberating Social Democracy is more than the figment of a dream.
>
> The vote of our party would have acted as a wet blanket upon the chauvinistic intoxication of the masses. It would have preserved the intelligent proletariat from delirium, would have made it more difficult for imperialism to poison and stupefy the minds of the people.
>
> And as the war went on, as the horror of endless massacre and bloodshed in all countries grew and grew, as its imperialistic hoof became more and more evident, as the exploitation

by bloodthirsty speculators became more and more shameless, every live, honest, progressive and humane element in the masses would have rallied to the standard of the social democracy.

Luxemburg managed to smuggle her pamphlet out of prison. However *Junius* still had not been printed when Luxemburg was eventually released on 22 January 1916. Her comrades had been unable to find a printer prepared to publish it in Germany. Nor had they established a disciplined underground organisation in the style of the Bolsheviks to cope with the repressive conditions.

By the time *Junius* was actually published in Zurich, Switzerland, almost a year after it was drafted, workers' opposition to the war was on the rise, stimulating divisions in the SPD. Included as an addendum to *Junius* were the *Theses on the Tasks of International Social Democracy*. Luxemburg had drafted them for the anti-war Zimmerwald conference, but they could not be smuggled out of prison in time. The *Theses* were subsequently adopted at the founding conference of the Internationale Group (later the Spartacus League) in January 1916. *Junius* could only be distributed in secret but according to Luxemburg's comrade and biographer, Paul Frölich, "it became the intellectual armour of thousands of illegal militants".[2] It had to be reprinted a number of times in quick succession to meet the demand of the comrades.

Lenin's criticisms of *Junius*

Lenin, who did not know that Rosa Luxemburg was the author of *Junius*, made a number of criticisms of the pamphlet. Its chief defect in his view was "its silence regarding the connection between social-chauvinism...and opportunism"; and in particular that it made no criticism of the Kautskyite centrist current in the SPD.

> This is wrong from the standpoint of theory, for it is impossible to *account* for the "betrayal" without linking it up with opportunism as a trend with a long history behind it, the history of the whole Second International...it is impossible either to understand the "crisis of Social-Democracy", or overcome it, without clarifying the meaning and the role of the two trends – the openly opportunist trend (Legien, David, etc.) and the tacitly opportunist trend (Kautsky and Co.)[3]

Lenin feared that the absence of criticism reflected a softening of the approach of the Internationale Group towards the centrists. Lenin was undoubtedly correct that elements of the German revolutionary left did not differentiate themselves sufficiently from the centrist swamp. However it was far from being the case that Luxemburg or her close ally Karl Liebknecht were softening their attitude, despite the lack of an explicit critique in the *Junius* pamphlet. Registering her utter contempt for the centrists' lack of principle, she wrote elsewhere:

---

2. Frölich 1972, p.217.
3. Lenin 1964, pp.306–7.

> I know thy works, that thou art neither cold nor hot: I would that that wert cold or hot. So then because thou art lukewarm, and neither cold nor hot, I will spew thee out of my mouth.[4]

Liebknecht was just as scathing:

> Whoever strays between armies locked in battle will get shot down in the crossfire, if he does not seek refuge on one side or the other. But then he arrives, not as a hero, but as a refugee.[5]

Luxemburg had in fact been a sharp critic of Kautsky from 1910 onwards. In the wake of the SPD's 1913 Jena Congress she argued that the left had to shift from concentrating its fire on the party's right-wing revisionists and instead launch a systematic offensive against the "swamp" (the Kautskyites).[6] Indeed, in those pre-war years Luxemburg had been far more critical of Kautsky than Lenin, a point Lenin acknowledged in a letter to Bolshevik activist Alexander Shlyapnikov in October 1914:

> Rosa Luxemburg was right when she wrote, long ago, that Kautsky has the "subservience of a theoretician" – servility, in plainer language, servility to the majority of the Party, to opportunism.[7]

However by 1915/1916 Luxemburg recognised that Kautsky was a declining figure. According to another of her biographers, JP Nettl, by then the "real leaders of the centrist opposition were not Kautsky, Eisner and Bernstein, but Haase, Dittman and Ledebour, a fact which Lenin did not realise until the end of 1917."[8] However it should be noted that Luxemburg did not attack Haase and Co. in *Junius* either.

Lenin's other major criticism of *Junius* was over the national question, in particular the argument that in the imperialist era *all* wars of national defence were reactionary. This echoed Lenin's longstanding dispute with Luxemburg over the question of the right of national self-determination for Poland, which he supported and she opposed.[9]

Junius fiercely polemicised against the SPD leadership's argument that Germany's war effort was supportable as a war of national defence against Russian barbarism. On this Luxemburg was undoubtedly correct, as she was in debunking the excuses raised by the rival imperialist powers of France, Britain and Russia and their smaller allies that they were waging a war of national defence against Prussian militarism. But to go from there to oppose *all* national wars was to over-generalise a correct argument. The imperialist nature of the world war did not, Lenin argued, rule out the necessity of Marxists supporting national revolts in the imperialist powers' colonies in Africa and Asia, or by oppressed national minorities in Europe itself. Such national revolts had the potential, alongside working-class revolts in the imperialist heartlands, to challenge the whole edifice of capitalist rule. World War I was to provoke a series of such revolts, foreshadowed by the Easter 1916 revolt against British rule in Dublin.

---

4. Nettl 2019, p.643.
5. Nettl 2019, p.646.
6. Riddell 1984, p.97.
7. Lenin 1965, p.168.
8. Nettl 2019, p.627.
9. For that debate see Luxemburg 2009 and Lenin 1914.

Despite these criticisms, Lenin recognised that while *Junius* had not completely rid itself of the "environment" of the German Social-Democrats: "There is no doubt that Junius is decidedly opposed to the imperialist war and is undoubtedly *in favour* of revolutionary tactics".[10] "On the whole", Lenin declared, "the *Junius* pamphlet is a splendid Marxist work, and its defects are, in all probability, to a certain extent accidental".[11]

Puncturing some misleading stereotypes

Luxemburg is often presented as being a softer figure, not a hard-nosed revolutionary leader and sharp polemicist like Lenin. This is quite misleading. Luxemburg was determined that the Spartacists demarcate themselves as an independent revolutionary force distinct from the centrist opposition within the SPD, which was to eventually form the Independent Social Democratic Party (USPD). In a letter on 8 December 1915 to her close comrade Leo Jogiches, she was highly critical of the comrades' intervention at the anti-war conference in Zimmerwald, Switzerland:

> I regret very much that I was not promptly informed...about the plan for Zimmerwald. I believe the affair was not only unsuccessful, but a nearly catastrophic mistake that has placed the further development of the opposition and the International on the wrong track... The problem is that our people believe that something must absolutely be done as soon as possible. So, in order to achieve this "something", they think it is vital not to scare away the flotsam and jetsam. This policy of going around and begging for crumbs, makes genuine clarity and action impossible.

And in words that could have been penned by Lenin she added:

> Our goal...should not be to bring the entire opposition under one roof, but rather to pull out of this mush the small, solid kernel, that is capable of action, and unite it around our platform.[12]

Luxemburg put forward the *Theses on the Tasks of International Social Democracy* for adoption at the formal founding conference of the Internationale Group. She argued that given the "passage" of the leaders of the Second International "to the political camp of the imperialist bourgeoisie; it is vitally necessary for socialism to build a new workers' International, which will take into its own hands the leadership and coordination of the revolutionary class struggle against world imperialism". Unlike the loose federation that was the old Socialist International, the new International needed to be a centralised and disciplined organisation in which, Luxemburg argued:

> The obligation to carry out the decisions of the International takes precedence over all else. National sections which do not conform with this place themselves outside the International.

The *Theses on the Tasks of International Social Democracy*, with their call for a disciplined, centralised International, cut sharply against the misconception that Luxemburg was a

10. Lenin 1964, p.318.
11. Lenin 1964, p.306.
12. Riddell 1984, p.414.

"spontaneist"; someone who worshipped the masses and downplayed the importance of decisive revolutionary leadership, supposedly the very opposite of Lenin. The *Theses* were actually criticised at the time by Karl Liebknecht as containing "altogether too much mention of discipline, not enough spontaneity" and as being "too mechanical and centralistic".[13]

The *Junius Pamphlet* itself is also anything but "spontaneist" in its approach. It emphasises both the extremely negative role the SPD leaders had played in confusing, demoralising and stifling the anti-war sentiments of the mass of workers and the need for an alternative revolutionary leadership that could provide "clearness concerning the political problems and interests of the proletariat in times of war". A decisive and determined leadership which puts forward precise slogans, Luxemburg argued, "will create in the masses assurance, self-confidence and a fearless fighting spirit".

A revolutionary leadership needed to utilise every available platform to advance the working-class struggle against the war and the whole capitalist system. In particular, as Frölich points out, Luxemburg highlights in *Junius* "how important parliament, as the one free tribune, could be for triggering off mass action if people like Liebknecht mastered its use in a systematic and determined way".[14]

This emphasis on the decisive role of revolutionary leadership was not some new stance by Luxemburg. In 1913, when attacking the conservative "attrition strategy" of Kautsky, she wrote:

> The task of Social Democracy and its leaders is not to be dragged along by events, but to be consciously ahead of them, to have an overall view of the trend of events, to shorten the period of development by conscious action, and to accelerate its progress.[15]

In other words, a strident argument for an organisation to *lead* the struggles. Again, Lenin could not have put it better.

Luxemburg concludes her pamphlet with a powerful call to action:

> This madness will not stop, and this bloody nightmare of hell will not cease until the workers of Germany, of France, of Russia and of England will wake up out of their drunken sleep; will clasp each others' hands in brotherhood and will drown the bestial chorus of war agitators and the hoarse cry of capitalist hyenas with the mighty cry of labour, "Proletarians of all countries, unite!"

This was no forlorn hope. By February 1917 the tsarist regime in Russia had been overthrown, and in October Russian workers took power into their own hands. Just over a year later the carnage of the World War was finally brought to an end by the November 1918 German revolution, and the revolutionary wave swept across Europe. Luxemburg, who had been incarcerated once again for her anti-war agitation, was liberated from her cell by the uprising. She set about founding a Communist Party to lead the revolution

---

13. Nettl 2019, p.630.
14. Frölich 1972, p.143.
15. Quoted in Frölich 1972, p.143.

forward and to challenge the baleful hold of the reformist SPD. But the powers-that-be were taking no chances. The SPD leaders, in cahoots with the German military, had Luxemburg and Liebknecht murdered on 15 January 1919, and two months later her long-term comrade Leo Jogiches.

Clara Zetkin wrote in her obituary of Rosa Luxemburg:

> Socialism was for Rosa Luxemburg a dominating passion which absorbed her whole life, a passion at once intellectual and ethical... This rare woman had but one ambition, one task in life – to prepare for the revolution which was to open the way to Socialism. Her greatest joy, her dream, was to live to see the revolution, to take her share in its struggles. Rosa Luxemburg gave to Socialism all she had to give; no words can ever express the strength of will, the disinterestedness, and the devotion, with which she served the cause. She offered up her life on the altar of Socialism, not alone in death, but in the long days of her labours, in the hours, the weeks and the years consecrated to the fight. Thus has she acquired the right to demand of others that they, too, shall sacrifice their all for Socialism – everything, life not excepted. She was the sword, she was the fire, of the revolution. Rosa Luxemburg will remain one of the greatest figures in the history of international Socialism.[16]

Mick Armstrong, January 2025

References

Armstrong, Mick 2023, "From Marx to Lenin: Debates that forged the socialist approach to war", *Marxist Left Review*, 26, Spring 2023.

Frölich, Paul 1972, *Rosa Luxemburg*, Pluto Press.

Lenin, VI 1914, "The Right of Nations to Self-Determination", *Collected Works*, Vol.20, Progress Publishers.

Lenin, 1964, "The Junius Pamphlet", *Collected Works*, Vol.22, Progress Publishers.

Lenin, 1965, "To A.G. Shlyapnikov", *Collected Works*, Vol.35, Progress Publishers.

Luxemburg, Rosa 2009, *The National Question. Selected Writings*, Aakar Books.

Nettl, JP 2019, *Rosa Luxemburg*, Verso.

Riddell, John (ed.) 1984, *Lenin's Struggle for a Revolutionary International. Documents: 1907–1916 The Preparatory Years*, Monad Press.

Zetkin, Clara 1919, *Rosa Luxemburg*, Introduction to the second edition of the *Junius Pamphlet*. https://www.marxists.org/archive/zetkin/1919/05/junius.htm

---

16. Zetkin 1919.

Chapter One

The scene has changed fundamentally. The six weeks' march to Paris has grown into a world drama.[17] Mass slaughter has become the tiresome and monotonous business of the day and the end is no closer. Bourgeois statecraft is held fast in its own vice. The spirits summoned up can no longer be exorcised.

Gone is the euphoria. Gone the patriotic noise in the streets, the chase after the gold-coloured automobile, one false telegram after another, the wells poisoned by cholera, the Russian students heaving bombs over every railway bridge in Berlin, the French airplanes over Nuremberg, the spy-hunting public running amok in the streets, the swaying crowds in the coffee shops with ear-deafening patriotic songs surging ever higher, whole city neighbourhoods transformed into mobs ready to denounce, to mistreat women, to shout hurrah and to induce delirium in themselves by means of wild rumours. Gone, too, is the atmosphere of ritual murder, the Kishinev air where the crossing guard is the only remaining representative of human dignity.[18]

The spectacle is over. German scholars, those "stumbling lemurs", have been whistled off the stage long ago. The trains full of reservists are no longer accompanied by virgins fainting from pure jubilation. They no longer greet the people from the windows of the train with joyous smiles. Carrying their packs, they quietly trot along the streets where the public goes about its daily business with aggrieved visages.

In the prosaic atmosphere of pale day there sounds a different chorus – the hoarse cries of the vulture and the hyenas of the battlefield. Ten thousand tarpaulins guaranteed up to regulations! A hundred thousand kilos of bacon, cocoa powder, coffee-substitute

---

17. Six weeks was the time allotted for victory on the Western Front by the Schlieffen Plan. The general staff was forced to scrap the plan in October 1914, as the war of movement swiftly evolved into grinding trench warfare.
18. For three days in April 1903, Kishinev, the provincial capital of Bessarabia in the Russian Empire, was the scene of an anti-Jewish riot. More than 50 Jews were killed and over 500 injured; hundreds of homes and shops were plundered and vandalised. Local authorities supported antisemitic organisations and deliberately maximised the carnage by holding back on the use of force to re-establish order. Luxemburg here uses the reference to the Kishinev pogrom and to "ritual murder" – the medieval belief that Jews used the blood of Christians, usually children, for ritual purposes – as the nadir of civilisation.

– COD, immediate delivery! Hand grenades, lathes, cartridge pouches, marriage bureaus for widows of the fallen, leather belts, jobbers for war orders – serious offers only! The cannon fodder loaded onto trains in August and September is mouldering in the killing fields of Belgium, the Vosges, and Masurian Lakes where the profits are springing up like weeds. It's a question of getting the harvest into the barn quickly. Across the ocean stretch thousands of greedy hands to snatch it up.

Business thrives in the ruins. Cities become piles of ruins; villages become cemeteries; countries, deserts; populations are beggared; churches, horse stalls. International law, treaties and alliances, the most sacred words and the highest authority have been torn into shreds. Every sovereign "by the grace of God" is called a rogue and lying scoundrel by his cousin on the other side. Every diplomat is a cunning rascal to his colleagues in the other party. Every government sees every other as dooming its own people and worthy only of universal contempt. There are food riots in Venice, in Lisbon, Moscow, Singapore. There is plague in Russia, and misery and despair everywhere.

Shamed, dishonoured, wading in blood and dripping with filth, thus capitalist society stands. Not as we usually see it, playing the roles of peace and righteousness, of order, of philosophy, of ethics – but as a roaring beast, as an orgy of anarchy, as a pestilential breath, devastating culture and humanity – so it appears in all its hideous nakedness.

In the midst of this witches' sabbath a catastrophe of world historical proportions has happened: international Social Democracy has capitulated. To deceive ourselves about it, to cover it up, would be the most foolish, the most fatal thing the proletariat could do. Marx says:

> [T]he democrat (that is, the petty-bourgeois revolutionary) [comes] out of the most shameful defeats as unmarked as he naively went into them; he comes away with the newly gained conviction that he must be victorious, not that he or his party ought to give up the old principles, but that conditions ought to accommodate him.[19]

The modern proletariat comes out of historical tests differently. Its tasks and its errors are both gigantic: no prescription, no schema valid for every case, no infallible leader to show it the path to follow. Historical experience is its only school mistress. Its thorny way to self-emancipation is paved not only with immeasurable suffering but also with countless errors. The aim of its journey – its emancipation depends on this – is whether the proletariat can learn from its own errors. Self-criticism, remorseless, cruel, and going to the core of things is the life's breath and light of the proletarian movement. The fall of the socialist proletariat in the present world war is unprecedented. It is a misfortune for humanity. But socialism will be lost only if the international proletariat fails to measure the depth of this fall, if it refuses to learn from it.

The last forty-five year period in the development of the modern labour movement now stands in doubt. What we are experiencing in this critique is a closing of accounts for what will soon be half a century of work at our posts. The grave of the Paris Commune

---

19. Karl Marx, *The Eighteenth Brumaire of Louis Bonaparte* (1852).

CHAPTER ONE

ended the first phase of the European labour movement as well as the First International. Since then there began a new phase. In place of spontaneous revolutions, risings and barricades, after which the proletariat each time fell back into passivity, there began the systematic daily struggle, the exploitation of bourgeois parliamentarianism, mass organisations, the marriage of the economic with the political struggle, and that of socialist ideals with stubborn defence of immediate daily interests. For the first time the pole star of strict scientific teachings lit the way for the proletariat and for its emancipation. Instead of sects, schools, utopias and isolated experiments in various countries, there arose a uniform, international theoretical basis which bound countries together like the strands of a rope. Marxist knowledge gave the working class of the entire world a compass by which it can make sense of the welter of daily events and by which it can always plot the right course to take to the fixed and final goal.

She who bore, championed, and protected this new method was German Social Democracy. The [Franco-Prussian] war and the defeat of the Paris Commune had shifted the centre of gravity for the European workers' movement to Germany. As France was the classic site of the first phase of proletarian class struggle and Paris the beating, bleeding heart of the European labouring classes of those times, so the German workers became the vanguard of the second phase. By means of countless sacrifices and tireless attention to detail, they have built the strongest organisation, the one most worthy of emulation; they created the biggest press, called the most effective means of education and enlightenment into being, gathered the most powerful masses of voters and attained the greatest number of parliamentary mandates. German Social Democracy was considered the purest embodiment of Marxist socialism. She had and laid claim to a special place in the Second International – its instructress and leader.

In his famous 1895 foreword to Marx's *The Class Struggles in France, 1848–1850*, Friedrich Engels wrote:

> No matter what happens in other countries, German Social Democracy has a special position and therefore a special task, at least for the time being. The two million voters it sends to the ballot box, and the young men and women who, although non-voters, stand behind them, constitute the most numerous and compact mass, the "decisive force" of the proletarian army.

German Social Democracy, as the Vienna *Arbeiterzeitung* wrote on August 5, 1914, was "the jewel of class-conscious proletarian organisations". In her footsteps trod the increasingly enthusiastic Social Democrats of France, Italy and Belgium, the labour movements of Holland, Scandinavia, Switzerland and the United States. The Slavic countries, the Russians, the Social Democrats of the Balkans looked upon German Social Democracy with limitless, nearly uncritical, admiration. In the Second International the German "decisive force" played the determining role. At the [international] congresses, in the meetings of the international socialist bureaus, all awaited the opinion of the Germans. Especially in the questions of the struggle against militarism and war, German Social Democracy always took the lead. "For us Germans that is unacceptable", regularly sufficed to decide the orientation of the Second International, which blindly bestowed its confidence upon the admired leadership of the mighty German Social Democracy: the pride of every socialist and the terror of the ruling classes everywhere.

And what did we in Germany experience when the great historical test came? The most precipitous fall, the most violent collapse. Nowhere has the organisation of the proletariat been yoked so completely to the service of imperialism. Nowhere is the state of siege borne so docilely.[20] Nowhere is the press so hobbled, public opinion so stifled, the economic and political class struggle of the working class so totally surrendered as in Germany.

But German Social Democracy was not merely the strongest vanguard troop, it was the thinking head of the International. For this reason, we must begin the analysis, the self-examination process, with its fall. It has the duty to begin the salvation of international socialism, that means unsparing criticism of itself. None of the other parties, none of the other classes of bourgeois society, may look clearly and openly into the mirror of their own errors, their own weaknesses, for the mirror reflects their historical limitations and the historical doom that awaits them. The working class can boldly look truth straight in the face, even the bitterest self-renunciation, for its weaknesses are only confusion. The strict law of history gives back its power, stands guarantee for its final victory.

Unsparing self-criticism is not merely an essential for its existence but the working class's supreme duty. On our ship we have the most valuable treasures of mankind, and the proletariat is their ordained guardian! And while bourgeois society, shamed and dishonoured by the bloody orgy, rushes headlong toward its doom, the international proletariat must and will gather up the golden treasure that, in a moment of weakness and confusion in the chaos of the world war, it has allowed to sink to the ground.

One thing is certain. The world war is a turning point. It is foolish and mad to imagine that we need only survive the war, like a rabbit waiting out the storm under a bush, in order to fall happily back into the old routine once it is over. The world war has altered the conditions of our struggle and, most of all, it has changed us. Not that the basic law of capitalist development, the life-and-death war between capital and labour, will experience any amelioration. But now, in the midst of the war, the masks are falling and the old familiar visages smirk at us. The tempo of development has received a mighty jolt from the eruption of the volcano of imperialism. The violence of the conflicts in the bosom of society, the enormousness of the tasks that tower up before the socialist proletariat – these make everything that has transpired in the history of the workers' movement seem a pleasant idyll.

Historically, this war was ordained to thrust forward the cause of the proletariat – to drive the German proletariat to the pinnacle of the nation and thereby begin to organise the international and universal conflict between capital and labour for political power

---

20. With mobilisation at the outbreak of the war, the country was divided into defence sectors and commanding generals within these took over all the functions of government; they could suspend civil rights, arrest individuals under the guise of protective custody, and exercised considerable powers of censorship. Thus they were able to stifle dissent and particularly to restrict news of the military failures.

within the state.

And did we envision a different role for the working class in the world war? Let us recall how we, only a short while ago, were accustomed to describe the future:

> Then comes the *catastrophe*. Then the great mobilisation will take place in Europe; 16–18 million men, the flower of the various nations, armed with the best tools of death, will enter the field as enemies. But, I am convinced, that behind the great mobilisation there stands the *great havoc*. It will not come through our agency, but rather yours. You are driving things to the limit. You are leading us to catastrophe. You will reap what you have sown. The *Götterdämmerung of the bourgeois world approaches. Believe it! It is approaching!* [All italics are Luxemburg's.]

Thus spoke our leader, August Bebel, during the Reichstag debate on the Morocco Crisis.[21]

Imperialism or Socialism?, the official party pamphlet distributed in hundreds of thousands of copies a few years ago, closes with these words:

> Thus the struggle against imperialism develops ever more into the decisive struggle between capital and labour. War crises, rising prices, capitalism vs. peace, welfare for all, socialism! Thus is the question stated. *History is moving toward great decisions.* The proletariat must work unceasingly at its world-historical task, strengthen its organisation, the clarity of its understanding. Then come what may, be it that [proletarian] power spares mankind the terrible cruelty of a world war, *or be it that the capitalist world sinks into history in the same way as it was born, in blood and violence.* [In either case] *the historical hour* will find the working class prepared – and *preparation is everything.* [All italics are Luxemburg's.]

The official *Handbook for Social-Democratic Voters* (1911), for the last Reichstag election, says on p.42 concerning the expected world war:

> *Do our rulers and ruling classes expect the peoples to permit this awful thing?* Will not a cry of horror, of scorn, of outrage not seize the peoples and cause them to put an end to this murder? Will they not ask: For whom? What's it all for? Are we mentally disturbed to be treated this way, to allow ourselves to be so treated? He who is calmly convinced of the probability of a great European war can come to no other conclusion than the following: The next European war will be such a desperate gamble as the world *has never seen. In all probability it will be the last war.*

With speeches and words such as these, our current Reichstag deputies acquired their 110 mandates.

In the summer of 1911, when the *Panther* made its lunge to Agadir[22] and the noisy agitation of the German imperialists put war in the immediate offing, an international

---

21. The Second Morocco Crisis of 1911 aroused fears of imminent European war. Its resolution entailed Germany's recognition of a French protectorate in exchange for a large, relatively worthless strip of French Equatorial Africa. While Britain supported its French ally, Germany had had to back down when its own allies were unwilling to go to war on behalf of overseas interests. Nationalists at home regarded the outcome as a humiliation. Socialists saw the crisis as ominous proof of the intentions of militarists and imperialists.
22. In July 1911, the German gunboat *Panther* sailed to Agadir, Morocco, "to protect German interests", i.e. to secure sources of iron ore for Mannesmann Steel. War almost broke out between France and Germany, but on Lloyd-George's threat of British intervention, Germany withdrew. At the Treaty of Berlin (November 1911) Germany was given a slice of the Cameroons and gave up her claims to Morocco.

meeting in London accepted the following resolution (August 4, 1911):

> The delegates of the German, Spanish, English, Dutch, and French workers' organisations declare themselves *to be ready to oppose any declaration of war with all the means at their disposal*. Every represented nation undertakes the obligation, according to the resolutions of national and international congresses, *to act* against all criminal machinations of the ruling classes.

When, in November 1912, the congress of the International met in the minster at Basel and when the long procession of worker representatives entered the cathedral, everyone present felt a presentiment of the greatness of the coming destiny and a heroic resolve.

The cool, sceptical Victor Adler spoke:

> Comrades, the most important thing is that we are here at the common source of our strength, that we can draw from this strength so that each can do in his own country what he can, according to the forms and means that we have, to oppose the crime of war with all the power we possess. And if it can be stopped, if it is really stopped, *then we must see to it that it becomes a cornerstone for the end* [of bourgeois society]. This is the moving spirit for the whole International. And if murder and arson and pestilence are unleashed throughout civilised Europe – we can only think of this with horror, outrage and indignation churning in our breasts. *And we ask ourselves: are we men, are the proletarians of today still sheep* that they can be led dumbly to slaughter?

And Jean Jaurès concluded the reading of the International Bureau's manifesto against the war with these words:

> The International represents all the moral force of the world! And if the tragic hour strikes and we must give ourselves up to it, the consciousness of this will support and strengthen us. We do not merely say "no" *but from the depth of our hearts we declare ourselves ready to sacrifice everything*.

It was reminiscent of the Oath of Ruetli.[23] The world directed its gaze to the church at Basel where the bell sounded solemnly for the future great battle between the army of labour and the power of capital...

Even a week before the outbreak of war, on July 26, 1914, German party newspapers wrote:

> *We are not marionettes.* We combat with all our energy a system that makes men into will-less tools of blind circumstance, this capitalism that seeks to transform a Europe thirsting for peace into a steaming slaughterhouse. If destruction has its way, if the united will to peace of the German, the international proletariat, which will make itself known in powerful demonstrations in the coming days, if the world war cannot be fended off, *then at least this should be the last war, it should become the Götterdämmerung of capitalism.* (*Frankfurter Volksstimme*)

Then on July 30, 1914, the central organ of German Social Democracy stated:

---

23. According to legend, Wilhelm Tell and representatives of three Swiss cantons met at Ruetli in 1307 to pledge resistance against Austrian tyranny, the traditional foundation of Swiss freedom.

CHAPTER ONE

> The socialist proletariat rejects any responsibility for the events being brought about by a blinded, a maddened ruling class. Let it be known that *a new life shall bloom from the ruins. All responsibility falls to the wielders of power today*! It is "to be or not to be!" "World-history is the world-court!"

And then came the awful, the incredible 4th of August 1914.

Did it *have* to come? An event of this scope is certainly no game of chance. It must have deep and wide-reaching objective causes. These causes can, however, also lie in the errors of the leader of the proletariat, the Social Democrats, in the waning of our fighting spirit, our courage and loyalty to our convictions. Scientific socialism has taught us to comprehend the objective laws of historical development. Men do not make history according to their own free will. But they make history nonetheless. Proletarian action is dependent upon the degree of maturity in social development. However, social development is not independent of the proletariat but is equally its driving force and cause, its effect and consequence. Proletarian action participates in history. And while we can as little skip a stage of historical development as escape our shadow, we can certainly accelerate or retard history.

Socialism is the first popular movement in world history that has set itself the goal of bringing human consciousness, and thereby free will, into play in the social actions of mankind. For this reason, Friedrich Engels designated the final victory of the socialist proletariat a leap of humanity from the animal world into the realm of freedom. This "leap" is also an iron law of history bound to the thousands of seeds of a prior torment-filled and all-too-slow development. But this can never be realised until the development of complex material conditions strikes the incendiary spark of conscious will in the great masses. The victory of socialism will not descend from heaven. It can only be won by a long chain of violent tests of strength between the old and the new powers. The international proletariat under the leadership of the Social Democrats will thereby learn to try to take its history into its own hands; instead of remaining a will-less football, it will take the tiller of social life and become the pilot to the goal of its own history.

Friedrich Engels once said: "Bourgeois society stands at the crossroads, either transition to socialism or regression into barbarism". What does "regression into barbarism" mean to our lofty European civilisation? Until now, we have all probably read and repeated these words thoughtlessly, without suspecting their fearsome seriousness. A look around us at this moment shows what the regression of bourgeois society into barbarism means. *This world war* is a regression into barbarism. The triumph of imperialism leads to the annihilation of civilisation. At first, this happens sporadically for the duration of a modern war, but then when the period of unlimited wars begins it progresses toward its inevitable consequences. Today, we face the choice exactly as Friedrich Engels foresaw it a generation ago: either the triumph of imperialism and the collapse of all civilisation as in ancient Rome, depopulation, desolation, degeneration – a great cemetery. Or the victory of socialism, that is, the conscious active struggle of the international proletariat against imperialism and its method of war. This is a dilemma of world history, an either/or; the scales are wavering before the decision of the class-conscious proletariat. The future of civilisation and humanity depends on whether or not the proletariat resolves manfully to throw its revolutionary broadsword into the scales. In this war imperialism has won. Its bloody sword of genocide has brutally tilted the scale toward the abyss of misery. The only compensation for all the misery and all the shame would be if we learn from the war how the proletariat can seize mastery of its own destiny and escape the role of the lackey to the ruling classes.

Dearly bought is the modern working class's understanding of its historic mission. Its emancipation as a class is sown with fearful sacrifices, a veritable path to Golgotha. The June days, the sacrifice of the Commune, the martyrs of the Russian revolution – a dance of bloody shadows without number.[24] All fell on the field of honour. They are, as Marx wrote about the heroes of the Commune, eternally "enshrined in the great heart of the working class". Now, millions of proletarians of all tongues fall upon the field of dishonour, of fratricide, lacerating themselves while the song of the slave is on their lips. This, too, we are not spared. We are like the Jews that Moses led through the desert. But we are not lost, and we will be victorious if we have not unlearned how to learn. And if the present leaders of the proletariat, the Social Democrats, do not understand how to learn, then they will go under "to make room for people capable of dealing with a new world".

---

24. In June 1848, four months after the revolutionary overthrow of the Orléanist monarchy in France, the conservative bourgeoisie regained control of Paris amid street-fighting and great bloodshed. The defeat of the Parisian communards in June 1871 was accompanied by mass executions and deportations. The Russian revolution referred to by Luxemburg took place in 1905. Workers' soviets (councils) briefly controlled St. Petersburg and Moscow, but tsarist forces were able to quell the revolutionaries and re-establish a somewhat modified autocracy.

Chapter Two

> We are now facing the irrevocable fact of war. We are threatened by the horrors of invasion. The decision, today, is not for or against war; for us there can be but one question: by what means is this war to be conducted? Much, aye everything, is at stake for our people and its future, if Russian despotism, stained with the blood of its own people, should be the victor. This danger must be averted, the civilisation and the independence of our people must be safeguarded. Therefore we will carry out what we have always promised: in the hour of danger we will not desert our fatherland. In this we feel that we stand in harmony with the International, which has always recognised the right of every people to its national independence, as we stand in agreement with the International in emphatically denouncing every war of conquest. Actuated by these motives, we vote in favour of the war credits demanded by the Government.

With these words the Reichstag group issued the countersign that determined and controlled the position of the German working class during the war. Fatherland in danger, national defence, people's war for existence, *Kultur*, liberty – these were the slogans proclaimed by the parliamentary representatives of the Social Democracy. What followed was but the logical sequence. The position of the party and the labour union press, the patriotic frenzy of the masses, the civil peace, the disintegration of the International, all these things were the inevitable consequence of that momentous orientation in the Reichstag.

If it is true that this war is really a fight for national existence, for freedom, if it is true that these priceless possessions can be defended only by the iron tools of murder, if this war is the holy cause of the people, then everything else follows as a matter of course, we must take everything that the war may bring as a part of the bargain. He who desires the purpose must be satisfied with the means. War is methodical, organised, gigantic murder. But in normal human beings this systematic murder is possible only when a state of intoxication has been previously created. This has always been the tried and proven method of those who make war. Bestiality of action must find a commensurate bestiality of thought and senses; the latter must prepare and accompany the former. Thus the *Wahre Jacob*[25] of August 28, 1914, with its brutal picture of the German thresher, the party papers of Chemnitz, Hamburg, Kiel, Frankfurt, Koburg and others, with their patriotic drive in poetry and prose, were the necessary narcotic for a proletariat that could rescue its existence and its liberty only by plunging the deadly steel into its French and English brothers. These chauvinistic papers are after all a great deal more logical and consistent than those others who attempted to unite hill and valley, war with humanity, murder with brotherly love, the voting for war credits with socialist internationalism.

If the stand taken by the German Reichstag group on the 4th of August was correct, then the death sentence of the proletarian International has been spoken, not only for this war, but forever. For the first time since the modern labour movement has existed there yawns an abyss between the commandments of international solidarity of the proletariat of the world and the interests of freedom and nationalist existence of the people; for the first time we discover that the independence and liberty of the nations command that working men kill and destroy each other. Up to this time we have cherished the belief that the interests of the peoples of all nations, that the class interests of the proletariat are a harmonious unit, that they are identical, that they cannot possibly come into conflict with one another. That was the basis of our theory and practice, the soul of our agitation. Were we mistaken in the cardinal point of our whole world philosophy? We are holding an inquest over international socialism.

This world war is not the first crisis through which our international principles have passed. Our party was first tried forty-five years ago. At that time, on the 21st of July, 1870, Wilhelm Liebknecht and August Bebel made the following historical declaration before the Reichstag:

> The present war is a dynastic war in the interest of the Bonaparte dynasty as the war of 1866 was conducted in the interest of the Hohenzollern dynasty.
>
> We cannot vote for the funds which are demanded from the Reichstag to conduct this war because this would be, in effect, a vote of confidence in the Prussian government. And we know that the Prussian government by its action in 1866 prepared this war. At the same time we cannot vote against the budget, lest this be construed to mean that we support the conscienceless and criminal policies of Bonaparte.
>
> As opponents, on principle, of every dynastic war, as socialist republicans and members of the International Workingmen's Association which, without regard to nationality, has fought all oppressors, has tried to unite all the oppressed into a great band of brothers, we cannot directly or indirectly lend support to the present war. We therefore refuse to vote, while expressing the earnest hope that the peoples of Europe, taught by the present unholy events, will strive to win the right to control their own destinies, to do away with the present rule of might and class as the cause of all social and national evil.

---

25. *Der Wahre Jacob* (The True Jacob) was a fortnightly satirical magazine produced by the SPD. Its goal was "to fight for the rights of the working classes in its peculiar and effective way".

With this declaration the representatives of the German proletariat put their cause clearly and unreservedly under the banner of the International and definitely repudiated the war against France as a national war of independence. It is well known that Bebel, many years later, in his memoirs, stated that he would have voted against the war loan had he known, when the vote was taken, the things that were revealed in the years that followed.

Thus, in a war that was considered by the whole bourgeois public, and by a powerful majority of the people under the influence of Bismarckian strategy, as a war in the national life interest of Germany, the leaders of the German Social Democracy held firmly to the conviction that the life interest of a nation and the class interest of the proletariat are one, that both are opposed to war. It was left to the present world war and to the Social Democratic Reichstag group to uncover, for the first time, the terrible dilemma: either you are for national liberty – or for international socialism.

Now the fundamental fact in the declaration of our Reichstag group was, in all probability, a sudden inspiration. It was simply an echo of the crown speech and of the chancellor's speech of August 4. "We are not driven by the desire for conquest", we hear in the crown speech, "we are inspired by the unalterable determination to preserve the land upon which God has placed us for ourselves, and for all coming generations. From the documents that have been presented to you, you will have seen how my government, and above all my chancellor strove, to the last, to avert the utmost. We grasp the sword in self-defence, with a clear conscience and a clean hand". And Bethmann-Hollweg declared:

> Gentlemen, we are acting in self-defence, and necessity knows no law. He who is threatened as we are threatened, he who is fighting for the highest aims can be guided by but one consideration, how best to beat his way out of the struggle. We are fighting for the fruits of our peaceful labour, for the heritage of our great past, for the future of our nation.

Wherein does this differ from the Social Democratic declaration? (1) We have done everything to preserve peace, the war was forced upon us by others. (2) Now that the war is here we must act in self-defence. (3) In this war the German people are in danger of losing everything. This declaration of our Reichstag group is an obvious rehashing of the government declaration. As the latter based their claims upon diplomatic negotiations and imperial telegrams, so the socialist group points to peace demonstrations of the Social Democracy before the war. Where the crown speech denies all aims of conquest, the Reichstag group repudiates a war of conquest by standing upon its socialism. And when the emperor and chancellor cry out, "We are fighting for the highest principles. We know no parties, we know only Germans", the Social Democratic declaration echoes: "Our people risk everything. In this hour of danger we will not desert our fatherland".

Only in one point does the Social Democratic declaration differ from its government model: it placed the danger of Russian despotism in the foreground of its orientation, as a danger to German freedom. The crown speech says, regarding Russia: "With a heavy heart I have been forced to mobilise against a neighbour with whom I have fought upon so many battlefields. With honest sorrow I have seen a friendship faithfully kept by

Germany fall to pieces". The Social Democratic group changed this sorrowful rupture of a true friendship with the Russian tsar into a fanfare for liberty against despotism, used the revolutionary heritage of socialism to give to the war a democratic mantle, a popular halo. Here alone the Social Democratic declaration gives evidence of independent thought on the part of our Social Democrats.

As we have said, all these things came to the Social Democracy as a sudden inspiration on the 4th of August. All that they had said up to this day, every declaration that they had made, down to the very eve of the war, was in diametrical opposition to the declaration of the Reichstag group. The *Vorwärts* wrote on July 25, when the Austrian ultimatum to Serbia was published:

> They want the war, the unscrupulous elements that influence and determine the Wiener Hofburg. They want the war – it has been ringing out of the wild cries of the black-yellow press for weeks. They want the war – the Austrian ultimatum to Serbia makes it plain and clear to the world.
>
> Because the blood of Franz Ferdinand and his wife flowed under the shots of an insane fanatic, shall the blood of thousands of workers and farmers be shed? Shall one insane crime be purged by another even more insane?... The Austrian ultimatum may be the torch that will set Europe in flames at all four corners.
>
> For this ultimatum, in its form and in its demands, is so shameless, that a Serbian government that should humbly retreat before this note, would have to reckon with the possibility of being driven out by the masses of the people between dinner and dessert...
>
> It was a crime of the chauvinistic press of Germany to egg on our dear ally to the utmost in its desire for war. And beyond a doubt, Herr von Bethmann-Hollweg promised Herr Berchtold our support. But Berlin is playing a game as dangerous as that being played by Vienna.

The *Leipziger Volkszeitung* wrote on July 24:

> The Austrian military party has staked everything on one card, for in no country in the world has national and military chauvinism anything to lose. In Austria chauvinistic circles are particularly bankrupt; their nationalistic howls are a frantic attempt to cover up Austria's economic ruin, the robbery and murder of war to fill its coffers...

The *Dresden Volkszeitung* said, on the same day:

> Thus far the war maniacs of the Wiener Ballplatz have failed to furnish proof that would justify Austria in the demands it has made upon Serbia. So long as the Austrian government is not in a position to do this, it places itself, by its provocative and insulting attacks upon Serbia, in a false position before all Europe. And even if Serbia's guilt was proven, even if the assassination in Sarajevo had actually been prepared under the eyes of the Serbian government, the demands made in the note are far in excess of normal bounds. Only the most unscrupulous war lust can explain such demands upon another state...

The *Münchener Post*, on July 25, wrote:

CHAPTER TWO

> This Austrian note is a document unequalled in the history of the last two centuries. Upon the findings of an investigation whose contents have, till now, been kept from the European public, without court proceedings against the murderer of the heir presumptive and his spouse, it makes demands on Serbia, the acceptance of which would mean national suicide to Serbia...

The *Schleswig-Holstein Volkszeitung* declared, on July 25:

> Austria is provoking Serbia. Austria-Hungary wants war, and is committing a crime that may drown all Europe in blood... Austria is playing *va banque*.[26] It dares a provocation of the Serbian state that the latter, if it is not entirely defenceless, will certainly refuse to tolerate...

> Every civilised person must protest emphatically against the criminal behaviour of the Austrian rulers. It is the duty of the workers above all, and of all other human beings who honour peace and civilisation, to try their utmost to prevent the consequences of the bloody insanity that has broken out in Vienna.

The *Magdeburger Volksstimme* of July 25 said:

> Any Serbian government that even pretended to consider these demands seriously would be swept out in the same hour by the parliament and by the people.

> The action of Austria is the more despicable because Berchtold is standing before the Serbian government and before Europe with empty hands.

> To precipitate a war such as this at the present time means to invite a world war. To act thus shows a desire to disturb the peace of an entire hemisphere. One cannot thus make moral conquests, or convince non-participants of one's own righteousness. It can be safely assumed that the press of Europe, and with it the European governments, will call the vainglorious and senseless Viennese statesmen energetically and unmistakably to order.

On July 24 the *Frankfurter Volksstimme* wrote:

> Upheld by the agitation of the clerical press, which mourns in Franz Ferdinand its best friend and demands that his death be avenged upon the Serbian people, upheld by German war patriots whose language becomes daily more contemptible and more threatening, the Austrian government has allowed itself to be driven to send an ultimatum to Serbia couched in language that, for presumptuousness, leaves little to be desired; containing demands whose fulfilment by the Serbian government is manifestly impossible.

On the same day the *Elberfelder Freie Presse* wrote:

> A telegram of the semi-official Wolff Bureau reports the terms of the demands made on Serbia by Austria. From these it may be gathered that the rulers in Vienna are pushing toward war with all their might. For the conditions imposed by the note that was presented in Belgrade last night are nothing short of a protectorate of Austria over Serbia. It is eminently necessary that the diplomats of Berlin make the war agitators of Vienna understand that Germany will not move a finger to support such outrageous demands, that a withdrawal of the threats would be advisable.

---

26. A gambling term meaning to put everything at stake.

The *Bergische Arbeiterstimme* of Solingen writes:

> Austria demands a conflict with Serbia, and uses the assassination at Sarajevo as a pretext for putting Serbia morally in the wrong. But the whole matter has been approached too clumsily to influence European public opinion.
>
> But if the war agitators of the Wiener Ballplatz believe that their allies of the Triple Alliance, Germany and Italy, will come to their assistance in a conflict in which Russia, too, will be involved, they are suffering from a dangerous illusion. Italy would welcome the weakening of Austria-Hungary, its rival on the Adriatic and in the Balkans, and would certainly decline to burn its fingers to help Austria. In Germany, on the other hand, the powers that be – even should they be so foolish as to wish it – would not dare to risk the life of a single soldier to satisfy the criminal lust for power of the Habsburgers without arousing the fury of the entire people.

Thus the entire working-class press, without exception, judged the war's causes a week before its outbreak. Obviously the question was one of neither the existence nor the freedom of Germany, but a shameful adventure of the Austrian war party; not a question of self-defence, national protection and a holy war forced upon us in the name of freedom, but a bold provocation, an abominable threat against foreign, Serbian independence and liberty.

What was it that happened on August 4 to turn this clearly defined and so unanimously accepted attitude of the Social Democracy upside down? Only one new factor had appeared – the *White Book* that was presented to the Reichstag by the German government on that day. And this contained, on page 4, the following:

> Under these circumstances Austria must say to itself that it is incompatible with the dignity and the safety of the monarchy to remain inactive any longer in the face of the occurrences across the border. The Austrian imperial government has notified us of this, their attitude, and has begged us to state our views. Out of a full heart we could but assure our ally of our agreement with this interpretation of conditions and assure him that any action that would seem necessary to put an end to Serbian attempts against the existence of the Austrian monarchy would meet with our approval. We fully realised that eventual war measures undertaken by Austria must bring Russia into the situation and that we, in order to carry out our duty as ally, might be driven into war. But we could not, realising as we did that the most vital interests of Austria-Hungary were threatened, advise our ally to adopt a policy of acquiescence, that could not possibly be brought into accord with its dignity, nor could we refuse to lend our aid in this attitude.
>
> And we were particularly prevented from taking this stand by the fact that the persistent subversive Serbian agitation seriously jeopardised us. If the Serbians had been permitted, with the aid of Russia and France, to continue to threaten the existence of the neighbouring monarchy, there would have ensued a gradual collapse of Austria and a subjection of all the Slavic races under the Russian sceptre, which would have rendered untenable the situation of the Germanic race in Central Europe. A morally weakened Austria, succumbing before the advance of Russian

Pan-Slavism, would no longer be an ally on which we could count and depend, as we are obliged to do in view of the increasingly menacing attitude of our neighbours to the East and to the West. We therefore gave Austria a free hand in her proceedings against Serbia. We have had no share in the preparations.

These were the words that lay before the Social Democratic Reichstag group on August 4, the only important and determining phrases in the entire *White Book*, a concise declaration of the German government beside which all other yellow, grey, blue, orange books on the diplomatic passages that preceded the war and its most immediate causes become absolutely irrelevant and insignificant. Here the Reichstag group had the key to a correct judgment of the situation in hand. The entire Social Democratic press, a week before, had cried out that the Austrian ultimatum was a criminal provocation of the world war and demanded preventive and pacific action on the part of the German government. The entire socialist press assumed that the Austrian ultimatum had descended upon the German government like a bolt from the blue as it had upon the German public.

But now the *White Book* declared, briefly and clearly:

1. That the Austrian government had requested German sanction before taking a final step against Serbia.

2. That the German government clearly understood that the action undertaken by Austria would lead to war with Serbia, and ultimately, to European war.

3. That the German government did not advise Austria to give in, but on the contrary declared that an acquiescent, weakened Austria could not be regarded as a worthy ally of Germany.

4. That the German government assured Austria, before it advanced against Serbia, of its assistance under all circumstances, in case of war, and finally,

5. That the German government, withal, had not reserved for itself control over the decisive ultimatum from Austria to Serbia, upon which the whole world war depended, but had left to Austria "an absolutely free hand".

All of this our Reichstag group learned on August 4. And still another fact it learned from the government – that German forces had already invaded Belgium. And from all this the Social Democratic group concluded that this is a war of defence against foreign invasion, for the existence of the fatherland, for "*Kultur*", a war for liberty against Russian despotism.

Was the obvious background of the war, and the scenery that so scantily concealed it, was the whole diplomatic performance that was acted out at the outbreak of the war, with its clamour about a world of enemies, all threatening the life of Germany, all moved the one desire to weaken, to humiliate, to subjugate the German people and nation – were all these things such a complete surprise? Did these factors actually call for more judgment, more critical sagacity than they possessed? Nowhere was this less true than of our party. It had already gone through two great German wars, and in both of them had received memorable lessons.

Even a poorly informed student of history knows that the war of 1866 against Austria was systematically prepared by Bismarck long before it broke out, and that his policies, from the very beginning, led inevitably to a rupture and to war with Austria. The crown prince himself, later Emperor Frederick, in his memoirs under the date of November 14 of that year, speaks of this purpose of the chancellor:

> He [Bismarck], when he went into office, was firmly resolved to bring Prussia to a war with Austria, but was very careful not to betray this purpose, either at that time or on any other premature occasion to His Majesty, until the time seemed favourable.

"Compare with this confession", says Auer in his brochure *Die Sedanfeier und die Sozialdemokratie* "the proclamation that King William sent out '*to my people*'".

> The fatherland is in danger! Austria and a large part of Germany have risen in arms against us.
>
> It is only a few years ago since I, of my own free will, without thinking of former misunderstandings, held out a fraternal hand to Austria in order to save a German nation from foreign domination. But my hopes have been blasted. Austria cannot forget that its lords once ruled Germany; it refuses to see in the younger, more virile Prussia an ally, but persists in regarding it as a dangerous rival. Prussia – so it believes – must be opposed in all its aims, because whatever favours Prussia harms Austria. The old unholy jealousy has again broken out; Prussia is to be weakened, destroyed, dishonoured. All treaties with Prussia are void, German lords are not only called upon, but persuaded, to sever their alliance with Prussia. Wherever we look in Germany, we are surrounded by enemies whose war cry is – Down with Prussia!

Praying for the blessings of heaven, Kaiser Wilhelm ordered a general day of prayer and penance for the 18th of July, saying: "It has not pleased God to crown with success my attempts to preserve the blessings of peace for my people".

Should not the official accompaniment to the outbreak of the war on August 4 have awakened in the minds of our group vivid memories of long remembered words and melodies? Had they completely forgotten their party history?

But not enough! In the year 1870 there came the war with France, and history has united its outbreak with an unforgettable occurrence: the Ems Dispatch,[27] a document that has become a classic byword for capitalist government art in war-making, and which marks a memorable episode in our party history. Was it not old [Wilhelm] Liebknecht, was it not the German Social Democracy who felt in duty bound, at that time, to disclose these facts and to show to the masses "how wars are made"?

Making war simply and solely for the protection of the fatherland was, by the way, not Bismarck's invention. He only carried out, with characteristic unscrupulousness, an old, well-known and truly international recipe of capitalist statesmanship. When and where has there been a war since so-called public opinion has played a role in governmental calculations, in which each and every belligerent party did not, with a heavy

---

27. The publication of this document on 13 July 1870 provoked the French Empire under Napoleon III to declare war on Prussia on 19 July 1870 – as Bismarck had intended.

heart, draw the sword from its sheath for the single and sole purpose of defending its fatherland and its own righteous cause from the shameful attacks of the enemy? This legend is as inextricably a part of the game of war as powder and lead. The game is old. Only that the Social Democratic Party could play it is new.

Chapter Three

Our party should have been prepared to recognise the real aims of this war, to meet it without surprise, to judge it by its deeper relationship according to their wide political experience. The events and forces that led to August 4, 1914, were no secrets. The world had been preparing for decades, in broad daylight, in the widest publicity, step by step, and hour by hour, for the world war. And if today a number of socialists threaten with horrible destruction the "secret diplomacy" that has brewed this devilry behind the scenes, they are ascribing to these poor wretches a magic power that they little deserve, just as the Botokude whips his fetish for the outbreak of a storm. The so-called captains of nations are, in this war, as at all times, merely chessmen, moved by all-powerful historic events and forces, on the surface of capitalist society. If ever there were persons capable of understanding these events and occurrences, it was the members of the German Social Democracy.

Two lines of development in recent history lead straight to the present war. One has its origin in the period when the so-called national states, i.e., the modern states, were first constituted, from the time of the Bismarckian war against France. The war of 1870, which, by the annexation of Alsace-Lorraine, threw the French republic into the arms of Russia, split Europe into two opposing camps and opened up a period of insane competitive armament, first piled up the firebrands for the present world conflagration.

Bismarck's troops were still stationed in France when Marx wrote to the *Braunschweiger Ausschuss:*

> He who is not deafened by the momentary clamour, and is not interested in deafening the German people, must see that the war of 1870 carries with it, of necessity, a war between Germany and Russia, just as the war of 1866 bore the war of 1870. I say of necessity, unless the unlikely should happen, unless a revolution breaks out in Russia before that time. If this does not occur, a war between Germany and Russia may even now be regarded as *un fait accompli*. It depends entirely upon the attitude of the German victor to determine whether

this war has been useful or dangerous. If they take Alsace-Lorraine, then France with Russia will arm against Germany. It is superfluous to point out the disastrous consequences.

At that time this prophecy was laughed down. The bonds which united Russia and Prussia seemed so strong that it was considered madness to believe in a union of autocratic Russia with republican France. Those who supported this conception were laughed at as madmen. And yet everything that Marx has prophesied has happened, to the last letter. "For that is", says Auer in his *Sedanfeier*, "Social Democratic politics, seeing things clearly as they are, and differing therein from the day-by-day politics of the others, bowing blindly down before every momentary success".

This must not be misunderstood to mean that the desire for revenge for the robbery accomplished by Bismarck has driven the French into a war with Germany, that the kernel of the present war is to be found in the much discussed "revenge for Alsace-Lorraine". This is the convenient nationalist legend of the German war agitator, who creates fables of a darkly brooding France that "cannot forget" its defeat, just as the Bismarckian press-servants ranted of the dethroned Princess Austria who could not forget her erstwhile superiority over the charming Cinderella Prussia. As a matter of fact revenge for Alsace-Lorraine has become the theatrical property of a couple of patriotic clowns, the "Lion de Belfort" nothing more than an ancient survival.

The annexation of Alsace-Lorraine long ago ceased to play a role in French politics, being superseded by new, more pressing cares; and neither the government nor any serious party in France thought of a war with Germany because of these territories. If, nevertheless, the Bismarck heritage has become the firebrand that started this world conflagration, it is rather in the sense of having driven Germany on the one hand, and France, and with it all of Europe, on the other, along the downward path of military competition, of having brought about the Franco-Russian alliance, of having united Austria with Germany as an inevitable consequence. This gave to Russian tsarism a tremendous prestige as a factor in European politics. Germany and France have systematically fawned before Russia for her favour. At that time the links were forged that united Germany with Austria-Hungary, whose strength, as the words quoted from the *White Book* show, lie in their "brotherhood in arms", in the present war.

Thus the war of 1870 brought in its wake the outward political grouping of Europe about the axes of the Franco-German antagonism, and established the rule of militarism in the lives of the European peoples. Historical development has given to this rule and to this grouping an entirely new content. The second line that leads to the present world war, and which again brilliantly justifies Marx's prophecy, has its origin in international occurrences that Marx did not live to see, in the imperialist development of the last twenty-five years.

The growth of capitalism, spreading out rapidly over a reconstituted Europe after the war period of the sixties and seventies, particularly after the long period of depression that followed the inflation and the panic of the year 1873, reaching an unnatural zenith in the prosperity of the nineties, opened up a new period of storm and danger among the nations of Europe. They were competing in their expansion toward the non-capitalist countries and zones of the world. As early as the eighties a strong tendency toward colonial expansion became apparent. England secured control of Egypt and created for itself, in South Africa, a powerful colonial empire, France took possession of Tunis in North Africa and Tonkin in East Asia; Italy gained a foothold in Abyssinia; Russia accomplished its conquests in Central Asia and pushed forward into Manchuria; Germany won its first colonies in Africa and in the South Sea, and the United States joined the circle when it procured the Philippines with "interests" in Eastern Asia. This period of feverish conquests has brought on, beginning with the Chinese-Japanese War in 1895, a practically uninterrupted chain of bloody wars, reaching its height in the Great Chinese Invasion, and closing with the Russo-Japanese War of 1904.

All these occurrences, coming blow upon blow, created new, extra-European antagonisms on all sides: between Italy and France in Northern Africa, between France and England in Egypt, between England and Russia in Central Asia, between Russia and Japan in Eastern Asia, between Japan and England in China, between the United States and Japan in the Pacific Ocean – a very restless ocean, full of sharp conflicts and temporary alliances, of tension and relaxation, threatening every few years to break out into a war between European powers. It was clear to everybody, therefore, (1) that the secret underhand war of each capitalist nation against every other, on the backs of Asiatic and African peoples, must sooner or later lead to a general reckoning, that the wind that was sown in Africa and Asia would return to Europe as a terrific storm, the more certainly since increased armament of the European states was the constant associate of these Asiatic and African occurrences; (2) that the European world war would have to come to an outbreak as soon as the partial and changing conflicts between the imperialist states found a centralised axis, a conflict of sufficient magnitude to group them, for the time being, into large, opposing factions. This situation was created by the appearance of German imperialism.

In Germany one may study the development of imperialism, crowded as it was into the shortest possible space of time, in concrete form. The unprecedented rapidity of German industrial and commercial development since the foundation of the empire brought out during the eighties two characteristically peculiar forms of capitalist accumulation: the most pronounced growth of monopoly in Europe and the best developed and most concentrated banking system in the whole world. The monopolies have organised the steel and iron industry, i.e., the branch of capitalist endeavour most interested in government orders, in militaristic equipment and in imperialistic undertakings (railroad building, the exploitation of mines, etc.) into the most influential factor in the nation. The latter has cemented the money interests into a firmly organised whole, with the greatest, most virile energy, creating a power that autocratically rules the industry, commerce and credit of the nation, dominant in private as well as public affairs, boundless in its powers of expansion, ever hungry for profit and activity, impersonal, and therefore, liberal-minded, reckless and unscrupulous, international by its very nature, ordained by its capacities to use the world as its stage.

Germany is under a personal regime, with strong initiative and spasmodic activity, with the weakest kind of parliamentarism, incapable of opposition, uniting all capitalist strata in the sharpest opposition to the working class. It is obvious that this live, unhampered imperialism, coming upon the world stage at a time when the world was practically divided up, with gigantic appetites, soon became an irresponsible factor of general unrest.

This was already foreshadowed by the radical upheaval that took place in the military policies of the empire at the end of the nineties. At that time two naval budgets were introduced which doubled the naval power of Germany and provided for a naval program covering almost two decades. This meant a sweeping change in the financial and trade policy of the nation. In the first place, it involved a striking change in the foreign policy of the empire. The policy of Bismarck was founded upon the principle that the empire is and must remain a land power, that the German fleet, at best, is but a very dispensable requisite for coastal defence. Even the secretary of state, Hollmann, declared in March 1897, in the Budget Commission of the Reichstag: "We need no navy for coastal defence. Our coasts protect themselves".

With the two naval bills an entirely new program was promulgated: on land and sea, Germany first. This marks the change from Bismarckian continental policies to *Weltpolitik*, from the defensive to the offensive as the end and aim of Germany's military program. The language of these facts was so unmistakable that the Reichstag itself furnished the necessary commentary. Lieber, the leader of the Centre[28] at that time, spoke on the 11th of March, 1896, after a famous speech of the emperor on the occasion of the twenty-fifth anniversary of the founding of the German empire, which had developed the new program as a forerunner to the naval bills, in which he mentioned "shoreless naval plans" – against which Germany must be prepared to enter into active opposition. Another Centre leader, Schädler, cried out in the Reichstag on March 23, 1898, when the first naval bill was under discussion, "The nation believes that we cannot be first on land and first on sea. You answer, gentlemen, that is not what we want! Nevertheless, gentlemen, you are at the beginning of such a conception, at a very strong beginning".

When the second bill came, the same Schädler declared in the Reichstag on the 5th of February, 1900, referring to previous promises that there would be no further naval bills, "and today comes this bill, which means nothing more and nothing less than the inauguration of a world fleet, as a basis of support for world policies, by doubling our navy and binding the next two decades by our demands". As a matter of fact the government openly defended the political program of its new course of action. On December 11, 1899, von Bülow, at that time state secretary of the foreign office, in a defence of the second naval bill stated:

---

28. The Centre Party (Deutsche Zentrumspartei), founded in 1870, was a political party representing Catholics.

CHAPTER THREE

> When the English speak of "a greater Britain", when the French talk of "The New France", when the Russians open up Asia for themselves, we too have a right to aspire to a greater Germany. If we do not create a navy sufficient to protect our trade, our natives in foreign lands, our missions and the safety of our shores, we are threatening the most vital interests of our nation. In the coming century the German people will be either the hammer or the anvil.

Strip this of its coastal defence ornamentation, and there remains the colossal program: greater Germany, as the hammer upon other nations.

It is not difficult to determine the direction toward which these provocations, in the main, were directed. Germany was to become the rival of the world's great naval force – England. And England did not fail to understand. The naval reform bills, and the speeches that ushered them in, created a lively unrest in England, an unrest that has never again subsided. In March 1910, Lord Robert Cecil said in the House of Commons during a naval debate: "I challenge any man to give me a plausible reason for the tremendous navy that Germany is building up, other than to take up the fight against England". The fight for supremacy on the ocean that lasted for one and a half decades on both sides and culminated in the feverish building of dreadnoughts and superdreadnoughts, was, in effect, the war between Germany and England. The naval bill of December 11, 1899, was a declaration of war by Germany, which England answered on August 4, 1914.

It should be noted that this fight for naval supremacy had nothing in common with the economic rivalry for the world market. The English "monopoly of the world market" which ostensibly hampered German industrial development, so much discussed at the present time, really belongs to the sphere of those war legends of which the evergreen French "revenge" is the most useful. This "monopoly" had become an old time fairy tale, to the lasting regret of the English capitalists. The industrial development of France, Belgium, Italy, Russia, India and Japan, and above all, of Germany and America, had put an end to this monopoly of the first half of the nineteenth century. Side by side with England, one nation after another stepped into the world market, capitalism developed automatically, and with gigantic strides, into world economy.

English supremacy on the sea, which has robbed so many Social Democrats of their peaceful sleep, and which, it seems to these gentlemen, must be destroyed to preserve international socialism, had, up to this time, disturbed German capitalism so little that the latter was able to grow up into a lusty youth, with bursting cheeks, under its "yoke". Yes, England itself, and its colonies, were the cornerstones for German industrial growth. And similarly, Germany became, for the English nation, its most important and most necessary customer. Far from standing in each other's way, British and German capitalist development were mutually highly interdependent, and united by a far-reaching system of division of labour, strongly augmented by England's free trade policy. German trade and its interests in the world market, therefore, had nothing whatever to do with a change of front in German politics and with the building of its fleet.

Nor did German colonial possessions at that time come into conflict with the English control of the seas. German colonies were not in need of protection by a first-class sea power. No one, certainly not England, envied Germany her possessions. That they were taken during the war by England and Japan, that the booty had changed owners, is but a generally accepted war measure, just as German imperialist appetites clamour for Belgium, a desire that no man outside of an insane asylum would have dared to express in time of peace. South-East and South-West Africa, Wilhelmsland or Tsingtau would never have caused any war, by land or by sea, between Germany and England. In fact, just before the war broke out, a treaty regulating a peaceable division of the Portuguese colonies in Africa between these two nations had been practically completed.

When Germany unfolded its banner of naval power and world policies it announced the desire for new and far-reaching conquest in the world by German imperialism. By means of a first-class aggressive navy, and by military forces that increased in a parallel ratio, the apparatus for a future policy was established, opening wide the doors for unprecedented possibilities. Naval building and military armaments became the glorious business of German industry, opening up a boundless prospect for further operations by trust and bank capital in the whole wide world. Thus, the acquiescence of all capitalist parties and their rallying under the flag of imperialism was assured. The Centre followed the example of the National Liberals, the staunchest defenders of the steel and iron industry, and, by adopting the naval bill it had loudly denounced in 1900, became the party of the government. The Progressives trotted after the Centre when the successor to the naval bill – the high-tariff party – came up; while the Junkers, the staunchest opponents of the "horrid navy" and of the canal brought up the rear as the most enthusiastic porkers and parasites of the very policy of sea-militarism and colonial robbery they had so vehemently opposed. The Reichstag election of 1907, the so-called Hottentot Elections, found the whole of Germany in a paroxysm of imperialistic enthusiasm, firmly united under one flag, that of the Germany of von Bülow, the Germany that felt itself ordained to play the role of the hammer in the world. These elections, with their spiritual pogrom atmosphere, were a prelude to the Germany of August 4, a challenge not only to the German working class, but to other capitalist nations as well, a challenge directed to no one in particular, a mailed fist shaken in the face of the entire world.

Chapter Four

Turkey became the most important field of operations of German imperialism; the Deutsche Bank, with its enormous Asiatic business interests, about which all German oriental policies centre, became its peacemaker. In the 1850s and '60s Asiatic Turkey worked chiefly with English capital, which built the railroad from Smyrna and leased the first stretch of the Anatolian railroad, up to Ismit. In 1888 German capital appeared upon the scene and procured from Abdul Hamid the control of the railroad that English capital had built and the franchise for the new stretch from Ismit to Angora and branch lines to Scutari, Bursa, Konya and Kaisarili. In 1899 the Deutsche Bank secured concessions for the building and operation of a harbour and improvements in Hardar Pasha, and the sole control over trade and tariff collections in the harbour. In 1901 the Turkish government turned over to the Deutsche Bank the concession for the Great Baghdad railroad[29] to the Persian Gulf, in 1907 for the drainage of the Sea of Karaviran and the irrigation of the Koma plain.

The reverse of this wonderful work of "peaceful culture" is the "peaceful" and wholesale ruin of the farming population of Asia Minor. The cost of this tremendous undertaking was advanced, of course, by the Deutsche Bank on the security of a widely diversified system of public indebtedness. Turkey will be, to all eternity, the debtor of Messrs. Siemens, Gwinner, Helfferich, etc., as it was formerly that of English, French and Austrian capital. This debtor, now, was forced not only to squeeze enormous sums out of the state to pay the interest on these loans, but, in addition, to guarantee a net income upon the railway, thus built. The most modern methods of transportation were grafted upon a primitive, in many cases purely agricultural, population. From the unfruitful soil of farming sections that had been exploited unscrupulously, for years, by an oriental despotism, producing scarcely enough to feed the population after the huge

---

29. The Berlin-Baghdad railroad, as a Eurasian axis with oil on both sides of it (Romania and Iraq) and a short route to the Indian Ocean, was mooted in 1871 by Wilhelm I and the Deutsche Bank. Abdul Hamid granted the concession in 1899. Britain had plans for a railroad from Cape to Cairo, while the Russians planned one from St. Petersburg to the Persian Gulf.

state debts had been paid, it is practically impossible to secure the profits demanded by the railroads. Freight and travelling are exceedingly undeveloped, since the industrial and cultural character of the region is most primitive, and can improve only at a slow rate. The deficit that must be paid to raise the required profit is, therefore, paid by the Turkish government in the form of a so-called kilometre guarantee.

European Turkey was built up according to this system by Austrian and French capital, and the same system has been adopted by the Deutsche Bank in its operations in Asiatic Turkey. As bond and surety that the subsidy will be paid, the Turkish government has handed over to the representatives of European capital, the so-called Executive Board in control of public debt, the main source of Turkish national income, which has given to the Deutsche Bank the right to collect the tithe from a number of provinces. In this way, for instance, the Turkish government paid, from 1893 to 1910, for the railroad to Angora and for the line from Eskishehir to Konya, a subsidy of about 9,090,000 Francs. The tithes thus leased by the Turkish government to its European creditors are ancient payments rendered in produce such as corn, sheep, silk, etc. They are not collected directly but through sub-lessees, somewhat similar to the famous tax-collectors, so notorious in pre-revolutionary France, the state selling the right to raise the amount required from each *vilayet* (province) by auction, against cash payment. When the speculator or company has thus procured the right to collect the tithe of a *vilayet*, it, in turn, sells the tithe of each individual *sanjak* (district) to other speculators, who again divide their portion among a veritable band of smaller agents. Since each one or these collectors must not only cover his own expenses but secure as large a profit as possible besides, the tithe grows like a landslide as it approaches the farmer; if the lessee has been mistaken in his calculation, he seeks to recompense himself at the expense of the farmer. The latter, practically always in debt, waits impatiently for the time when he can sell his crop. But after his grain is cut he must frequently wait for weeks before the tithe collector comes to take his portion. The collector, who is usually grain dealer as well, exploits this need of the farmer whose crop threatens to rot in the field, and persuades him to sell at a reduced price, knowing full well that it will be easy to secure the assistance of public officials and particularly of the *muktar* (town mayor) against the dissatisfied. When no tax-collector can be found the government itself collects the tithe in produce, puts it into storage houses and turns it over as part payment to the capitalists. This is the inner mechanism of the "industrial regeneration of Turkey" by European capital.

Thus a twofold purpose is accomplished. The farming population of Asia Minor becomes the object of a well organised process of exploitation in the interest of European, in this case German, financial and industrial capital. This again promotes the growth of the German sphere of interest in Turkey and lays the foundation for Turkey's "political protection". At the same time the instrument that carries out the exploitation of the farming population, the Turkish government, becomes the willing tool and vassal of Germany's foreign policies. For many years Turkish finance, tariff policies, taxation and state expenditures have been under European control. German influence has made itself particularly felt in the Turkish military organisation.

It is obvious from the foregoing that the interests of German imperialism demand the protection of the Turkish state, to the extent at least of preventing its complete disintegration. The liquidation of Turkey would mean its division between England, Russia, Italy and Greece among others, and the basis for a large-scale operation by German capital would vanish. Moreover, an extraordinary increase in the power of Russia, England and the Mediterranean states would result. For German imperialism, therefore, the preservation of this accommodating apparatus of the "independent Turkish state", the "integrity" of Turkey is a matter of necessity. And this necessity will exist until such time as this state will fall, having been consumed from within by German capital, as was Egypt by England and more recently Morocco by France, into the lap of Germany. The well-known spokesman of German imperialism, Paul Rohrbach, expressed this candidly and honestly when he said:

> In the very nature of things Turkey, surrounded on all sides by envious neighbours, must seek the support of a power that has practically no territorial interests in the Orient. That power is Germany. We, on the other hand, would be at a disadvantage if Turkey should disappear. If Russia and England fall heir to the Turkish state, obviously it will mean to both of these states a considerable increase in power. But even if Turkey should be so divided that we should also secure an extensive portion, it would mean for us endless difficulties. Russia, England, and in a certain sense France and Italy as well, are neighbours of present Turkish possessions and are in a position to hold and defend their portion by land and by sea. But we have no direct connection with the Orient. A German Asia Minor or Mesopotamia can become a reality only if Russia, and in consequence France as well, should be forced to relinquish their present political aims and ideals, i.e., if the world war should take a decisive turn in favour of German interests. (*The War and German Policy*, p.36).

Germany swore solemnly on November 8, 1898, in Damascus, by the shade of the great Saladin, to protect and to preserve the Mohammedan world and the green flag of the Prophet, and in so doing strengthened the regime of the bloody Sultan Abdul Hamid for over a decade, It has been able, after a short period of estrangement, to exert the same influence upon the Young Turk regime.[30] Aside from conducting the profitable business of the Deutsche Bank, the German mission busied itself chiefly with the reorganisation and training of Turkish militarism, under German instructors, with von der Goltz Pasha at the head. The modernisation of the army, of course, piled new burdens upon the Turkish farmers, but it was a splendid business arrangement for Krupp and the Deutsche Bank. At the same time Turkish militarism became entirely dependent upon Prussian militarism, and became the centre of German ambitions in the Mediterranean

---

30. The Young Turks, or the Committee of Union and Progress, were an essentially military organisation. On 23 July 1908 they compelled Sultan Abdul Hamid II to proclaim a constitution. Following the Sultan's attempt early in 1909 to stage a counter-revolution with the help of the Muslim Brotherhood, he was deposed on 23 April. In May–June 1912, "Saviour Officers", another counter-revolutionary group, was formed, and on 17 July they compelled the government to resign. The Young Turks were ousted. On 23 January 1913, a *coup d'état* took place and Turkey was from then till 1922 under the dictatorship of a triumvirate of Pashas.

and in Asia Minor.

That this "regeneration" of Turkey is a purely artificial attempt to galvanise a corpse, the fate of the Turkish revolutions best shows. In the first stage, while ideal considerations still predominated in the Young Turkish movement, when it was still fired with ambitious plans and illusions of a real springtime of life and of a rejuvenation for Turkey, its political sympathies were decidedly in favour of England. This country seemed to them to represent the ideal state of modern liberal rule, while Germany, which has so long played the role of protector of the holy regime of the old Sultan, was felt to be its natural opponent. For a while it seemed as if the revolution of 1908 would mean the bankruptcy of German oriental policies. It seemed certain that the overthrow of Abdul Hamid would go hand in hand with the downfall of German influence. As the Young Turks assumed power, however, and showed their complete inability to carry out any modern industrial, social or national reform on a large scale, as the counter-revolutionary hoof became more and more apparent, they turned of necessity to the tried and proven methods of Abdul Hamid, which meant periodic bloody massacres of oppressed peoples, goaded on until they flew at each other's throats, boundless, truly oriental exploitation of the farming population became the foundation of the nation. The artificial restoration of rule by force again became the most important consideration for "Young Turkey" and the traditional alliance of Abdul Hamid with Germany was re-established as the deciding factor in the foreign policy of Turkey.

The multiplicity of national problems that threaten to disrupt the Turkish nation make its regeneration a hopeless undertaking. The Armenian, Kurdian, Syrian, Arabian, Greek and (up to the most recent times) the Albanian and Macedonian questions, the manifold economic and social problems that exist in the different parts of the realm, are a serious menace. The growth of a strong, a hopeful, capitalism in the neighbouring Balkan states and the long years of destructive activity of international capital and international diplomacy stamp every attempt to hold together this rotting pile of timber as nothing but a reactionary undertaking. This has long been apparent, particularly to the German Social Democracy. As early as 1896, at the time of the Cretan uprising,[31] the German party press was filled with long discussions on the Oriental problem, that led to a revision of the attitude taken by Marx at the time of the Crimean War[32] and to definite repudiation of the "integrity of Turkey" as a heritage of European reaction. Nowhere was the Young Turkish regime, its inner sterility and its counter-revolutionary character, so quickly and so thoroughly recognised as in the German Social Democratic press. It was a real Prussian idea, this building of strategic railroads for rapid mobilisation, this sending of capable military instructors to prop up the crumbling edifice of the Turkish state.

In 1912 the Young Turkish regiment was forced to abdicate to the counter-revolution.

---

31. In 1897, the Christian peoples of Crete, which had been conquered by Turkey in 1645–69, rose against their rulers with the help of Greece, and the Turks were forced to withdraw in November 1898. Crete was placed under European trusteeship. In March 1905, another insurrection took place under the leadership of Veniselos. In 1907 a new constitution was proclaimed, and the island annexed to Greece.
32. Britain, France and Turkey fought Russia in 1854–56 for the control of Crimea. Piedmont (Italy) joined them in 1855. On 8 September 1855 Sebastopol was taken from the Russians and they were soon defeated.

CHAPTER FOUR

Characteristically, the first act of "Turkish regeneration" in this war was a *coup d'état*, the annihilation of the constitution. In this respect too there was a formal return to the rule of Abdul Hamid.

The first Balkan war[33] brought bankruptcy to Turkish militarism, in spite of German training. And the present war, into which Turkey was precipitated as Germany's "charge", will lead, with inevitable fatality, to the further or to the final liquidation of the Turkish Empire.

The position of German militarism – and its essence, the interests of the Deutsche Bank – has brought the German Empire in the Orient into opposition to all other nations. Above all to England. The latter had not only rival business relations and fat profits in Mesopotamia and Anatolia which were forced to retreat before their German rivals. This was a situation that English capitalism grudgingly accepted. But the building of a strategic railroad, and the strengthening of Turkish militarism under German influence was felt by England to be a sore point, in a strategic question of its world political relations; lying as it did at the cross roads between Central Asia, Persia and India, on the one side, and Egypt on the other.

"England", writes Rohrbach in his *Baghdadbahn*, "can be attacked and mortally wounded on land in Egypt. The loss of Egypt will mean to England not only the loss of control over the Suez Canal and its connections with India and Asia, but probably the sacrifice of its possessions in Central and Eastern Africa as well. A Mohammedan power like Turkey, moreover, could exercise a dangerous influence over the 60 millions of Mohammedan subjects of England in India, in Afghanistan and Persia, should Turkey conquer Egypt. But Turkey can subjugate Egypt only if it possesses an extended system of railroads in Asia Minor and Syria, if by an extension of the Anatolian Railway it is able to ward off an English attack upon Mesopotamia, if it increases and improves its army, if its general economic and financial conditions are improved".

And in his *The War and German Policy*, which was published after the outbreak of the war, he says:

> The Baghdad Railroad was destined from the start to bring Constantinople and the military strongholds of the Turkish Empire in Asia Minor into direct connection with Syria and the provinces on the Euphrates and on the Tigris. Of course it was to be foreseen that this railway, together with the projected and, partly or wholly, completed railroads in Syria and Arabia, would make it possible to use Turkish troops in the direction of Egypt. No one will deny that, should the Turkish-German alliance remain in force, and under a number of other important conditions whose realisation will be even more difficult than this alliance, the Baghdad railway is a political life insurance policy for Germany.

Thus the semi-official spokesman of German imperialism openly revealed its plan and

---

33. The first Balkan war broke out in October 1912. The Turks were pushed back to Constantinople. It ended with the Treaty of London (30 May 1913). Turkey was forced to give up all claims to its former European possessions. Albania was created as a new state. In June 1913, the second Balkan war began: Bulgaria attacked Serbia and Greece, and Romania and Turkey opposed Bulgaria. It ended with the Treaty of Bucharest (30 July 1913). Italy invaded Albania in 1914.

its aims in the Orient. Here German policies were clearly marked out, and an aggressive fundamental tendency most dangerous for the existing balance of world power, with a clearly defined point against England, was disclosed. German oriental policies became the concrete commentary to the naval policy inaugurated in 1899.

With its program for Turkish integrity, Germany came into conflict with the Balkan states, whose historic completion and inner growth are dependent upon the liquidation of European Turkey. It came into conflict with Italy, finally, whose imperialistic appetite was likewise longing for Turkish possessions. At the Morocco Conference at Algeciras[34] in 1905, Italy already sided with England and France. Six years later the Italian expedition to Tripoli,[35] which followed the Austrian annexation of Bosnia and gave the signal for the Balkan War, already indicated a withdrawal of Italy, foreshadowed the disruption of the Triple Alliance[36] and the isolation of German policies on this side as well. The other tendency of German expansionist desires in the West became evident in the Morocco affair.[37]

Nowhere was the negation of the Bismarck policy in Germany more clearly shown. Bismarck, as is well known, supported the colonial aspirations of France in order to distract its attention from Alsace-Lorraine. The new course of Germany, on the other hand, ran exactly counter to French colonial expansion. Conditions in Morocco were quite different from those that prevailed in Asiatic Turkey. Germany had few legitimate interests in Morocco. To be sure, German imperialists puffed up the claims of the German firm of Mannesmann, which had made a loan to the Moroccan Sultan and demanded mining concessions in return, into a national issue. But the well known fact that both of these rival groups in Morocco, the Mannesmann as well as the Krupp-Schneider Company, are a thoroughly international mixture of German, French and Spanish capitalists, prevents anyone from seriously speaking of a German sphere of interest. The more symptomatic was the determination and the decisiveness with which the German Empire, in 1905, suddenly announced its claim to participation in the regulation of Moroccan affairs, and protested against French rule in Morocco. This was the first world-political clash with France. In 1895 Germany, together with France and Russia, assumed a threatening attitude toward victorious Japan to prevent it from exploiting its victory over China at Shimonoseki.[38] Five years later it went arm in arm with France all along the line on a plundering expedition against China.

---

34. When a crisis threatened between France and Britain (who had entered into an "Entente Cordiale" in 1904) on the one hand, and Germany and Austro-Hungary on the other with the Kaiser's personal attempt to lead an expedition to Tangier, Morocco, in March 1905, US President Theodore Roosevelt organised a conference in Algeciras, Spain, on 16 January 1906. An agreement was signed on 7 April 1906, but the Morocco crisis was to brew again.
35. Tripoli, which had been under Turkish rule since 1551, was attacked by Italy in September 1911. Turkey was defeated, despite courageous resistance by the local population. Under the Treaty of Lausanne (October 1912), Tripoli and Cyrenaica became Italian colonies and remained so till 1943.
36. Following the Dual Alliance of 1979 (Germany and Austro-Hungary) the Triple Alliance was formed in 1882 between Germany, Austro-Hungary and Italy. Romania joined in 1883. It was repudiated by Italy in 1906 at the Algeciras Conference and Italy finally joined the "Entente" nations (Britain, France, Russia) in 1915.
37. i.e., the despatch of the German gunboat *Panther* to Agadir, Morocco.
38. The Treaty of Shimonoseki ended the Sino-Japanese war of 1895 and foreigners were granted the right to invest in China.

CHAPTER FOUR

Morocco caused a radical reorientation in Germany's relations with France. The Morocco crisis, which in seven years of its duration, twice brought Europe to the verge of war between France and Germany, was not a question of "revenge" for continental conflicts between the two nations. An entirely new conflict had arisen, German imperialism had come into competition with that of France. In the end, Germany was satisfied with the French Congo region, and in accepting this admitted that it had no special interests to protect in Morocco itself. This very fact gave to the German attack in Morocco a far reaching political significance. The very indefinitiveness of its tangible aims and demands betrayed its insatiable appetite, the seeking and feeling for prey – it was a general imperialistic declaration of war against France. The contrast between the two nations here was brought into the limelight. On the one hand, a slow industrial development, a stagnant population, a nation living on its investments, concerned chiefly with foreign financial business, burdened with a large number of colonial possessions that it could hold together only with the utmost difficulty. On the other hand, a mighty young giant, a capitalism forging toward the first place among nations, going out into the world to hunt for colonies. English colonies were out of the question. So the hunger of German imperialism, besides feeding on Asiatic Turkey, turned at once to the French heritage. The French colonies moreover were a convenient bait with which Italy might eventually be attracted and repaid for Austrian desires of expansion on the Balkan peninsula, and be thus more firmly welded into the Triple Alliance by mutual business interests. The demands Germany made upon French imperialism were exceedingly disturbing, especially when it is remembered that Germany, once it had taken a foothold in any part of Morocco, could at any time set fire to the entire French North African possessions, whose inhabitants were in a chronic state of incipient warfare with the French conquerors, by supplying them with ammunition. Germany's final withdrawal for suitable compensation did away with this immediate danger. But they could not allay the general disturbance in France and the world-political conflict that had been created.

Its Morocco policy not only brought Germany into conflict with France but with England as well. Here in Morocco, in the immediate neighbourhood of Gibraltar, the second important centre of world-political interests of the British government, the sudden appearance of German imperialism with its demands, and the drastic impressiveness with which these demands were supported, were regarded as a demonstration against England as well. Furthermore the first formal protest of 1911 was directed specifically against the agreement of 1904 between England and France concerning Egypt and Morocco.[39] Germany insisted briefly and definitely that England be disregarded in all further regulations of Moroccan affairs. The effect that such a demand was certain to have on German-English relations is obvious. The situation was commented upon in the *Frankfurter Zeitung* of November 8, 1911, by a London correspondent:

---

39. Under the terms of the Entente Cordiale between Britain and France in 1904, France was given a free hand in Morocco in exchange for a free hand for Britain in Egypt.

> This is the outcome: a million negroes in Congo, a great *Katzenjammer* [caterwaul] and a furious resentment against *perfides Albion*.⁴⁰ The *Katzenjammer* Germany will live down. But what is to become of our relations with England? As they stand today matters are untenable. According to every historic probability they will either lead to something worse, that is war, or they will have to be speedily patched up... The trip of the *Panther* was, as a Berlin correspondent said so well in the *Frankfurter Zeitung* the other day, a dig into the ribs of France to show that Germany is still here... Concerning the effect that this event would create here, Berlin cannot possibly entertain the slightest doubt. Certainly no correspondent in London was for a moment in doubt that England would stand energetically on the side of France. How can the *Norddeutsche Allgemeine Zeitung* still insist that Germany must treat with France alone? For several hundred years Europe has been the scene of a steadily increasing interweaving of political interests. The misfortune of one, according to the laws of politics, fills some with joy, others with apprehension. When two years ago Austria had its difficulties with Russia, Germany appeared upon the scene with shimmering armour, although Vienna, as was afterwards stated, would have preferred to settle matters without German intervention. It is very unlikely that England, having just emerged from a period of anti-German feeling, should consider that our dealings with France are none of its business. In the last analysis, it was a question of might; for a dig in the ribs, be it ever so friendly, it is a very tangible matter. For no one can be quite sure when a blow on the teeth may follow. Since then the situation has become less critical. At the moment when Lloyd George spoke, the danger of a war between Germany and England was acute. Are we justified in expecting a different attitude from Sir Edward Grey after the policies that he and his followers have been pursuing? If Berlin entertained such ideas then it seems to me that the German foreign policies have been weighed and found wanting.

Thus did our imperialistic policies create sharp conflicts in Asia Minor and Morocco, between England and Germany, between Germany and France. But what of German relations with Russia? In the murderous spirit that took possession of the German public during the first weeks of the war everything seemed credible. The German populace believed that Belgian women had gouged out the eyes of the German wounded, that Cossacks ate tallow candles, that they had taken infants by the legs and torn them to pieces; they believed that Russia aspired to the annexation of the German Empire, to the destruction of German "*Kultur*", to the introduction of absolutism from Kiel to Munich, from the Warthe to the Rhine. The Social Democratic *Chemnitzer Volksstimme* wrote on August 2nd:

> At this moment we all feel it our duty to fight first against the Russian knout. German women and children shall not become the victims of Russian bestiality, German territory must not fall into the hands of the Cossacks. For if the Entente is victorious, not the French Republicans, but the Russian Tsar will rule over Germany. In this moment we defend everything that we possess of German culture and German freedom against a pitiless and barbarous foe.

On the same day the *Fränkische Tagespost* cried out:

---

40. *Perfides Albion*: "perfidious Albion" – a pejorative phrase referring to the duplicity or treachery of British monarchs or governments. (Albion is an ancient poetic name for Great Britain.)

CHAPTER FOUR

> Shall the Cossacks, who have already taken possession of our border towns, in their onrush on our country, bring destruction to our cities? Shall the Russian Tsar, whose love of peace the Social Democrats refused to trust even on the day when his peace manifesto was published, who is the worst enemy of the Russian people themselves, rule over one man of German blood?

And the *Königsberger Volkszeitung* wrote on August 3rd:

> Not one of us can doubt, whether he is liable for military service or not, that he must do everything to keep these worthless vandals from our borders so long as the war may last. For if they should be victorious, thousands of our comrades will be condemned to horrible prison sentences. Under the Russian sceptre there is no such thing as self-expression of the people, no Social Democratic press is allowed to exist, Social Democratic meetings and organisations are prohibited. We cannot conceive for a moment the possibility of a Russian victory. While still upholding our opposition to war, we will all work together to protect ourselves against these vandals that rule the Russian nation.

We shall later enter a little more fully into the relations that exist between German culture and Russian tsarism. They form a chapter by itself in the position of the German Social Democracy on the war. This much may be said now: one might with as much justification assume that the tsar desires to annex Europe or the moon, as to speak of his desire to annex Germany. In the present war only two nations are threatened in their national existence, Belgium and Serbia. While we howled about safeguarding the national existence of Germany, our cannon were directed against these two states. It is impossible to discuss with people who still believe in the possibility of ritual murder. But to those who do not act from mob instinct, who do not think in terms of clumsy slogans that are invented to catch the rabble, who guide their thoughts by historic facts, it must be obvious that Russian tsarism cannot have such intentions. Russia is ruled by desperate criminals, but not by maniacs. And after all, the policies of absolutism, in spite of all their characteristic differences, have this similarity in all nations, that they live not on thin air but upon very real possibilities, in a realm where concrete things come into the closest contact with each other. We need have no fear of the arrest of our German comrades and their banishment to Siberia, nor of the introduction of Russian absolutism into Germany. For the statesmen of the bloody tsar, with all their mental inferiority, have a clearer materialistic conception of the situation than some of our party editors. These statesmen know very well that political forms of government cannot be "introduced" anywhere and everywhere according to the desire of the rulers; they know full well that every form of government is the outcome of certain economic and social foundations, they know from bitter experience that even in Russia itself conditions are almost beyond their power to control; they know, finally, that reaction in every country can use only the forms that are in accord with the nature of the country, and that the absolutism that is in accord with our class and party conditions is the Hohenzollern police state and the Prussian three-class electoral system. A dispassionate consideration of the whole situation will show that we need not fear that Russian tsarism, even if it should win a complete victory over Germany, would feel called upon to do away with these products of German culture.

In reality the conflicts that exist between Germany and Russia are of an entirely different nature. These differences are not to be found in the field of inner politics. Quite the contrary: their mutual tendencies and internal relationships have established a century-old traditional friendship between the two nations. But in spite of and notwithstanding their solidarity on questions of inner policy, they have come to blows in the field of foreign, world-political hunting grounds.

Russian imperialism, like that of western nations, consists of widely diversified elements. Its strongest strain is not, however, as in Germany or England, the economic expansion of capital, hungry for territorial accumulation, but the political interests of the nation. To be sure, Russian industry can show a considerable export to the Orient, to China, Persia and Central Asia, and the tsarist government seeks to encourage this export trade because it furnishes a desirable foundation for its sphere of interest. But national policies here play an active, not a passive, role. On the one hand, the traditional tendencies of a conquest-loving tsardom, ruling over a mighty nation whose population today consists of 172 millions of human beings, demand free access to the ocean, to the Pacific Ocean on the East, to the Mediterranean on the South, for industrial as well as for strategic reasons. On the other hand, the very existence of absolutism, and the necessity of holding a respected place in the world-political field, and finally the need of financial credit in foreign countries without which tsarism cannot exist, all play their important part. We must add to these, as in every other monarchy, the dynastic interest. Foreign prestige and temporary forgetfulness of inner problems and difficulties are well known family remedies in the art of ruling, when a conflict arises between the government and the great mass of the people.

But modern capitalist interests are becoming more and more a factor in the imperialist aims of the tsarist nation. Russian capitalism, still in its earliest youth, cannot hope to perfect its development under an absolutist regime. On the whole it has advanced little beyond the primitive stage of home industry. But it sees a gigantic future before its eyes in the exploitation of the nation's natural resources. As soon as Russia's absolutism is swept away, of this there can be no doubt, Russia will develop rapidly into the foremost capitalist nation, provided always that the international situation will give it the time necessary for such development. It is this hope, and the appetite for foreign markets that will mean increased capitalistic development even at the present time, that has filled the Russian bourgeoisie with imperialistic desires and led them to eagerly voice their demands in the coming division of the world's resources.

This historic desire is actively supported by very tangible immediate interests. There are, in the first place, the armament industry and its purveyors. In the second place the conflicts with the "enemy within", the revolutionary proletariat, have given to the Russian bourgeoisie an increased appreciation of the powers of militarism and the distracting efforts of a world-political evangel. It has bound together the various capitalist groups and the nobility under one counter-revolutionary regime. The imperialism of bourgeois Russia, particularly among the liberals, has grown enormously in the stormy atmosphere of the revolutionary period, and has given to the traditional foreign policies of the Romanovs a modern stamp. Chief among the aims of the traditional policies of monarchic Russia, as well as of the more modern appetites of the Russian bourgeoisie, are the Dardanelles. They are, according to the famous remark made by Bismarck, the latchkey to the Russian possessions on the Black Sea. Since the eighteenth century, Russia has waged a number of bloody wars against Turkey, has undertaken its mission as the liberator of the Balkans, for the realisation of this goal. For this ideal, Russia has piled up mountains of dead in Ismail, in Navarin, in Sinope, Silistria and Sevastopol, in Plevna and Shipka. To the Russian *muzhik* [peasant], the defence of his Slavic and Christian brothers from the horrors of Turkish oppression has become as potent a war legend as the defence of German culture and freedom against the horrors of Russia has become to the German Social Democracy.

But the Russian bourgeoisie also was much more enthusiastic over the Mediterranean prospect than for its Manchurian and Mongolian "mission". The liberal bourgeoisie of Russia criticised the Japanese war so severely as a senseless adventure, because it distracted the attention of Russian politics from the problem that was to them more important, the Balkans. And in another way, the unfortunate war with Japan had the same effect. The extension of Russian power into Eastern and Central Asia, to Tibet and down into Persia necessarily aroused a feeling of discomfort in the minds of English imperialists. England, fearing for its enormous Indian empire, viewed the Asiatic movements of Russia with growing suspicion. In fact, at the beginning of the present century the English-Russian conflict in Asia was the strongest world-conflict in the international situation. Moreover this will be, in all probability, the most critical issue in future world-political developments when the present war is over. The crushing defeat of Russia in 1904 and the subsequent outbreak of the Russian revolution only temporarily changed the situation. The apparent weakening of the empire of the tsar brought about a relaxation of the tension between England and Russia. In 1907 a treaty was signed between the two nations providing for a mutual control of Persia[41] that established, for the time being, friendly neighbourly relations in Central Asia. This kept Russia from undertaking great projects in the East, and her energies reverted all the more vigorously to their old occupation, Balkan politics. Here the Russia of the tsar came for the first time into sharp conflict with German culture, after a century of faithful and well-founded friendship. The road to the Dardanelles leads over the corpse of Turkey. But for more than a decade Germany has regarded the "integrity" of this corpse as its most important world-political task. Russian methods in the Balkans had changed at various times. Embittered by the ingratitude of the liberated Balkan Slavs who tried to escape from their position as vassals to the

---

41. The Anglo-Russian Treaty of 31 August 1907 divided Persia into three zones for development. Britain lost in the deal, as oil was soon discovered in the area she had abandoned. However, the Anglo-Persian Oil Company was soon formed.

tsarist government, Russia for a time supported the program of Turkish integrity with the silent understanding that the division of that country should be postponed to some more auspicious time. But today the final liquidation of Turkey coincides with the plans of both Russian and English politics. The latter aims to unite Arabia and Mesopotamia and the Russian territories that lie between Egypt and India, under British rule, into a great Mohammedan empire, thus conserving its own position in India and Egypt. In this way Russian imperialism, as in earlier times English imperialism, came into opposition with that of Germany. For this privileged exploiter of Turkish disintegration had taken up her position as sentinel on the Bosphorus.

Russian interests came to a clash in the Balkans not only directly with Germany but with Austria as well. Austrian imperialism is the political complement of German imperialism, at the same time its Siamese twin brother and its fate.

Germany, having isolated herself on all sides by her world policy, has in Austria her only ally. The alliance with Austria is old, having been founded by Bismarck in 1879. But since that time it has completely changed its character. Like the enmity toward France, the alliance with Austria received an entirely new content through the development of the last decades. In 1879 its chief purpose was the mutual defence of the possessions gained in the wars of 1864–70. The Bismarck Triple Alliance was conservative in character, especially since it signified Austria's final renunciation of admission to the German federation of states, its acceptance of the state of affairs created by Bismarck, and the military hegemony of Greater Prussia. The Balkan aspirations of Austria were as distasteful to Bismarck as the South African conquests of Germany. In his *Gedanken und Erinnerungen* [*Reflections and Reminiscences*, written in 1896–98] he says:

> It is natural that the inhabitants of the Danube region should have needs and aspirations that extend beyond the present boundaries of their monarchy. The German national constitution points out the way along which Austria can form a union of the political and material interests that exist between the most eastern Rumanian tribe and the Bay of Cattaro. But the duty of the German Empire does not demand that it satisfy the desires of its neighbours for increased territory with the blood and wealth of its subjects.

He expressed the same thought still more drastically when he uttered the well known sentiment that, to him, the whole of Bosnia was not worth the bone of a Pomeranian grenadier. Indeed, a treaty drawn up with Russia in 1884 proves conclusively that Bismarck never desired to place the Triple Alliance at the service of Austrian annexationist desires. By this treaty, the German Empire promised, in the event of a war between Austria and Russia, not to support the former, but rather to observe a "benevolent neutrality".

But since imperialism has taken hold of German politics, its relations to Austria have changed as well. Austria-Hungary lies between Germany and the Balkans, in other words, on the road over the critical point in German Oriental politics. To make Austria its enemy at this time would mean complete isolation, and complete abdication by Germany of its world-political plan. But the weakening of Austria, which would signify the final liquidation of Turkey, with a consequent strengthening of Russia, the Balkan states and England, would probably accomplish the national unification of Germany, but would, at the same time, wipe out, forever, its imperialistic aspirations. The safety of the Hapsburg monarchy has therefore logically become a necessary complement to German imperialism, the preservation of Turkey its chief problem.

But Austria means a constant latent state of war in the Balkans. For Turkish disintegration has promoted the existence and growth of the Balkan states in the immediate neighbourhood of the Hapsburg monarchy, and the resulting state of chronic incipient warfare. Obviously the existence of virile and independent national states on the border of a monarchy that is made up of fragments of these same nationalities, which it can rule only by the whip-lash of dictatorship, must hasten its downfall. Austrian Balkan politics and particularly its Serbian relations have plainly revealed its inner decay. Although its imperialistic appetites wavered between Salonika and Durazzo, Austria was not in a position to annex Serbia, even before the latter had grown in strength and size through the two Balkan wars. For the forcible annexation of Serbia would have dangerously strengthened in its interior one of the most refractory South Slavic nationalities, a people that even now, because of Austria's stupid regime of reaction, can scarcely be held in check. But neither can Austria tolerate the normal independent development of Serbia or profit from it by normal commercial relations. For the Hapsburg monarchy is not the political expression of a capitalist state, but a loose syndicate of a few parasitic cliques, striving to grasp everything within reach, utilising the political powers of the nation so long as this weak edifice still stands. For the benefit of Hungarian agrarians, and for the purpose of increasing the prices of agricultural products, Austria has forbidden Serbia to send cattle and fruits into Austria, thus depriving this nation of farmers of its most important market. In the interest of Austrian monopolies it has forced Serbia to import industrial products exclusively from Austria, and at the highest prices. To keep Serbia in a state of economic and political dependence, it prevented Serbia from uniting on the East with Bulgaria, to secure access to the Black Sea, and from securing access to the Adriatic, on the West, by prohibiting the acquisition of a harbour in Albania. In short, the Balkan policy of Austria was nothing more than a barefaced attempt to choke off Serbia. Also it was directed against the establishment of mutual relations between and against the inner growth of the Balkan states, and was, therefore, a constant menace for them.

Austrian imperialism constantly threatened the existence and development of the Balkan states, now by the annexation of Bosnia, now by its demands upon the Sanjak of Novibazar and on Saloniki, now by its encroachments upon the Albanian coast. To satisfy these tendencies on the part of Austria, and to meet the competition of Italy as well, the caricature of an independent Albania under the rule of a German nobleman was created after the second Balkan war, a country which was, from the first hour, little more than the plaything of the intrigues of imperialistic rivals.

Thus the imperialistic policies of Austria during the last decade were a constant hindrance to the normal progressive development of the Balkans, and led to the inevitable alternative: either the Hapsburg monarchy or the capitalist development of the Balkan states.

Emancipated from Turkish rule, the Balkans now faced its new hindrance, Austria, and the necessity of removing it from its path. Historically the liquidation of Austria-Hungary is the logical sequence of Turkish disintegration, and both are in direct line with the process of historical development.

There was but one solution: war – a world war. For behind Serbia stood Russia, unable to sacrifice its influence in the Balkans and its role of "protector" without giving up its whole imperialistic program in the Orient as well. In direct conflict with Austrian politics, Russia aimed to unite the Balkan states, under a Russian protectorate, to be sure. The Balkan union that had almost completely annihilated European Turkey in the victorious war of 1912 was the work of Russia, and was directly and intentionally aimed against Austria. In spite of Russian efforts, the Balkan union was smashed in the second Balkan war. But Serbia, emerging the victor, became dependent upon the friendship of Russia in the same degree as Austria had become Russia's bitter enemy. Germany, whose fate was firmly linked to that of the Hapsburg monarchy, was obliged to back up the stupid Balkan policy of the latter, step by step, and was thus brought into a doubly aggravated opposition to Russia.

But the Balkan policies of Austria, furthermore, brought Austria into conflict with Italy, which was actively interested in the dissolution of the Turkish and Austrian empires. The imperialism of Italy has found in the Italian possessions of Austria a most popular cloak for its own annexationist desires. Its eyes are directed especially toward the Albanian coast of the Adriatic, should a new regulation of Balkan affairs take place. The Triple Alliance, having already sustained a severe blow in the Tripolitan war, was destroyed by the acute crisis in the Balkans during the two Balkan wars. The Central Powers were thus brought into conflict with the entire outside world. German imperialism, chained to two decaying corpses, was steering its course directly toward a world war.

Moreover, Germany embarked upon this course with a full realisation of its consequences. Austria, as the motive power, was rushing blindly into destruction. Its clique of clerical-militarist rulers, with the Archduke Franz Ferdinand and his right-hand man Baron von Chlumezki at the head, fairly jumped at every excuse to strike the first blow. In 1909 Austria framed up the famous documents by Professor Friedmann, exposing what purported to be a widespread, criminal conspiracy of the Serbs against the Hapsburg monarchy for the sole purpose of infusing the German nations with the necessary war enthusiasm. These papers had only one slight drawback – they were forged from beginning to end. A year later the rumour of the horrible martyrdom of the Austrian consul Prohaska in Ueskub was busily spread for days to serve as the spark that would ignite the keg of powder, while Prohaska roamed unmolested and happy through the streets of Ueskub. Then came the assassination at Sarajevo, a long desired, truly shameful crime.[42]

---

42. On 28 June 1914 Archduke Franz Ferdinand, Crown Prince of Austria, and his wife, who were visiting Sarajevo

CHAPTER FOUR

"If ever blood sacrifice has had a liberating, releasing effect, it was the case here", rejoiced the spokesman of German imperialism. Among Austrian imperialists the rejoicing was still greater, and they decided to use the noble corpses while they were still warm. After a hurried conference with Berlin, war was virtually decided and the ultimatum sent out as a flaming torch that was to set fire to the capitalist world at all four corners.

But the occurrence at Sarajevo only furnished the immediate pretext. Causes and conflicts for the war had been overripe for a long time. The conjuncture that we witness today was ready a decade ago. Every year, every political occurrence of recent years has but served to bring war a step nearer: the Turkish revolution, the annexation of Bosnia, the Morocco crisis, the Tripoli expedition, the two Balkan wars. All military bills of the last years were drawn up in direct preparation for this war; the countries of Europe were preparing, with open eyes, for the inevitable final contest. Five times during recent years this war was on the verge of an outbreak: in the summer of 1905, when Germany for the first time made her decisive demands in the Morocco crisis; in the summer of 1908, when England, Russia and France threatened with war after the conference of the monarchs in Reval over the Macedonian question, and war was prevented only by the sudden outbreak of the Turkish revolution; at the beginning of 1909 when Russia replied to the Bosnian annexation with a mobilisation, when Germany in Petersburg formally declared its readiness to go to war on the side of Austria; in the summer of 1911 when the *Panther* was sent to Agadir, an act that would certainly have brought on war if Germany had not finally acquiesced in the Morocco question and allowed itself to be compensated with the Congo concession; and finally, at the beginning of 1913, when Germany, in view of the proposed Russian invasion of Albania, a second time threatened Petersburg with its readiness for warlike measures.

Thus the world war has been hanging fire for eight years. It was postponed again and again only because always one of the two sides in question was not yet ready with its military preparations.

So, for instance, the present world war was imminent at the time of the *Panther* adventure in 1911 – without a murdered Grand Duke, without French fliers over Nuremberg, without a Russian invasion into East Prussia. Germany simply put it off for a more favourable moment – one need only read the frank explanation of a German imperialist:

> The German government has been accused by the so-called pan-Germans of weakness in the Morocco crisis in 1911. Let them disabuse their minds of this false impression. It is a fact that, at the time when we sent the *Panther* to Agadir, the reconstruction of the North-East Sea Canal was still in progress, that building operations on Helgoland for the construction of a great fort were nowhere near completion, that our fleet of dreadnoughts and accessories, in comparison with the English sea power, was in a far more unfavourable position than was the case three years later.

(then part of Austro-Hungary) were killed by a Serbian patriot, Gavrilo Princip.

> Compared to the present time, 1914, the canal as well as Helgoland were in a deplorable state of unreadiness, were partially absolutely useless for war purposes. Under such circumstances, where one knows that one's chances will be far more favourable in a few years, it would be worse than foolish to provoke a war. First the German fleet had to be put in order; the great military bill had to be pushed through the Reichstag. In the summer of 1914 Germany was prepared for war, while France was still labouring over its three years military service program, while in Russia neither the army nor the naval program were ready. It was up to Germany to utilise the auspicious moment.

The same Rohrbach, who is not only the most serious representative of imperialism in Germany, but is also in intimate touch with the leading circles in German politics and is their semi-official mouthpiece, comments upon the situation in July 1914, as follows: "At this time there was only one danger, that we might be morally forced, by an apparent acquiescence on the part of Russia, to wait until Russia and France were really prepared". In other words, Germany feared nothing so much as that Russia might give in. "With deep pain we saw our untiring efforts to preserve world peace shipwrecked, etc., etc."[43]

The invasion of Belgium, therefore, and the accomplished fact of war was not a bolt from the blue. It did not create a new, unheard of situation. Nor was it an event that came, in its political associations, as a complete surprise to the Social Democratic group. The world war that began officially on August 4, 1914, was the same world war toward which German imperialism had been driving for decades, the same war whose coming the Social Democracy and prophesied year after year. This same war has been denounced by Social Democratic parliamentarians, newspapers and leaflets a thousand times as a frivolous imperialistic crime, as a war that is against every interest of culture and against every interest of the nation.

And, indeed, not the existence and the independent development of Germany in this war are at stake, in spite of the reiterations of the Social Democratic press, but the immediate profits of the Deutsche Bank in Asiatic Turkey and the future profits of the Mannesmann and Krupp interests in Morocco, the existence and the reactionary character of Austria, "this heap of organised decay, that calls itself the Hapsburg monarchy", as the *Vorwärts* wrote on 25 July, 1914.

Our party press was filled with moral indignation over the fact that Germany's foes should drive black men and barbarians, Negroes, Sikhs and Maoris into the war. Yet these peoples play a role in this war that is approximately identical with that played by the socialist proletariat in the European states. If the Maoris of New Zealand were eager to risk their skulls for the English king, they showed only as much understanding of their own interests as the German Social Democratic group that traded the existence, the freedom and the civilisation of the German people for the existence of the Hapsburg

---

43. The words quoted are those of Kaiser Wilhelm II.

CHAPTER FOUR

monarchy, for Turkey and for the vaults of the Deutsche Bank.

One difference there is between the two. A generation ago, Maori were still cannibals and not students of Marxist philosophy.

Chapter Five

But tsarism! In the first moments of the war this was undoubtedly the factor that decided the position of our party. In its declaration, the Social Democratic group had given the slogan: Against tsarism! And out of this the socialist press has made a fight for European culture.

The *Frankfurter Volksstimme* wrote on July 31:

> The German Social Democracy has always hated tsardom as the bloody guardian of European reaction: from the time that Marx and Engels followed, with far-seeing eyes, every movement of this barbarian government, down to the present day, where its prisons are filled with political prisoners, and yet it trembles before every labour movement. The time has come when we must square accounts with these terrible scoundrels, under the German flag of war.

The *Pfälzische Post* of Ludwigshafen wrote on the same day:

> This is a principle that was first established by our August Bebel. This is the struggle of civilisation against barbarism, and in this struggle the proletariat will do its share.

The *Münchener Post* of August 1:

> When it comes to defending our country against the bloody tsardom we will not be made citizens of the second class.

The *Halle Volksblatt* wrote on August 5:

> If this is so, if we have been attacked by Russia, and everything seems to corroborate this statement – then the Social Democracy, as a matter of course, must vote in favour of all means of defence. With all our strength we must fight to drive tsarism from our country!

And on August 18:

> Now that the die is cast in favour of the sword, it is not only the duty of national defence and national existence that puts the weapon into our hands as into the hands of every German, but also the realisation that in the enemy whom we are fighting in the east we are striking

a blow at the foe of all culture and all progress... The overthrow of Russia is synonymous with the victory of freedom in Europe.

On August 5, the *Braunschweiger Volksfreund* wrote:

> The irresistible force of military preparation drives everything before it. But the class-conscious labour movement obeys, not an outside force, but its own conviction, when it defends the ground upon which it stands from attack in the east.

The *Essener Arbeiterzeitung* cried out on August 3:

> If this country is threatened by Russia's determination, then the Social Democrats, since the fight is against Russian blood – tsarism, against the perpetrator of a million crimes against freedom and culture, will allow none to excel them in the fulfilment of their duty, in their willingness to sacrifice. Down with tsarism! Down with the home of barbarism! Let that be our slogan!

Similarly the *Bielefelder Volkswacht* writes on August 4: "Everywhere the same cry: against Russian despotism and faithlessness".

The Elberfeld party organ on August 5:

> All Western Europe is vitally interested in the extermination of rotten murderous tsarism. But this human interest is crushed by the greed of England and France to check the profits that have been made possible by German capital.

The *Rheinische Zeitung* in Cologne:

> Do your duty, friends, wherever fate may place you. You are fighting for the civilisation of Europe, for the independence of your fatherland, for your own welfare.

The *Schleswig-Holstein Volkszeitung* of August 7 writes:

> Of course we are living in an age of capitalism. Of course we will continue to have class struggles after the great war is over. But these class struggles will be fought out in a freer state, they will be far more confined to the economic field than before. In the future the treatment of socialists as outcasts, as citizens of the second class, as politically rightless will be impossible, once the tsardom of Russia has vanished.

On August 11, the *Hamburger Echo* cried:

> We are fighting to defend ourselves not so much against England and France as against tsarism. But this war we carry on with the greatest enthusiasm, for it is the war for civilisation.

And the Lübeck party organ declared, as late as September 4:

> If European liberty is saved, then Europe will have German arms to thank for it. Our fight is a fight against the worst enemy of all liberty and all democracy.

Thus the chorus of the German party press sounded and resounded.

In the beginning of the war the German government accepted the proffered assistance. Nonchalantly it fastened the laurels of the liberator of European culture to

CHAPTER FIVE

its helmet. Yes, it endeavoured to carry through the role of the "liberator of nations", though often with visible discomfort and rather awkward grace. It flattered the Poles and the Jews in Russia, and egged one nation on against the other, using the policies that had proven so successful in their colonial warfare, where again and again they played up one chief against the other. And the Social Democrats followed each leap and bound of German imperialism with remarkable agility. While the Reichstag group covered up every shameful outrage with a discreet silence, the Social Democratic press filled the air with jubilant melodies, rejoicing in the liberty that "German rifle butts" had brought to the poor victims of tsarism.

Even the theoretical organ of the party, *Neue Zeit*, wrote on August 28:

> The border population of the "little father's" realm greeted the coming of the German troops with cries of joy. For these Poles and Jews have but one conception of their fatherland, that of corruption and rule by the knout. Poor devils, really fatherlandless creatures, these downtrodden subjects of bloody Nicholas. Even should they desire to do so, they could find nothing to defend but their chains. And so they live and toil, hoping and longing that German rifles, carried by German men, will crush the whole tsarist system... A clear and definite purpose still lives in the German working class, though the thunder of a world war is crashing over its head. It will defend itself from the allies of Russian barbarism in the west to bring about an honourable peace. It will give to the task of destroying tsarism the last breath of man and beast.

After the Social Democratic group had stamped the war as a war of defence for the German nation and European culture, the Social Democratic press proceeded to hail it as the "saviour of the oppressed nations". Hindenburg became the executor of Marx and Engels.

The memory of our party has played it a shabby trick. It forgot all its principles, its pledges, the decision of international congresses, just at the moment when they should have found their application. And to its great misfortune, it remembered the heritage of Karl Marx and dug it out of the dust of passing years at the very moment when it could serve only to decorate Prussian militarism, for whose destruction Karl Marx was willing to sacrifice "the last breath of man and beast". Long forgotten chords that were sounded by Marx in the *Neue Rheinische Zeitung* against the vassal state of Nicholas I, during the German March Revolution of 1848, suddenly reawakened in the ears of the German Social Democracy in the year of Our Lord 1914, and called them to arms, arm in arm with Prussian junkerdom, against the Russia of the Great Revolution of 1905.

This is where a revision should have been made; the slogans of the March Revolution should have been brought into accord with the historical experiences of the last seventy years.

In 1848 Russian tsarism was, in truth, "the guardian of European reaction". The product of Russian social conditions, firmly rooted in its medieval, agricultural state, absolutism was the protector and at the same time the mighty director of monarchical reaction. This was weakened, particularly in Germany where a system of small states still obtained. As late as 1851 it was possible for Nicholas I to assure Berlin through the Prussian consul von Rochow "that he would, indeed, have been pleased to see the revolution destroyed by the roots when General von Wrangel advanced upon Berlin in November, 1848". At another time, in a warning to Manteuffel, the tsar stated "that he relied upon the imperial ministry, under the leadership of His Highness, to defend the rights of the crown against the chambers, and give to the principles of conservatism their due". It was possible for the same Nicholas I to bestow the Order of Alexander Nevski on a Prussian ministerial president in recognition of his "constant efforts to preserve legal order in Prussia".

The Crimean War worked a noticeable change in this respect. It ended with the military and therefore with the political bankruptcy of the old system. Russian absolutism was forced to grant reforms, to modernise its rule, to adjust itself to capitalist conditions. In so doing, it gave its little finger to the devil who already holds it firmly by the arm, and will eventually get it altogether. The Crimean War was, by the way, an instructive example of the kind of liberation that can be brought to a downtrodden people "at the point of a gun". The military overthrow at Sedan [in 1871] brought France its republic. But this republic was not the gift of the Bismarck soldiery. Prussia, at that time as today, can give to other peoples nothing but its own Junker rule. Republican France was the ripe fruit of inner social struggles and of the three revolutions that had preceded it. The crash at Sevastopol was in effect similar to that of Jena. But because there was no revolutionary movement in Russia, it led to the outward renovation and reaffirmation of the old regime.

But the reforms that opened the road for capitalist development in Russia during the 1860s were possible only with the money of a capitalist system. This money was furnished by western European capital. It came from Germany and France, and has created a new relationship that has lasted down to the present day. Russian absolutism is now subsidised by the western European bourgeoisie. No longer does the Russian rouble "roll in diplomatic chambers" as Prince William of Prussia bitterly complained in 1854, "into the very chambers of the king". On the contrary, German and French money is rolling to Petersburg to feed a regime that would long ago have breathed its last without this life-giving juice. Russian tsarism is today no longer the product of Russian conditions; its root lies in the capitalist conditions of western Europe. And the relationship is shifting from decade to decade. In the same measure as the old root of Russian absolutism in Russia itself is being destroyed, the new, west European root is growing stronger and stronger. Besides lending their financial support, Germany and France, since 1870, have been vying with each other to lend Russia their political support as well. As revolutionary forces arise from the womb of the Russian people itself to fight against Russian absolutism, they meet with an ever growing resistance in western Europe, which stands ready to lend to threatened tsarism its moral and political support. So when, in the beginning of the eighties, the older Russian socialist movement severely shook the tsarist government and partly destroyed its authority within and without, Bismarck made his treaty with Russia and strengthened its position in international politics.

Capitalist development, tenderly nurtured by tsarism with its own hands, finally bore fruit: in the nineties the revolutionary movement of the Russian proletariat began. The erstwhile "guardian of reaction" was forced to grant a meaningless constitution, to seek a new protector from the rising flood in its own country. And it found this protector – in Germany. The Germany of von Bülow must pay the debt of gratitude that the Prussia of Wrangel and Manteuffel had incurred. Relations were completely reversed. Russian support against the revolution in Germany is superseded by German aid against the revolution in Russia. Spies, outrages, betrayals – a demagogic agitation, like that which blessed the times of the Holy Alliance, was unleashed in Germany against the fighters for the cause of Russian freedom, and followed to the very doorsteps of the Russian Revolution. In the Königsberg trial of 1904 this wave of persecution was at its height. This trial threw a scathing light upon a whole historical development since 1848 and showed the complete change of relations between Russian absolutism and European reaction. "*Tua res agitur*" [Your problem is being attended to!] cried a Prussian minister of justice to the ruling classes of Germany, pointing to the tottering foundation of the tsarist regime. "The establishment of a democratic republic in Russia would strongly influence Germany", declared First District Attorney Schulze in Königsberg. "When my neighbour's home burns my own is also in danger." And his assistant Casper also emphasised: "It is naturally not indifferent to Germany's public interests whether this bulwark of absolutism stands or falls. Certainly the flames of a revolutionary movement may easily spring over into Germany...".

The revolution was overthrown, but the very causes that led to its temporary downfall are valuable in a discussion of the position taken by the German Social Democracy in this war. That the Russian uprising in 1905–6 was unsuccessful in spite of its unequalled expenditure of revolutionary force, its clearness of purpose and tenacity can be ascribed to two distinct causes. The one lies in the inner character of the revolution itself, in its enormous historical program, in the mass of economic and political problems that it was forced to face. Some of them, for instance, the agrarian problem, cannot possibly be solved within capitalist society. There was the difficulty furthermore of creating a class state for the supremacy of the modern bourgeoisie against the counter-revolutionary opposition of the bourgeoisie as a whole. To the onlooker it would seem that the Russian revolution was doomed to failure because it was a proletarian revolution with bourgeois duties and problems, or if you wish, a bourgeois revolution waged by socialist proletarian methods, a crash of two generations amid lightning and thunder, the fruit of the delayed industrial development of class conditions in Russia and their over-ripeness in western Europe. From this point of view its downfall in 1906 signifies not its bankruptcy, but the natural closing of the first chapter, upon which the second must follow with the inevitability of a natural law.

The second cause was of external nature; it lay in western Europe. European reaction once more hastened to help its endangered protégé; not with lead and bullets, although "German guns" were in German fists even in 1905 and only waited for a signal from Petersburg to attack the neighbouring Poles. Europe rendered an assistance that was equally valuable: financial subsidy and political alliances were arranged to help tsarism in Russia. French money paid for the armed forces that broke down the Russian Revolution; from Germany came the moral and political support that helped the Russian government to clamber out from the depths of shame into which Japanese torpedoes and Russian proletarian fists had thrust it. In 1910, in Potsdam, official Germany received Russian tsarism with open arms. The reception of the blood-stained monarch at the gates of the German capital was not only the German blessing for the throttling of Persia, but above all for the hangman's work of the Russian counter-revolution. It was the official banquet of German and European "*Kultur*" over what they believed to be the grave of the Russian Revolution.

And strange! At that time, when this challenging feast upon the grave of the Russian revolution was held in its own home, the German Social Democracy remained silent, and had completely forgotten "the heritage of our masters" from 1848. At that time, when the hangman was received in Potsdam, not a sound, not a protest, not an article vetoed this expression of solidarity with the Russian counter-revolution. Only since this war has begun, since the police permits it, the smallest party organ intoxicates itself with bloodthirsty attacks upon the hangman of Russian liberty. Yet nothing could have disclosed more clearly than did this triumphal tour of the tsar in 1910 that the oppressed Russian proletariat was the victim, not only of domestic reaction, but of western European reaction as well. Their fight, like that of the March revolutionists of 1848, was against reaction, not only in their own country, but against its guardians in all other European countries.

After the inhuman crusades of the counter-revolution had somewhat subsided, the revolutionary ferment in the Russian proletariat once more became active. The flood began to rise and to boil. Economic strikes in Russia, according to the official reports, involved 46,623 workers and 256,386 days in 1910; 96,730 workers and 768,556 days in 1911; and 89,771 workers and 1,214,881 days in the first five months of 1912. Political mass strikes, protests and demonstrations comprised 1,005,000 workers in 1912, 1,272,000 in 1913. In 1914 the flood rose higher and higher. On January 22, the anniversary of the beginning of the revolution, there was a demonstration mass strike of 200,000 workers. As in the days before the revolution of 1905, the flame broke out in June, in the Caucasus. In Baku, 40,000 workers were on a general strike. The flames leaped over to Petersburg. On the 17th of June 80,000 workers in Petersburg laid down their tools, on the 20th of July, 200,000 were out; by July 23 the general strike movement was spreading out all over Russia, barricades were being built, the revolution was on its way. A few more

CHAPTER FIVE

months and it would have come, its flags fluttering in the wind. A few more years, and perhaps the whole world political constellation would have been changed, imperialism, perhaps would have received a firm check on its mad impulse.

But German reaction checked the revolutionary movement. From Berlin and Vienna came declarations of war, and the Russian revolution was buried beneath its wreckage. "German guns" are shattering, not tsarism, but its most dangerous enemy. The hopefully fluttering flag of the revolution sank down amid a wild whirlpool of war. But it sank honourably, and it will rise again out of the horrible massacre, in spite of "German guns", in spite of victory or defeat for Russia on the battlefields.

The national revolts in Russia which the Germans tried to foster, too, were unsuccessful. The Russian provinces were evidently less inclined to fall for the bait of Hindenburg's cohorts than the German Social Democracy. The Jews, practical people that they are, were able to count on their fingers that "German fists" which have been unable to overthrow their own Prussian reaction, can hardly be expected to smash Russian absolutism. The Poles, exposed to the triple-headed war, were not in a position to answer their "liberators" in audible language. But they will have remembered that Polish children were taught to say the Lord's Prayer in the German language with bloody welts on their backs, will not have forgotten the liberality of Prussian anti-Polish laws. All of them, Poles, Jews and Russians, had no difficulty in understanding that the "German gun", when it descends upon their heads, brings not liberty, but death.

To couple the legend of Russian liberation with its Marxian heritage is worse than a poor joke on the part of the German Social Democracy. It is a crime. To Marx, the Russian revolution was a turning point in the history of the world. Every political and historical perspective was made dependent upon the one consideration: "provided the Russian revolution has not already broken out". Marx believed in the Russian revolution and expected it even at a time when Russia was only a state of vassals. When the war broke out the Russian revolution had occurred. Its first attempt had not been victorious; but it could not be ignored; it is on the order of the day. And yet our German Social Democrats came with "German guns," declaring the Russian revolution null and void, struck it from the pages of history. In 1848 Marx spoke from the German barricades; in Russia there was a hopeless reaction. In 1914 Russia was in the throes of a revolution; while its German "liberators" were cowed by the fists of Prussian Junkerdom.

But the liberating mission of the German armies was only an episode. German imperialism soon raised its uncomfortable mask and turned openly against France and England. Here, too, it was supported valiantly by a large number of the party papers. They ceased railing against the bloody tsar, and held up "perfidious Albion" and its merchant soul to the public disdain. They set out to free Europe, no longer from Russian absolutism, but from English naval supremacy. The hopeless confusion in which the party had become entangled found a drastic illustration in the desperate attempt made by the more thoughtful portion of our party press to meet this new change of front.

In vain they tried to force the war back into its original channels, to nail it down to the "heritage of our masters" – that is, to the myth that they, the Social Democracy, had themselves created. "With heavy heart I have been forced to mobilise the army against a neighbour at whose side I have fought on so many battlefields. With honest sorrow I saw a friendship, truly served by Germany, break." That was simple, open, honest. But when the rhetoric of the first weeks of war backed down before the lapidary language of imperialism, the German Social Democracy lost its only plausible excuse.

Chapter Six

Of equal importance in the attitude of the Social Democracy was the official adoption of a program of civil peace, i.e., the cessation of the class struggle for the duration of the war. The declaration that was read by the Social Democratic group in the Reichstag on the 4th of August had been agreed upon in advance with representatives of the government and the capitalist parties. It was little more than a patriotic grandstand play, prepared behind the scenes and delivered for the benefit of the people at home and in other nations.

To the leading elements in the labour movement, the vote in favour of the war credits by the Reichstag group was a cue for the immediate settlement of all labour controversies. Nay more, they announced this to the manufacturers as a patriotic duty incurred by labour when it agreed to observe a civil peace. These same labour leaders undertook to supply city labour to farmers in order to assure a prompt harvest. The leaders of the Social Democratic women's movement united with capitalist women for "national service" and placed the most important elements that remained after the mobilisation at the disposal of national Samaritan work. Socialist women worked in soup kitchens and on advisory commissions instead of carrying on agitation work for the party.

Under the anti-socialist laws the party had utilised parliamentary elections to spread its agitation and to keep a firm hold upon the population in spite of the state of siege that had been declared against the party and the persecution of the socialist press. In this crisis the Social Democratic movement has voluntarily relinquished all propaganda and education in the interest of the proletarian class struggle, during Reichstag and Landtag elections. Parliamentary elections have everywhere been reduced to the simple bourgeois formula; the catching of votes for the candidates of the party on the basis of an amicable and peaceful settlement with its capitalist opponents. When the Social Democratic representatives in the Landtag and in the municipal commissions – with the laudable exceptions of the Prussian and Alsatian Landtag – with high-sounding references to the existing state of civil peace, voted their approval of the war credits that had been demanded, it only emphasised how completely the party had broken with things as they were before the war.

The Social Democratic press, with a few exceptions, proclaimed the principle of national unity as the highest duty of the German people. It warned the people not to withdraw their funds from the savings banks lest by so doing they unbalance the economic life of the nation, and hinder the savings banks in liberally buying war-loan bonds. It pleaded with proletarian women that they should spare their husbands at the front the tales of suffering that they and their children were being forced to undergo, to bear in silence the neglect of the government, to cheer the fighting warriors with happy stories of family life and favourable reports of prompt assistance through government agencies. They rejoiced that the educational work that had been conducted for so many years in and through the labour movement had become a conspicuous asset in conducting the war. Something of this spirit the following example will show:

> A friend in need is a friend indeed. This old adage has once more proven its soundness. The Social Democratic proletariat that has been prosecuted and clubbed for its opinions went, like one man, to protect our homes. German labour unions that had so often suffered both in Germany and in Prussia report unanimously that the best of their members have joined the colours. Even capitalist papers like the *General-Anzeiger* note the fact and express the conviction that "these people" will do their duty as well as any man, that blows will rain most heavily where they stand.

> As for us, we are convinced that our labour unionists can do more than deal out blows. Modern mass armies have by no means simplified the work of their generals. It is practically impossible to move forward large troop divisions in close marching order under the deadly fire of modern artillery. Ranks must be carefully widened, must be more accurately controlled. Modern warfare requires discipline and clearness of vision not only in the divisions but in every individual soldier. The war will show how vastly human material has been improved by the educational work of the labour unions, how well their activity will serve the nation in these times of awful stress. The Russian and the French soldier may be capable of marvellous deeds of bravery. But in cool, collected consideration none will surpass the German labour unionists. Then too, many of our organised workers know the ways and byways of the borderland as well as they know their own pockets, and not a few of them are accomplished linguists. The Prussian advance in 1866 has been termed a schoolmasters' victory. This will be a victory of labour union leaders. (*Frankfurter Volksstimme*, August 18, 1914)

In the same strain *Neue Zeit*, the theoretical organ of the party, declared (number 23, 25 September 1914):

> Until the question of victory or defeat has been decided, all doubts must disappear, even as to the causes of the war. Today there can be no difference of party, class and nationality within the army or the population.

And in number 8, 27 November 1914, the same *Neue Zeit* declared in a chapter on "The

Limitations of the International":

> The world war divides the socialists of the world into different camps and especially into different national camps. The International cannot prevent this. In other words, the International ceases to be an effective instrument in times of war. It is, on the whole, a peace instrument. Its great historic problem is the struggle for peace and the class struggle in times of peace.

Briefly, therefore, beginning with the 4th of August until the day when peace shall be declared, the Social Democracy has declared the class struggle extinct. The first thunder of Krupp cannons in Belgium welded Germany into a wonderland of class solidarity and social harmony.

How is this miracle to be understood? The class struggle is known to be not a Social Democratic invention that can be arbitrarily set aside for a period of time whenever it may seem convenient to do so. The proletarian class struggle is older than the Social Democracy, is an elementary product of class society. It flamed up all over Europe when capitalism first came into power. The modern proletariat was not led by the Social Democracy into the class struggle. On the contrary, the international Social Democratic movement was called into being by the class struggle to bring a conscious aim and unity into the various local and scattered fragments of the class struggle.

What then has changed in this respect when the war broke out? Have private property, capitalist exploitation and class rule ceased to exist? Or have the propertied classes in a spell of patriotic fervour declared: in view of the needs of the war we hereby turn over the means of production, the earth, the factories and the mills therein, into the possession of the people? Have they relinquished the right to make profits out of these possessions? Have they set aside all political privileges, will they sacrifice them upon the altar of the fatherland, now that it is in danger? It is, to say the least, a rather naive hypothesis, and sounds almost like a story from a kindergarten primer. And yet the declaration of our official leaders that the class struggle has been suspended permits no other interpretation. Of course nothing of the sort has occurred. Property rights, exploitation and class rule, even political oppression in all its Prussian thoroughness, have remained intact. The cannons in Belgium and in Eastern Prussia have not had the slightest influence upon the fundamental social and political structure of Germany.

The cessation of the class struggle was, therefore, a deplorably one-sided affair. While capitalist oppression and exploitation, the worst enemies of the working class, remain; socialist and labour union leaders have generously delivered the working class, without a struggle, into the hands of the enemy for the duration of the war. While the ruling classes are fully armed with the property and supremacy rights, the working class, on the advice of the Social Democracy, has laid down its arms.

Once before, in 1848 in France, the proletariat experienced this miracle of class harmony, this fraternity of all classes of a modern capitalist state of society. In his *Class Struggles in France*, Karl Marx writes:

> In the eyes of the proletariat, who confused the moneyed aristocracy with the bourgeoisie, in the imagination of republican idealists, who denied the very existence of classes, or attributed them to a monarchical form of government, in the deceitful phrases of those bourgeois who had hitherto been excluded from power, the rule of the bourgeoisie was ended when the republic was proclaimed. At that time all royalists became republican, all millionaires in Paris became labourers. In the word *Fraternité*, the brotherhood of man, this imaginary destruction of classes found official expression. This comfortable abstraction from class differences, this sentimental balancing of class interests, this utopian disregard of the class struggle, this *Fraternité* was the real slogan of the February Revolution... The Parisian proletariat rejoiced in an orgy of brotherhood... The Parisian proletariat, looking upon the republic as its own creation, naturally acclaimed every act of the provisional bourgeois government. Willingly it permitted Caussidière to use its members as policemen to protect the property of Paris. With unquestioning faith it allowed Louis Blanc to regulate wage differences between workers and masters. In their eyes it was a matter of honour to preserve the fair name of the republic before the peoples of Europe.

Thus in February 1848, a naive Parisian proletariat set aside the class struggle. But let us not forget that even they committed this mistake only after the July monarchy had been crushed by their revolutionary action, after a republic had been established. The 4th of August, 1914, is an inverted February Revolution. It is the setting aside of class differences, not under a republic, but under a military monarchy, not after a victory of the people over reaction, but after a victory of reaction over the people, not with the proclamation of *Liberté, Égalité, Fraternité*, but with the proclamation of a state of siege, after the press had been choked and the constitution annihilated.

Impressively the government of Germany proclaimed a civil peace. Solemnly the parties promised to abide by it. But as experienced politicians these gentlemen know full well that it is fatal to trust too much in promises. They secured civil peace for themselves by the very real measure of a military dictatorship. This too the Social Democratic group accepted without protest or opposition. In the declarations of August 4 and December 2 there is not a syllable of indignation over the affront contained in the proclamation of military rule. When it voted for civil peace and war credits, the Social Democracy silently gave its consent to military rule as well, and laid itself, bound and gagged, at the feet of the ruling classes. The declaration of military rule was purely an anti-socialist measure. From no other side were resistance, protest, action and difficulties to be expected. As a reward for its capitulation the Social Democracy merely received what it would have received under any circumstances, even after an unsuccessful resistance, namely, military rule. The impressive declaration of the Reichstag group emphasises the old socialist principle of the right of nations to self-determination, as an explanation of their vote in favour of war credits. Self-determination for the German proletariat was the straitjacket of a siege. Never in the history of the world has a party made itself more ridiculous.

But, more! In refuting the existence of the class struggle, the Social Democracy has denied the very basis of its own existence. What is the very breath of its body, if not the class struggle? What role could it expect to play in the war, once having sacrificed the class struggle, the fundamental principle of its existence? The Social Democracy has destroyed its mission, for the period of the war, as an active political party, as a representative of working-class politics. It has thrown aside the most important weapon it possessed, the power of criticism of the war from the peculiar point of view of the working class. Its only mission now is to play the role of the gendarme over the working class under a state of military rule.

German freedom, that same German freedom for which, according to the declaration of the Reichstag group, Krupp cannons are now fighting, has been endangered by this attitude of the Social Democracy far beyond the period of the present war. The leaders of the Social Democracy are convinced that democratic liberties for the working class will come as a reward for its allegiance to the fatherland. But never in the history of the world has an oppressed class received political rights as a reward for service rendered to the ruling classes. History is full of examples of shameful deceit on the part of the ruling classes, even when solemn promises were made before the war broke out. The Social Democracy has not assured the extension of liberty in Germany. It has sacrificed those liberties that the working class possessed before the war broke out.

The indifference with which the German people have allowed themselves to be deprived of the freedom of the press, of the right of assembly and of public life, the fact that they not only calmly bore, but even applauded, the state of siege is unexampled in the history of modern society. In England the freedom of the press has nowhere been violated, in France there is incomparably more freedom of public opinion than in Germany. In no country has public opinion so completely vanished, nowhere has it been so completely superseded by official opinion, by the order of the government, as in Germany. Even in Russia there is only the destructive work of a public censor who effectively wipes out opposition of opinion. But not even there have they descended to the custom of providing articles ready for the press to the opposition papers.

In no other country has the government forced the opposition press to express in its columns the politics that have been dictated and ordered by the government in "Confidential Conferences". Such measures were unknown even in Germany during the war of 1870. At that time the press enjoyed unlimited freedom, and accompanied the events of the war, to Bismarck's active resentment, with criticism that was often exceedingly sharp. The newspapers were full of active discussion on war aims, on questions of annexation and constitutionality. When Johann Jacobi was arrested, a storm of indignation swept over Germany, so that even Bismarck felt obliged to disavow all responsibility for this "mistake" of the powers of reaction. Such was the situation in Germany at a time when Bebel and Liebknecht, in the name of the German working class, had declined all community of interests with the ruling jingoes. It took a Social Democracy with four and a half million votes to conceive of the touching *Burgfrieden*,[44]

[44.] Literally meaning "fortress peace", this refers to the political truce the SPD agreed to at the outbreak of the war. The SPD would vote for war credits in the Reichstag and not criticise the government, and the trade unions would refrain from striking.

to assent to war credits, to bring upon us the worst military dictatorship that was ever suffered to exist. That such a thing is possible in Germany today, had not only the bourgeois press, but the highly developed and influential socialist press as well, permits these things without even the pretence of opposition bears a fatal significance for the future of German liberty. It proves that society in Germany today has within itself no foundation for political freedom, since it allows itself to be thus lightly deprived of its most sacred rights.

Let us not forget that the political rights that existed in Germany before the war were not won, as were those of France and England, in great and repeated revolutionary struggles, are not firmly anchored in the lives of the people by the power of revolutionary tradition. They are the gift of a Bismarckian policy granted after a period of victorious counter-revolution that lasted over twenty years. German liberties did not ripen on the field of revolution, they are the product of diplomatic gambling by Prussian military monarchy, they are the cement with which this military monarchy has united the present German Empire. Danger threatens the free development of German freedom not, as the German Reichstag group believes, from Russia, but in Germany itself. It lies in the peculiar counter-revolutionary origin of the German constitution, and looms dark in the reactionary powers that have controlled the German state since the Empire was founded, conducting a silent but relentless war against these pitiful "German liberties".

The Junkers of East of the Elbe, the business jingoes, the arch-reactionaries of the Centre, the degraded "German liberals", the personal rulership, the sway of the sword, the Zabern policy[45] that triumphed all over Germany before the war broke out, these are the real enemies of culture and liberty; and the war, the state of siege and the attitude of the Social Democracy are strengthening the powers of darkness all over the land. The liberal, to be sure, can explain away this graveyard quietly in Germany with a characteristically liberal explanation; to him it is only a temporary sacrifice, for the duration of the war. But to a people that are politically ripe, a sacrifice of their rights and their public life, even temporarily, is as impossible as for a human being to give up, for a time, his right to breathe. A people that gives silent consent to military government in times of war thereby admits that political independence at any time is superfluous. The passive submission of the Social Democracy to the present state of siege and its vote for war credits without attaching the slightest condition thereto, its acceptance of a civil peace, has demoralised the masses, the only existing pillar of German constitutional government, has strengthened the reaction of its rulers, the enemies of constitutional government.

By sacrificing the class struggle, our party has moreover, once and for all, given up the possibility of making its influence effectively felt in determining the extent of the war and the terms of peace. To its own official declaration, its acts have been a stinging blow. While protesting against all annexations, which are, after all, the logical consequences

---

45. This term has its origins in the arbitrary and illegal acts by the Prussian military against the population of Zabern (Saverne) in Alsace-Lorraine in 1913; it came to refer to the abuse of military authority or to tyrannical, aggressive conduct in general.

of an imperialist war that is successful from the military point of view, it has handed over every weapon that the working class possessed that might have empowered the masses to mobilise public opinion in their own direction, to exert an effective pressure upon the terms of war and of peace. By assuring militarism of peace and quiet at home, the Social Democracy has given its military rulers permission to follow their own course without even considering the interests of the masses, has unleashed in the hearts of the ruling classes the most unbridled imperialistic tendencies. In other words, when the Social Democracy adopted its platform of civil peace, and the political disarmament of the working class, it condemned its own demand of no annexations to impotence.

Thus the Social Democracy has added another crime to the heavy burden it already has to bear, namely the lengthening of the war. The commonly accepted dogma that we can oppose the war only so long as it is threatened has become a dangerous trap. As an inevitable consequence, once the war has come, Social Democratic political action is at an end. There can be, then, but one question, victory or defeat, i.e., the class struggle must stop for the period of the war. But actually the greatest problem for the political movement of the Social Democracy begins only after the war has broken out. At the International congresses held in Stuttgart in 1907 and in Basel in 1912, the German party and labour union leaders unanimously voted in favour of a resolution which says:

> Should war nevertheless break out, it shall be the duty of the Social Democracy to work for a speedy peace, and to strive with every means in its power to utilise the industrial and political crisis to accomplish the awakening of the people, thus hastening the overthrow of the capitalist class rule.

What has the Social Democracy done in this war? Exactly the contrary. By voting in favour of war credits and entering upon a civil peace, it has striven, by all the means in its power, to prevent the industrial and political crisis, to prevent an awakening of the masses by the war. It strives "with all the means in its power" to save the capitalist state from its own anarchy to reduce the number of its victims. It is claimed – we have often heard this argument used by Reichstag deputies – that not one man less would have fallen upon the battlefields if the Social Democratic group had voted against the war credits. Our party press has steadfastly maintained that we must support and join in the defence of our country in order to reduce the number of bloody victims that this war shall cost.

But the policy that we have followed has had exactly the opposite effect. In the first place, thanks to the civil peace, and the patriotic attitude of the Social Democracy, the imperialist war unleashed its furies without fear. Hitherto, fear of restiveness at home, fear of the fury of the hungry populace, have been a load upon the minds of the ruling classes that effectively checked them in their bellicose desires. In the well-known words of von Bülow: "They are trying to put off the war chiefly because they fear the Social Democracy". Rohrbach says in his *Krieg und die Deutsche Politik*, page 7, "unless elemental catastrophes intervene, the only power that can force Germany to make peace is the hunger of the breadless". Obviously, he meant a hunger that attracts attention, that forces itself unpleasantly upon the ruling classes in order to force them to pay heed to its demands. Let us see, finally, what a prominent military theoretician, General Bernhardi, says, in his great work *Vom Heutigen Kriege*:

> Thus modern mass armies make war difficult for a variety of reasons. Moreover they constitute, in and of themselves, a danger that must never be underestimated.
>
> The mechanism of such an army is so huge and so complicated, that it can remain efficient and flexible only so long as its cogs and wheels work, in the main, dependably, and obvious moral confusion is carefully prevented. These are things that cannot be completely avoided, as little as we can conduct a war exclusively with victorious battles. They can be overcome if they appear only within certain restricted limits. But when great, compact masses once shake off their leaders, when a spirit of panic becomes widespread, when a lack of sustenance becomes extensively felt, when the spirit of revolt spreads out among the masses of the army, then the army becomes not only ineffectual against the enemy, it becomes a menace to itself and to its leaders. When the army bursts the bands of discipline, when it voluntarily interrupts the course of military operation, it creates problems that its leaders are unable to solve.
>
> War, with its modern mass armies, is, under all circumstances, a dangerous game, a game that demands the greatest possible sacrifice, personal and financial sacrifice the state can offer. Under such circumstances it is clear that provision must be made everywhere that the war, once it has broken out, be brought to an end as quickly as possible, to release the extreme tension that must accompany this supreme effort on the part of whole nations.

Thus capitalist politicians and military authorities alike believe war, with its modern mass armies, to be a dangerous game. And therein lay for the Social Democracy the most effectual opportunity to prevent the rulers of the present day from precipitating war and to force them to end it as rapidly as possible. But the position of the Social Democracy in this war cleared away all doubts, has torn down the dams that held back the storm-flood of militarism. In fact it has created a power for which neither Bernhardi nor any other capitalist statesman dared hope in his wildest dreams. From the camp of the Social Democrats came the cry: "*Durchhalten*" [see it through], i.e., the continuation of this human slaughter. And so the thousands of victims that have fallen for months on battlefields lie upon our conscience.

Chapter Seven

> But since we have been unable to prevent the war, since it has come in spite of us, and our country is facing invasion, shall we leave our country defenceless! Shall we deliver it into the hands of the enemy? Does not socialism demand the right of nations to determine their own destinies? Does it not mean that every people is justified, nay more, is in duty bound, to protect its liberties, its independence? "When the house is on fire, shall we not first try to put out the blaze before stopping to ascertain the incendiary?"

These arguments have been repeated, again and again in defence of the attitude of the social democracy in Germany and in France.

Even in the neutral countries this argument has been used. Translated into Dutch we read for instance: "When the ship leaks must we not seek, first of all, to stop the hole?"

To be sure. Fie upon a people that capitulates before invasion and fie upon a party that capitulates before the enemy within.

But there is one thing that the firemen in the burning house have forgotten: that in the mouth of a socialist, the phrase "defending one's fatherland" cannot mean playing the role of cannon fodder under the command of an imperialistic bourgeoisie.

Is an invasion really the horror of all horrors, before which all class conflict within the country must subside as though spellbound by some supernatural witchcraft? According to the police theory of bourgeois patriotism and military rule, every evidence of the class struggle is a crime against the interests of the country because they maintain that it constitutes a weakening of the stamina of the nation. The Social Democracy has allowed itself to be perverted into this same distorted point of view. Has not the history of modern capitalist society shown that in the eyes of capitalist society, foreign invasion is by no means the unmitigated terror as it is generally painted; that on the contrary, it is a measure to which the bourgeoisie has frequently and gladly resorted as an effective weapon against the enemy within? Did not the Bourbons and the aristocrats of France invite foreign invasion against the Jacobins? Did not the Austrian counter-revolution in 1849 call out the French invaders against Rome, the Russian against Budapest? Did not the "Party of Law and Order" in France in 1850 openly threaten an invasion of the Cossacks in order to bring the National Assembly to terms? And was not the Bonaparte army released, and the support of the Prussian army against the Paris Commune assured, by the famous contract between Jules Favre, Thiers and Co. and Bismarck?

This historical evidence led Karl Marx, forty-five years ago, to expose the "national wars" of modern capitalist society as miserable frauds. In his famous address to the General Council of the International on the downfall of the Paris Commune, he said:

> That, after the greatest war of modern times the belligerent armies, the victor and the vanquished, should unite for the mutual butchery of the proletariat – this incredible event proves, not as Bismarck would have us believe, the final overthrow of the new social power, but the complete disintegration of the old bourgeois society. The highest heroic accomplishment of which the old order is capable is the national war. And this has now proved to be a fraud perpetrated by government for no other purpose than to put off the class struggle, a fraud that is bared as soon as the class struggle flares up in a civil war. Class rule can no longer hide behind a national uniform. The national governments are united against the proletariat.

In capitalist history, invasion and class struggle are not opposites, as the official legend would have us believe, but one is the means and the expression of the other. Just as invasion is the true and tried weapon in the hands of capital against the class struggle, so on the other hand the fearless pursuit of the class struggle has always proven the most effective preventive of foreign invasions. On the brink of modern times are the examples of the Italian cities, Florence and Milan, with their century of bitter struggle against the Hohenstaufen. The stormy history of these cities, torn by inner conflicts, proves that the force and the fury of inner class struggles not only does not weaken the defensive powers of the community, but that, on the contrary, from their fires shoot the only flames that are strong enough to withstand every attack from a foreign foe.

But the classic example of our own times is the Great French Revolution. In 1793 Paris, the heart of France, was surrounded by enemies. And yet Paris and France at that time did not succumb to the invasion of a stormy flood of European coalition; on the contrary, it welded its force in the face of the growing danger to a more gigantic opposition. If France, at that critical time, was able to meet each new coalition of the enemy with a new miraculous and undiminished fighting spirit, it was only because of the impetuous loosening of the inmost forces of society in the great struggle of the classes of France. Today, in the perspective of a century, it is clearly discernible that only this intensification of the class struggle, that only the dictatorship of the French people and their fearless radicalism, could produce means and forces out of the soil of France, sufficient to defend and to sustain a newborn society against a world of enemies, against the intrigues of a dynasty, against the traitorous machinations of the aristocrats, against the attempts of the clergy, against the treachery of their generals, against the opposition of sixty departments and provincial capitals, and against the united armies and navies of monarchical Europe. The centuries have proven that not the state of siege, but relentless class struggle, is the power that awakens the spirit of self-sacrifice, the moral strength of the masses; that the class struggle is the best protection and the best defence against a foreign enemy.

This same tragic *quid pro quo* victimised the Social Democracy when it based its attitude in this war upon the doctrine of the right of national self-determination.

It is true that socialism gives to every people the right of independence and the freedom of independent control of its own destinies. But it is a veritable perversion of socialism to regard present-day capitalist society as the expression of this self-determination of nations. Where is there a nation in which the people have had the right to determine the form and conditions of their national, political and social existence? In Germany the determination of the people found concrete expression in the demands formulated by the German revolutionary democrats of 1848; the first fighters of the German proletariat, Marx, Engels, Lassalle, Bebel and Liebknecht, proclaimed and fought for a united German Republic. For this ideal the revolutionary forces in Berlin and in Vienna, in those tragic days of March, shed their heart's blood upon the barricades. To carry out this program, Marx and Engels demanded that Prussia take up arms against tsarism. The foremost demand made in the national program was for the liquidation of "the heap of organised decay, the Habsburg monarchy", as well as of two dozen other dwarf monarchies within Germany itself. The overthrow of the German revolution, the treachery of the German bourgeoisie to its own democratic ideals, led to the Bismarck regime and to its creature, present-day Greater Prussia, twenty-five fatherlands under one helm, the German Empire.

Modern Germany is built upon the grave of the March Revolution [of 1848], upon the wreckage of the right of self-determination of the German people. The present war, supporting Turkey and the Habsburg monarchy and strengthening German military autocracy, is a second burial of the March revolutionists, and of the national program of the German people. It is a fiendish jest of history that the Social Democrats, the heirs of the German patriots of 1848, should go forth in this war with the banner of "self-determination of nations" held aloft in their hands. But, perhaps the Third French Republic, with its colonial possessions in four continents and its colonial horrors in two, is the expression of the self-determination of the French nation? Or the British nation, with its India, with its South African rule of a million whites over a population of five million coloured people? Or perhaps Turkey, or the empire of the tsar?

Capitalist politicians, in whose eyes the rulers of the people and the ruling classes are the nation, can honestly speak of the "right of national self-determination" in connection with such colonial empire. To the socialist, no nation is free whose national existence is based upon the enslavement of another people, for to him colonial peoples, too, are human beings, and, as such, parts of the national state. International socialism recognises the right of free independent nations, with equal rights. But socialism alone can create such nations, can bring self-determination of their peoples. This slogan of socialism is like all its others, not an apology for existing conditions, but a guidepost, a spur for the revolutionary, regenerative, active policy of the proletariat. So long as capitalist states exist, i.e., so long as imperialistic world policies determine and regulate the inner and the outer life of a nation, there can be no "national self-determination" either in war or in peace.

In the present imperialistic milieu there can be no wars of national self-defence. Every socialist policy that depends upon this determining historic milieu, that is willing to fix its policies in the world whirlpool from the point of view of a single nation, is built upon a foundation of sand.

We have already attempted to show the background for the present conflict between Germany and her opponents. It was necessary to show up more clearly the actual forces and relations that constitute the motive power behind the present war, because this legend of the defence of the existence, the freedom and civilisation of Germany plays an important part in the attitude of our group in the Reichstag and our socialist press. Against this legend historical truth must be emphasised to show that this is a war that has been prepared by German militarism and its world political ideas for years, that it was brought about in the summer of 1914, by Austrian and German diplomacy, with a full realisation of its import.

In a discussion of the general causes of the war, and of its significance, the question of the "guilty party" is completely beside the issue. Germany certainly has not the right to speak of a war of defence, but France and England have little more justification. They too are protecting, not their national, but their world political existence, their old imperialistic possessions, from the attacks of the German upstart. Doubtless the raids of German and Austrian imperialism in the Orient started the conflagration, but French imperialism, by devouring Morocco, and English imperialism, in its attempts to rape Mesopotamia, and all the other measures that were calculated to secure its rule of force in India, Russia's Baltic policies, aiming toward Constantinople, all of these factors have carried together and piled up, brand for brand, the firewood that feeds the conflagration. If capitalist armaments have played an important role as the mainspring that times the outbreak of the catastrophe, it was a competition of armaments in all nations. And if Germany laid the cornerstone for European competitive armaments by Bismarck's policy of 1870, this policy was furthered by that of the second empire and by the military-colonial policies of the third empire, by its expansions in East Asia and in Africa.

The French socialists have some slight foundation for their illusion of "national defence", because neither the French government nor the French people entertained the slightest warlike desires in July 1914. "Today everyone in France is honestly, uprightly and without reservation for peace", insisted Jaurès in the last speech of his life, on the eve of the war, when he addressed a meeting in the People's House in Brussels. This was absolutely true, and gives the psychological explanation for the indignation of the French socialists when this criminal war was forced upon their country. But this fact was not sufficient to determine the socialist attitude on the world war as a historic occurrence.

The events that bore the present war did not begin in July 1914 but reach back for decades. Thread by thread they have been woven together on the loom of an inexorable natural development until the firm net of imperialist world politics has encircled five continents. It is a huge historical complex of events, whose roots reach deep down into the Plutonic deeps of economic creation, whose outermost branches spread out and point away into a dimly dawning new world, events before whose all-embracing immensity, the conception of guilt and retribution, of defence and offence, sink into pale nothingness.

Imperialism is not the creation of any one or of any group of states. It is the product of a particular stage of ripeness in the world development of capital, an innately international condition, an indivisible whole, that is recognisable only in all its relations, and from which no nation can hold aloof at will. From this point of view only is it possible to understand correctly the question of "national defence" in the present war.

The national state, national unity and independence were the ideological shield under which the capitalist nations of central Europe constituted themselves in the past century. Capitalism is incompatible with economic and political divisions, with the accompanying splitting up into small states. It needs for its development large, united territories, and a state of mental and intellectual development in the nation that will lift the demands and needs of society to a plane corresponding to the prevailing stage of capitalist production, and to the mechanism of modern capitalist class rule. Before capitalism could develop, it sought to create for itself a territory sharply defined by national limitations. This program was carried out only in France at the time of the great revolution, for in the national and political heritage left to Europe by the feudal middle ages, this could be accomplished only by revolutionary measures. In the rest of Europe this nationalisation, like the revolutionary movement as a whole, remained the patchwork of half-kept promises. The German empire, modern Italy, Austria-Hungary, Turkey, the Russian empire and the British world empire are all living proofs of this fact. The national program could play a historic role only so long as it represented the ideological expression of a growing bourgeoisie, lusting for power, until it had fastened its class rule, in some way or other, upon the great nations of central Europe and had created within them the necessary tools and conditions of its growth. Since then, imperialism has buried the old bourgeois democratic program completely by substituting expansionist activity irrespective of national relationships for the original program of the bourgeoisie in all nations. The national phase, to be sure, has been preserved, but its real content, its function, has been perverted into its very opposite. Today the nation is but a cloak that covers imperialistic desires, a battle cry for imperialistic rivalries, the last ideological measure with which the masses can be persuaded to play the role of cannon fodder in imperialistic wars.

This general tendency of present-day capitalist policies determines the policies of the individual states as their supreme blindly operating law, just as the laws of economic competition determine the conditions under which the individual manufacturer shall produce.

Let us assume for a moment, for the sake of argument, for the purpose of investigating this phantom of "national wars" that controls Social Democratic politics at the present time, that in one of the belligerent states, the war at its outbreak was purely one of national defence. Military success would immediately demand the occupation of foreign territory. But the existence of influential capitalist groups interested in imperialistic annexations will awaken expansionist appetites as the war goes on. The imperialistic tendency that, at the beginning of hostilities, may have been existent only in embryo, will shoot up and expand in the hothouse atmosphere of war until they will in a short time determine its character, its aims and its results.

Furthermore, the system of alliance between military states that has ruled the political relations of these nations for decades in the past makes it inevitable that each of the belligerent parties, in the course of war, should try to bring its allies to its assistance, again purely from motives of self-defence. Thus one country after another is drawn into the war, inevitably new imperialistic circles are touched and others are created. Thus England drew in Japan, and, spreading the war into Asia, has brought China into the circle of political problems and has influenced the existing rivalry between Japan and the United States, between England and Japan, thus heaping up new material for future conflicts. Thus Germany has dragged Turkey into the war, bringing the question of Constantinople, of the Balkans and of Western Asia directly into the foreground of affairs.

Even he who did not realise at the outset that the world war, in its causes, was purely imperialistic, cannot fail to see after a dispassionate view of its effects that war, under the present conditions, automatically and inevitably develops into a process of world division. This was apparent from the very first. The wavering balance of power between the two belligerent parties forces each, if only for military reasons, in order to strengthen its own position, or in order to frustrate possible attacks, to hold the neutral nations in check by intensive deals in peoples and nations, such as the German-Austrian offers to Italy, Rumania, Bulgaria and Greece on the one hand, and the English-Russian bids on the other. The "national war of defence" has the surprising effect of creating, even in the neutral nations, a general transformation of ownership and relative power, always in direct line with expansionist tendencies. Finally the fact that all modern capitalist states have colonial possessions that will, even though the war may have begun as a war of national defence, be drawn into the conflict from purely military considerations, the fact that each country will strive to occupy the colonial possessions of its opponent, or at least to create disturbances therein, automatically turns every war into an imperialistic world conflagration.

Thus the conception of even that modest, devout fatherland-loving war of defence that has become the ideal of our parliamentarians and editors is pure fiction, and shows,

CHAPTER SEVEN

on their part, a complete lack of understanding of the whole war and its world relations. The character of the war is determined, not by solemn declaration, not even by the honest intentions of leading politicians, but by the momentary configuration of society and its military organisations. At the first glance the term "national war of defence" might seem applicable in the case of a country like Switzerland. But Switzerland is no national state, and, therefore, no object of comparison with other modern states. Its very "neutral" existence, its luxury of a militia are after all only the negative fruits of a latent state of war in the surrounding great military states. It will hold this neutrality only so long as it is willing to oppose this condition. How quickly such a neutral state is crushed by the military heel of imperialism in a world war the fate of Belgium shows.

This brings us to the peculiar position of the "small nation". A classic example of such "national wars" is Serbia. If ever a state, according to formal considerations, had the right of national defence on its side, that state is Serbia. Deprived through Austrian annexations of its national unity, threatened by Austria in its very existence as a nation, forced by Austria into war, it is fighting, according to all human conceptions, for existence, for freedom, and for the civilisation of its people. But if the Social Democratic group is right in its position, then the Serbian Social Democrats who protested against the war in the parliament at Belgrade and refused to vote war credits are actually traitors to the most vital interests of their own nation. In reality the Serbian socialists Laptchevic and Kaclerovic have not only enrolled their names in letters of gold in the annals of the international socialist movement, but have shown a clear historical conception of the real causes of the war. In voting against war credits they therefore have done their country the best possible service. Serbia is formally engaged in a national war of defence. But its monarchy and its ruling classes are filled with expansionist desires as are the ruling classes in all modern states. They are indifferent to ethnic lines, and thus their warfare assumes an aggressive character. Thus Serbia is today reaching out toward the Adriatic coast where it is fighting out a real imperialistic conflict with Italy on the backs of the Albanians, a conflict whose final outcome will be decided not by either of the powers directly interested, but by the great powers that will speak the last word on terms of peace. But above all this we must not forget: behind Serbian nationalism stands Russian imperialism. Serbia itself is only a pawn in the great game of world politics. A judgment of the war in Serbia from a point of view that fails to take these great relations and the general world political background into account is necessarily without foundation.

The same is true of the recent Balkan war. Regarded as an isolated occurrence, the young Balkan states were historically justified in defending the old democratic program of the national state. In their historical connection, however, which makes the Balkans the burning point and the centre of imperialistic world policies, these Balkan wars, also, were objectively only a fragment of the general conflict, a link in the chain of events that led, with fatal necessity, to the present world war. After the Balkan war the international Social Democracy tendered to the Balkan socialists, for their determined refusal to offer moral or political support to the war, a most enthusiastic ovation at the peace congress at Basel. In this act alone the International condemned in advance the position taken by the German and French socialists in the present war.

All small states, as for instance Holland, are today in a position like that of the Balkan states. "When the ship leaks, the hole must be stopped"; and what, forsooth, could little Holland fight for but for its national existence and for the independence of its people? If we consider here merely the determination of the Dutch people, even of its ruling classes, the question is doubtlessly one purely of national defence. But again proletarian politics cannot judge according to the subjective purposes of a single country. Here again it must take its position as a part of the International, according to the whole complexity of the world's political situation. Holland, too, whether it wishes to be or not, is only a small wheel in the great machine of modern world politics and diplomacy. This would become clear at once, if Holland were actually torn into the maelstrom of the world war. Its opponents would direct their attacks against its colonies. Automatically Dutch warfare would turn to the defence of its present possessions. The defence of the national independence of the Dutch people on the North Sea would expand concretely to the defence of its rule and right of exploitation over the Malays in the East Indian Archipelago. But not enough: Dutch militarism, if forced to rely upon itself, would be crushed like a nutshell in the whirlpool of the world war. Whether it wished to or not it would become a member of one of the great national alliances. On one side or the other it must be the bearer and the tool of purely imperialistic tendencies.

Thus it is always the historic milieu of modern imperialism that determines the character of the war in the individual countries, and this milieu makes a war of national self-defence impossible.

Kautsky also expressed this, only a few years ago, in his pamphlet *Patriotism and Social Democracy*, (Leipzig 1907, pages 12–14):

> Though the patriotism of the bourgeoisie and of the proletariat are two entirely different, actually opposite, phenomena, there are situations in which both kinds of patriotism may join forces for united action, even in times of war. The bourgeoisie and the proletariat of a nation are equally interested in their national independence and self-determination, in the removal of all kinds of oppression and exploitation at the hands of a foreign nation. In the national conflicts that have sprung from such attempts, the patriotism of the proletariat has always united with that of the bourgeoisie. But the proletariat has become a power that may become dangerous to the ruling classes at every great national upheaval; revolution looms dark at the end of every war, as the Paris Commune of 1871 and Russian terrorism after the Russo-Japanese war have proven.
>
> In view of this the bourgeoisie of those nations which are not sufficiently united have actually sacrificed their national aims where these can be maintained only at the expense of the government, for they hate and fear the revolution even more than they love national independence and greatness. For this reason, the bourgeoisie sacrifices the independence of Poland and permits ancient constellations like Austria and Turkey to remain in existence,

though they have been doomed to destruction for more than a generation. National struggles as the bringers of revolution have ceased in civilised Europe. National problems that today can be solved only by war or revolution will be solved in the future only by the victory of the proletariat. But then, thanks to international solidarity, they will at once assume a form entirely different from that which prevails today in a social state of exploitation and oppression. In capitalist states this problem needs no longer to trouble the proletariat in its practical struggles. It must divert its whole strength to other problems.

Meanwhile the likelihood that proletarian and bourgeois patriotism will unite to protect the liberty of the people is becoming more and more rare.

Kautsky then goes on to say that the French bourgeoisie has united with tsarism, that Russia has ceased to be a danger for western Europe because it has been weakened by the revolution.

> Under these circumstances a war in defence of national liberty in which bourgeois and proletarian may unite is nowhere to be expected. (ibid., p.16)

> We have already seen that conflicts which, in the nineteenth century, might still have led some liberty-loving peoples to oppose their neighbours, by warfare, have ceased to exist. We have seen that modern militarism nowhere aims to defend important popular rights, but everywhere strives to support profits. It activities are dedicated not to assure the independence and invulnerability of its own nationality, that is nowhere threatened, but to the assurance and the extension of overseas conquests that again only serve the aggrandisement of capitalist profits. At the present time the conflicts between states can bring no war that proletarian interests would not, as a matter of duty, energetically oppose. (ibid., p.23)

In view of all these considerations, what shall be the practical attitude of the Social Democracy in the present war? Shall it declare: since this is an imperialist war, since we do not enjoy in our country, any socialist self-determination, its existence or non-existence is of no consequence to us, and we will surrender it to the enemy? Passive fatalism can never be the role of a revolutionary party like the Social Democracy. It must neither place itself at the disposal of the existing class state, under the command of the ruling classes, nor can it stand silently by to wait until the storm is past. It must adopt a policy of active class politics, a policy that will whip the ruling classes forward in every great social crisis and that will drive the crisis itself far beyond its original extent. That is the role that the Social Democracy must play as the leader of the fighting proletariat.

Instead of covering this imperialist war with a lying mantle of national self-defence, the Social Democracy should have demanded the right of national self-determination seriously, should have used it as a lever against the imperialist war.

The most elementary demand of national defence is that the nation takes its defence into its own hands. The first step in this direction is the militia; not only the immediate armament of the entire adult male populace, but above all, popular decision in all questions of peace and war. It must demand, furthermore, the immediate removal of every form of political oppression, since the greatest political freedom is the best basis for national defence. To proclaim these fundamental measures of national defence, to demand their realisation, that was the first duty of the Social Democracy.

For forty years we have tried to prove to the ruling classes as well as to the masses of the people that only the militia is really able to defend the fatherland and to make it invincible. And yet, when the first test came, we turned over the defence of our country, as a matter of course, into the hands of the standing army to be cannon fodder under the club of the ruling classes. Our parliamentarians apparently did not even notice that the fervent wishes with which they sped these defenders of the fatherland to the front were, to all intents and purposes, an open admission that the imperial Prussian standing army is the real defender of the fatherland. They evidently did not realise that by this admission they sacrificed the fulcrum of our political program, that they gave up the militia and dissolved the practical significance of forty years of agitation against the standing army into thin air. By the act of the Social Democratic group our military program became a utopian doctrine, a doctrinaire obsession, that none could possibly take seriously.

The masters of the international proletariat saw the idea of the defence of the fatherland in a different light. When the proletariat of Paris, surrounded by Prussians in 1871, took the reins of the government into its own hands, Marx wrote enthusiastically:

> Paris, the centre and seat of the old government powers, and simultaneously the social centre of gravity of the French working class, Paris has risen in arms against the attempt of Monsieur Thiers and his Junkers to reinstate and perpetuate the government of the old powers of imperial rule. Paris was in a position to resist only, because through a state of siege, it was rid of its army, because in its place there had been put a national guard composed chiefly of working men. It was necessary that this innovation be made a permanent institution. The first act of the Commune was, therefore, the suppression of the standing army and the substitution of an armed people... If now, the Commune was the true representative of all healthy elements of French society and, therefore, a true national government, it was likewise, as a proletarian government, as the daring fighter for the liberation of labour, international in the truest sense of that word. Under the eyes of the Prussian army, which has annexed two French provinces to Germany, the Commune has annexed the workers of a whole world to France. (*Address of the General Council of the International*)

But what did our masters say concerning the role to be played by the Social Democracy in the present war? In 1892 Friedrich Engels expressed the following opinion concerning the fundamental lines along which the attitude of proletarian parties in a great war should follow:

> A war in the course of which Russians and Frenchmen should invade Germany would mean for the latter a life and death struggle. Under such circumstances it could assure its national existence only by using the most revolutionary methods. The present government, should it not be forced to do so, will certainly not bring on the revolution, but we have a strong party that may force its hand, or that, should it be necessary, can replace it, the Social Democratic Party.

CHAPTER SEVEN

> We have not forgotten the glorious example of France in 1793. The one hundredth anniversary of 1793 is approaching. Should Russia's desire for conquest, or the chauvinistic impatience of the French bourgeoisie check the victorious but peaceable march of the German socialists, the latter are prepared – be assured of that – to prove to the world that the German proletarians of today are not unworthy of the French *sans culottes*, that 1893 will be worthy of 1793. And should the soldiers of Monsieur Constans set foot upon German territory we will meet them with the words of the *Marseillaise*:
>
> Shall hateful tyrants, mischief breeding,
>
> With hireling host, a ruffian band,
>
> Affright and desolate the land?
>
> In short, peace assures the victory of the Social Democratic Party in about ten years. The war will bring either victory in two or three years or its absolute ruin for at least fifteen or twenty years.

When Engels wrote these words, he had in mind a situation entirely different from the one existing today. In his mind's eye, ancient tsarism still loomed threateningly in the background. We have already seen the great Russian Revolution. He thought, furthermore, of a real national war of defence, of a Germany attacked on two sides, on the east and on the west by two enemy forces. Finally, he overestimated the ripeness of conditions in Germany and the likelihood of a social revolution, as all true fighters are wont to overrate the real tempo of development. But for all that, his sentences prove with remarkable clearness, that Engels meant by national defence, in the sense of the Social Democracy, not the support of a Prussian Junker military government and its *Generalstab* [general staff], but a revolutionary action after the example of the French Jacobins.

Yes, socialists should defend their country in great historical crises, and here lies the great fault of the German Social Democratic Reichstag group. When it announced on the 4th of August, "in this hour of danger, we will not desert our fatherland", it denied its own words in the same breath. For truly it has deserted its fatherland in its hour of greatest danger. The highest duty of the Social Democracy toward its fatherland demanded that it expose the real background of this imperialist war, that it rend the net of imperialist and diplomatic lies that covers the eyes of the people. It was their duty to speak loudly and clearly, to proclaim to the people of Germany that in this war victory and defeat would be equally fatal, to oppose the gagging of the fatherland by a state of siege, to demand that the people alone decide on war and peace, to demand a permanent session of parliament for the period of the war, to assume a watchful control over the government by parliament, and over parliament by the people, to demand the immediate removal of all political inequalities, since only a free people can adequately govern its country, and finally, to oppose to the imperialist war, based as it was upon the most reactionary forces in Europe, the program of Marx, of Engels and of Lassalle.

That was the flag that should have waved over the country. That would have been truly national, truly free, in harmony with the best traditions of Germany and the international class policy of the proletariat.

The great historical hour of the world war obviously demanded unanimous political accomplishment, a broad-minded, comprehensive attitude that only the Social Democracy is destined to give. Instead, there followed, on the part of the parliamentary representatives of the working class, a miserable collapse. The Social Democracy did not adopt the wrong policy – it had no policy whatsoever. It has wiped itself out completely as a class party with a world conception of its own, has delivered the country, without a word of protest, to the fate of imperialist war without, to the dictatorship of the sword within. Nay more, it has taken the responsibility for the war upon its own shoulders. The declaration of the Reichstag group says: "We have voted only the means for our country's defence. We decline all responsibility for the war". But as a matter of fact, the truth lies in exactly the opposite direction. The means for "national defence", i.e., for imperialistic mass butchery by the armed forces of the military monarchy, were not voted by the Social Democracy. For the availability of the war credits did not in the least depend upon the social Democracy. They, as a minority, stood against a compact three-quarters majority of the capitalist Reichstag. The Social Democratic group accomplished only one thing by voting in favour of the war credits. It placed upon the war the stamp of democratic fatherland defence, and supported and sustained the fictions that were propagated by the government concerning the actual conditions and problems of the war.

Thus the serious dilemma between the national interests and international solidarity of the proletariat, the tragic conflict that made our parliamentarians fall "with heavy heart" to the side of imperialistic warfare, was a mere figment of the imagination, a bourgeois nationalist fiction. Between the national interests and the class interests of the proletariat, in war and in peace, there is actually complete harmony. Both demand the most energetic prosecution of the class struggle, and the most determined insistence on the Social Democratic program.

But what action should the party have taken to give to our opposition to the war and to our war demands weight and emphasis? Should it have proclaimed a general strike? Should it have called upon the soldiers to refuse military service? Thus the question is generally asked. To answer with a simple yes or no were just as ridiculous as to decide: "When war breaks out we will start a revolution". Revolutions are not "made" and great movements of the people are not produced according to technical recipes that repose in the pockets of the party leaders. Small circles of conspirators may organise a riot for a certain day and a certain hour, can give their small group of supporters the signal to begin. Mass movements in great historical crises cannot be initiated by such primitive measures.

The best prepared mass strike may break down miserably at the very moment when the party leaders give the signal, may collapse completely before the first attack. The success of the great popular movements depends on, aye, the very time and circumstance of their inception is decided by, a number of economic, political and psychological factors. The existing degree of tension between the classes, the degree of intelligence of the masses and the degree or ripeness of their spirit of resistance – all these factors, which are incalculable, are premises that cannot be artificially created by any party. That is the difference between the great historical upheavals and the small show-demonstrations that a well-disciplined party can carry out in times of peace, orderly, well-trained performances, responding obediently to the baton in the hands of the party leaders. The great historical hour itself creates the forms that will carry the revolutionary movements to a successful outcome, creates and improvises new weapons, enriches the arsenal of the people with weapons unknown and unheard of by the parties and their leaders.

What the Social Democracy as the advance guard of the class-conscious proletariat should have been able to give was not ridiculous precepts and technical recipes, but a political slogan, clearness concerning the political problems and interests of the proletariat in times of war.

For what has been said of mass strikes in the Russian revolution is equally applicable to every mass movement:

> While the revolutionary period itself commands the creation and the computation and payment of the cost of a mass strike, the leaders of the Social Democracy have an entirely different mission to fill. Instead of concerning itself with the technical mechanism of the mass movement, it is the duty of the Social Democracy to undertake the political leadership even in the midst of a historical crisis. To give the slogan, to determine the direction of the struggle, to so direct the tactics of the political conflict that in its every phase and movement the whole sum of available and already mobilised active force of the proletariat is realised and finds expression in the attitude of the party, that the tactics of the Social Democracy in determination and vigour shall never be weaker than is justified by the actual power at its back, but shall rather hasten in advance of its actual power, that is the important problem of the party leadership in a great historical crisis. Then this leadership will become, in a sense, the technical leadership. A determined, consistent, progressive course of action on the part of the Social Democracy will create in the masses assurance, self-confidence and a fearless fighting spirit. A weakly vacillating course, based upon a low estimate of the powers of the proletariat, lames and confuses the masses. In the first case mass action will break out "of its own accord" and "at the right time"; in the second, even a direct call to action on the part of the leaders often remains ineffectual. (*The Mass Strike, The Political Party and the Trade Unions*)

Far more important than the outward, technical form of the action is its political content. Thus the parliamentary stage, for instance, the only far reaching and internationally conspicuous platform, could have become a mighty motive power for the awakening of the people, had it been used by the Social Democratic representatives to proclaim loudly and distinctly the interests, the problems and the demands of the working class.

"Would the masses have supported the Social Democracy in its attitude against the war?" That is a question that no one can answer. But neither is it an important one. Did our parliamentarians demand an absolute assurance of victory from the generals of the Prussian army before voting in favour of war credits? What is true of military armies is equally true of revolutionary armies. They go into the fight, wherever necessity demands it, without previous assurance of success. At the worst, the party would have been doomed, in the first few months of the war, to political ineffectuality.

Perhaps the bitterest persecutions would have been inflicted upon our party for its manly stand, as they were, in 1870, the reward of Liebknecht and Bebel. "But what does that matter", said Ignaz Auer, simply, in his speech on the Sedanfeier in 1895. "A party that is to conquer the world must bear its principles aloft without counting the dangers that this may bring. To act differently is to be lost!" Said the older Liebknecht:

> It is never easy to swim against the current. And when the stream rushes on with the rapidity and the power of a Niagara it does not become easier. Our older comrades still remember the hatred of that year of greatest national shame, under the socialist exception laws of 1878. At that time millions looked upon every Social Democrat as having played the part of a murderer and vile criminal in 1870; the socialist had been in the eyes of the masses a traitor and an enemy. Such outbreaks of the "popular soul" are astounding, stunning, crushing in their elemental fury. One feels powerless, as before a higher power. It is a real *force majeure*. There is no tangible opponent. It is like an epidemic, in the people, in the air, everywhere.
>
> The outbreak of 1878 cannot, however, be compared with the outbreak in 1870. This hurricane of human passions, breaking, bending, destroying all that stands in its way – and with it the terrible machinery of militarism, in fullest, most horrible activity; and we stand between the crushing iron wheels, whose touch means instant death, between iron arms, that threaten every moment to catch us. By the side of this elemental force of liberated spirits stood the most complete mechanism of the art of murder the world had hitherto seen; and all in the wildest activity, every boiler heated to the bursting point. At such a time, what is the will and the strength of the individual? Especially, when one feels that one represents a tiny minority, that one possesses no firm support in the people itself.
>
> At that time our party was still in a period of development. We were placed before the most serious test, at a time when we did not yet possess the organisation necessary to meet it. When the anti-socialist movement came in the year of shame of our enemies, in the year of honour for the Social Democracy, then we had already a strong, widespread organisation. Each and every one of us was strengthened by the feeling that he possessed a mighty support in the organised movement that stood behind him, and no sane person could conceive of the downfall of the party.
>
> So it was no small thing at that time to swim against the current. But what is to be done, must be done. And so we gritted our teeth in the face of the inevitable. There was no time for fear... Certainly Bebel and I...never for a moment thought of the warning. We did not retreat. We had to hold our posts, come what might!

They stuck to their posts, and for forty years the Social Democracy lived upon the moral strength with which it had opposed a world of enemies.

The same thing would have happened now. At first we would perhaps have accomplished nothing but to save the honour of the proletariat, and thousands upon thousands of proletarians who are dying in the trenches in mental darkness would not have died in spiritual confusion, but with the one certainty that that which has been everything in their lives, the international, liberating Social Democracy is more than the figment of a dream.

The voice of our party would have acted as a wet blanket upon the chauvinistic intoxication of the masses. It would have preserved the intelligent proletariat from delirium, would have it more difficult for imperialism to poison and to stupefy the minds of the people. The crusade against the Social Democracy would have awakened the masses in an incredibly short time.

And as the war went on, as the horror of endless massacre and bloodshed in all countries grew and grew, as its imperialistic hoof became more and more evident, as the exploitation by bloodthirsty speculators became more and more shameless, every live, honest, progressive and humane element in the masses would have rallied to the standard of the Social Democracy. The German Social Democracy would have stood in the midst of this mad whirlpool of collapse and decay, like a rock in a stormy sea, would have been the lighthouse of the whole International, guiding and leading the labour movements of every country of the earth. The unparalleled moral prestige that lay in the hands of the German socialists would have reacted upon the socialists of all nations in a very short time. Peace sentiments would have spread like wildfire and the popular demand for peace in all countries would have hastened the end of the slaughter, would have decreased the number of its victims.

The German proletariat would have remained the lighthouse keeper of socialism and of human emancipation.

Truly this was a task not unworthy of the disciples of Marx, Engels and Lassalle.

Chapter Eight

In spite of the military dictatorship and censorship of the press, in spite of the abdication of the Social Democrats, in spite of the fratricidal war, the class struggle rises with elemental force from out of the *Burgfrieden*; and the international solidarity of labour from out of the bloody mists of the battlefield. Not in the weak and artificial attempts to galvanise the old International, not in pledges renewed here and there to stand together again *after* the war. No! Now in and from the war the fact emerges with a wholly new power and energy that the proletarians of all lands have one and the same interests. The war itself dispels the illusion it has created.

Victory or defeat? Thus sounds the slogan of the ruling militarism in all the warring countries, and, like an echo, the Social Democratic leaders have taken it up. Supposedly, victory or defeat on the battlefield should be for the proletarians of Germany, France, England or Russia exactly the same as for the ruling classes of these countries. As soon as the cannons thunder, every proletarian should be interested in the victory of his own country and, therefore, in the defeat of the other countries. Let us see what such a victory can bring to the proletariat.

According to the official version, adopted uncritically by the Social Democratic leaders, German victory holds the prospect of unlimited economic growth, while defeat means economic ruin. This conception rests upon the pattern of the war of 1870. However, the flourishing capitalism following that war was not the consequence of the war but of the political unification, even though this came in the crippled form of Bismarck's German Empire. Economic growth proceeded out of unification *despite* the war and the many reactionary obstacles that came in its wake. What the victorious war contributed to all this was the entrenchment of the military monarchy in Germany and the rule of the Prussian Junkers; the defeat of France helped liquidate the [Second] Empire and establish the [Third] Republic.

But today matters are quite different in the belligerent states. Today war does not function as a dynamic method of procuring for rising young capitalism the preconditions of its "national" development. War has this character only in the isolated and fragmentary case of Serbia. Reduced to its historically objective essence, today's world war is entirely a competitive struggle among fully mature capitalisms for world domination, for the exploitation of the remaining zones of the world not yet capitalistic. That is why this war is totally different in character and effects. The high degree of economic development in the capitalist world is expressed in the extraordinarily advanced technology, that is, in the destructive power of the weaponry which approaches the same level in all the warring nations. The international organisation of the murder industry is reflected now in the military balance, the scales of which always right themselves after partial decisions and momentary changes; a general decision is always and again pushed into the future. The indecisiveness of military results leads to ever new reserves from the population masses of warring and hitherto neutral nations being sent into fire. The war finds abundant material to feed imperialist appetites and contradictions, creates its own supplies of these, and spreads like wildfire. But the mightier the masses and the more numerous the nations dragged into the war on all sides, the more drawn out its existence will be.

Considered all together, and before any decision regarding military victory or defeat has been taken, the effect of the war will be unlike any phenomenon of earlier wars in the modern age: the economic ruin of all belligerents and to an increasing degree that of the formally neutral as well. Every additional month of the war affirms and extends this result and postpones the expected fruits of military success for decades. In the last analysis, neither victory nor defeat can change any of this. On the contrary, it makes a purely military decision extremely unlikely and leads one to conclude the greater probability that the war will end finally with the most general and mutual exhaustion.

In these circumstances a victorious Germany would win but a Pyrrhic victory, even should its imperialistic warmongers succeed in the total defeat of all its enemies through mass murder and thus realise its audacious dream. Germany's trophies would be: a few beggared and depopulated territories to annex. Under its own roof would be a leering ruin. And once the stage scenery of war loan financing and the Potemkin villages[46] of war contracts and unshakeable national prosperity are pushed aside it will be immediately seen as the ruin it is. It must be clear even to the most superficial observer that the most victorious state can not expect any reparations that would even come close to healing the wounds inflicted by this war. A replacement for this and a complement of "victory" would be the perhaps even greater economic ruin of the conquered side: France and England, the very countries most closely connected economically to Germany and upon whose welfare she is most dependent for her own recovery. After a "victorious" war the German people would have to pay back the war credits granted by the patriotic parliament, that is, in reality have to bear an immense burden of taxation while enduring a strengthened military reaction – the only lasting, tangible fruit of "victory".

---

46. Count Gregory Alexandrovich Potemkin was said to have deceived Catherine the Great of Russia with cardboard façades of new villages he was supposed to have constructed.

CHAPTER EIGHT

If we seek to imagine the worst results of a military defeat, then, aside from the imperialist annexations, they present feature for feature essentially the same consequences as would have issued from victory. The consequences of waging war are today so deeply embedded and far-reaching in nature that the military outcome has only minimal effects upon it.

Nevertheless, let us accept for the moment that the victorious state would understand how to throw off the burden of great ruin from itself onto its defeated opponent and to hamstring its economic development with all sorts of obstacles. Can the trade union struggles of the German working class go forward after the war if the union action of the French, English, Belgian, and Italian workers is thwarted by economic regression? Until 1870 the workers' movement operated independently in each country; sometimes key decisions were taken in individual cities. It was in Paris on whose cobblestones the battles of the proletariat were joined and decided. The labour movement of today, because of its more arduous daily economic struggle, bases its mass organisation on cooperation with worker movements in all capitalist countries. If the principle is valid that the workers' cause can flourish only on the basis of a healthy, powerfully pulsating economic life, then it is valid not only for Germany but also for France, England, Belgium, Russia, Italy. And if the workers' movement stagnates in all the capitalist countries of Europe, if there exist low wages, weak unions and slight resistance to exploitation, then it will be impossible for the trade union movement to thrive in Germany. From this standpoint and in the last analysis, it is exactly the same loss for the situation of the proletariat if German capitalism enriches itself at the cost of the French or the English at the cost of the German.

Let us turn, however, to the political results of the war. Here differentiation ought to be easier than in the economic area. Historically, the sympathies and partisanship of the socialists have been on the side fighting for historical progress and against reaction. Which side in the present war represents progress and which reaction? Clearly, this question cannot be answered on the basis of the superficial labels of the warring states, such as "democracy" or "absolutism". Rather, the question should be judged on the actual objective tendencies they represent in world politics. Before we can judge what benefits a German victory would bring to the German proletariat, we must see what the effects of such a victory would have upon the overall shape of European political relationships.

The definitive victory of Germany would result in the immediate annexation of Belgium, as well as additional strips of territory in east and west, wherever feasible, and a part of the French colonies. The Habsburg monarchy would be preserved and enriched with new regions. Finally, Turkey, retaining a fictional "integrity", would become a German protectorate, which would mean the simultaneous transformation of the Middle East into *de facto* German provinces, whatever the form. The actual military and economic hegemony of Germany in Europe would logically follow these results.

These results of a decisive German military victory will come about, not because they correspond to the wishes of imperialist agitators in this war, but because they are the wholly inevitable consequences emanating from Germany's position in the world and from the original conflicts with England, France and Russia that have grown tremendously beyond their initial dimensions during the course of the war. It will suffice to put these results into context by understanding that under no circumstances will it be possible to maintain any sort of balance of power in the world.

The war means ruin for all the belligerents, although more so for the defeated. On the day after the concluding of peace, preparations for a new world war will be begun under the leadership of England in order to throw off the yoke of Prusso-German militarism burdening Europe and the Near East. A German victory would be only a prelude to a soon-to-follow second world war; and this would be the signal for a new, feverish arms race as well as the unleashing of the blackest reaction in all countries, but first and foremost in Germany itself.

On the other hand, an Anglo-French victory would most probably lead to the loss of at least some German colonies, as well as Alsace-Lorraine. Quite certain would be the bankruptcy of German imperialism on the world stage. But that also means the partition of Austria-Hungary and the total liquidation of Turkey. The fall of such arch-reactionary creatures as these two states is wholly in keeping with the demands of progressive development. But the fall of the Habsburg monarchy as well as Turkey, in the concrete situation of world politics, can have no other effect than to put their peoples in pawn to Russia, England, France and Italy. Add to this grandiose redrawing of the world map power shifts in the Balkans and the Mediterranean and a further one in Asia. The liquidation of Persia and a new dismemberment of China will inevitably follow.

In the wake of these changes the English-Russian, as well as the English-Japanese, conflict will move into the foreground of world politics. And directly upon the liquidation of this world war, these conflicts may lead to a new world war, perhaps over Constantinople, and would certainly make it likely. Thus, from this side, too, an Anglo-French victory would lead to a new feverish armaments race among all the states – with defeated Germany obviously in the forefront. An era of unalloyed militarism and reaction would dominate all Europe with a new world war as its ultimate goal.

Thus proletarian policy is locked in a dilemma when trying to decide on which side it ought to intervene, which side represents progress and democracy in this war. In these circumstances, and from the perspective of international politics as a whole, victory or defeat, in political as well as economic terms, comes down to a hopeless choice between two kinds of beatings for the European working classes. Therefore, it is nothing but fatal madness when the French socialists imagine that the military defeat of Germany will strike a blow at the head of militarism and imperialism and thereby pave the way for peaceful democracy in the world. Imperialism and its servant, militarism, will calculate their profits from every victory and every defeat in this war – except in one case: if the international proletariat intervenes in a revolutionary way and puts an end to such calculations.

This war's most important lesson for the policy of the proletariat is the unassailable fact that it cannot parrot the slogan *Victory or Defeat*, not in Germany or in France, not in England or in Russia. Only from the standpoint of imperialism does this slogan have any real content. For every Great Power it is identical to the question of gain or loss of political standing, of annexations, colonies and military predominance. From the standpoint of class for the European proletariat as a whole the victory and defeat of any of the warring camps is equally disastrous.

It is war as such, no matter how it ends militarily, that signifies the greatest defeat for Europe's proletariat. It is only the overcoming of war and the speediest possible enforcement of peace by the international militancy of the proletariat that can bring victory to the workers' cause. And in reality this victory alone can simultaneously rescue Belgium as well as democracy in Europe.

The class-conscious proletariat cannot identify with any of the military camps in this war. Does it follow that proletarian policy ought to demand maintenance of the status quo, that we have no other action program beyond the wish that everything should be as it was before the war? But existing conditions have never been our ideal; they have never expressed the self-determination of peoples. Furthermore, the earlier conditions are no longer to be saved; they no longer exist, even if historic state borders continue to exist. Even before its results have been formally established, the war has already brought about immense confusion in power relationships, the reciprocal estimate of forces, of alliances and conflicts. It has sharply revised the relations between states and of classes within society. So many old illusions and potencies have been destroyed, so many new forces and problems have been created that a return to the old Europe as it existed before August 4, 1914 is out of the question. It is as out of the question as a return to pre-revolutionary conditions even after a defeated revolution.

Proletarian policy knows no retreat; it can only struggle forward. It must always go beyond the existing and the newly created. In this sense alone, it is legitimate for the proletariat to confront both camps of imperialists in the world war with a policy of its own.

But this policy cannot consist of Social Democratic parties holding international conferences where they individually or collectively compete to discover ingenious recipes with which bourgeois diplomats ought to make the peace and ensure the further peaceful development of democracy. All demands for complete or partial "disarmament", for the dismantling of secret diplomacy, for the partition of all multinational great states into small national ones, and so forth, are part and parcel utopian as long as capitalist class domination holds the reins. Capitalism cannot, under its current imperialist course, dispense with present-day militarism, secret diplomacy, or the centralised multinational state. In fact, it would be more pertinent for the realisation of these postulates to make just one simple "demand": abolition of the capitalist class state.

It is not through utopian advice and schemes to tame, ameliorate or reform imperialism within the framework of the bourgeois state that proletarian policy can reconquer its leading place. The actual problem that the world war has posed to the socialist parties, upon the solution of which the destiny of the workers' movement depends, is this: *the capacity of the proletarian masses for action in the battle against imperialism*. The proletariat does not lack for postulates, prognoses, slogans; it lacks deeds, the capacity for effective resistance to imperialism at the decisive moment, to intervene against it during, not after, the war and to convert the old slogan "war against war" into practice. Here is the crux of the matter, the Gordian knot of proletarian politics and its long-term future.

Imperialism and all its political brutality, the chain of incessant social catastrophes that it has let loose, is undoubtedly an historical necessity for the ruling classes of the contemporary capitalist world. Nothing would be more fatal for the proletariat than to delude itself into believing that it were possible after this war to rescue the idyllic and peaceful continuation of capitalism. However, the conclusion to be drawn by proletarian policy from the historical necessity of imperialism is that surrender to imperialism will mean living forever in its victorious shadow and eating from its leftovers.

The historical dialectic moves forward by contradiction, and establishes in the world the antithesis of every necessity. Bourgeois class domination is undoubtedly an historical necessity, but, so too, the rising of the working class against it. Capital is an historical necessity, but, so too, its grave-digger, the socialist proletariat. Imperialist world domination is an historical necessity, but, so too, its destruction by the proletarian international. Step for step there are two historical necessities in conflict with one another. Ours, the necessity of socialism, has the greater stamina. Our necessity enters into its full rights the moment that the other – bourgeois class domination – ceases to be the bearer of historical progress, when it becomes an obstacle, a danger to the further development of society. The capitalist world order, as revealed by the world war, has today reached this point.

The expansionist imperialism of capitalism, the expression of its highest stage of development and its last phase of existence, produces the following economic tendencies: it transforms the entire world into the capitalist mode of production; all outmoded, pre-capitalist forms of production and society are swept away; it converts all the world's riches and means of production into capital, the working masses of all zones into wage slaves. In Africa and Asia, from the northernmost shores to the tip of South America and the South Seas, the remnant of ancient primitive communist associations, feudal systems of domination, patriarchal peasant economies, traditional forms of craftsmanship are annihilated, crushed by capital; whole peoples are destroyed and ancient cultures flattened. All are supplanted by profit-mongering in its most modern form.

This brutal victory parade of capital through the world, its way prepared by every means of violence, robbery and infamy, has its light side. It creates the preconditions for its own final destruction. It put into place the capitalist system of world domination, the indispensable precondition for the socialist world revolution. This alone constitutes the cultural, progressive side of its reputed "great work of civilisation" in the primitive lands. For bourgeois-liberal economists and politicians, railroads, Swedish matches, sewer systems and department stores are "progress" and "civilisation". In themselves these works grafted onto primitive conditions are neither civilisation nor progress, for they are bought with the rapid economic and cultural ruin of peoples who must experience simultaneously the full misery and horror of two eras: the traditional natural economic system and the most modern and rapacious capitalist system of exploitation. Thus, the capitalist victory parade and all its works bear the stamp of progress in the historical sense only because they create the material preconditions for the abolition of capitalist domination and class society in general. And in this sense imperialism ultimately works for us.

The world war is a turning point. For the first time, the ravening beasts set loose upon all quarters of the globe by capitalist Europe have broken into Europe itself. A cry of horror went through the world when Belgium, that precious jewel of European civilisation, and when the most august cultural monuments of northern France fell into shards under the impact of the blind forces of destruction. This same "civilised world" looked on passively as the same imperialism ordained the cruel destruction of ten thousand Herero tribesmen and filled the sands of the Kalahari with the mad shrieks and death rattles of men dying of thirst;[47] the "civilised world" looked on as forty thousand men on the Putumayo River (Columbia) were tortured to death within ten years by a band of European captains of industry, while the rest of the people were made into cripples;[48] as in China where an age-old culture was put to the torch by European mercenaries, practised in all forms of cruelty, annihilation and anarchy; as Persia was strangled, powerless to resist the tightening noose of foreign domination; as in Tripoli where fire and sword bowed the Arabs beneath the yoke of capitalism, destroyed their culture and habitations. Only today has this "civilised world" become aware that the bite of the imperialist beast brings death, that its very breath is infamy. Only now has the "civilised world" recognised this, after the beast's ripping talons have clawed its own mother's lap, the bourgeois civilisation of Europe itself. And even this knowledge is grappled with in the distorted form of bourgeois hypocrisy. Every people recognises the infamy only in the national uniform of the enemy. "German barbarians!" – as though every people that marches out to do organised murder were not transformed instantly into a barbarian horde. "Cossack atrocities!" – as though war itself were not the atrocity of atrocities, as though the praising of human slaughter as heroism in a socialist youth paper were not the purest example of intellectual Cossackdom!

Nonetheless, the imperialist bestiality raging in Europe's fields has one effect about which the "civilised world" is not horrified and for which it has no breaking heart: that is *the mass destruction of the European proletariat*. Never before on this scale has a war

---
47. The Herero tribesmen rebelled against German control of their homeland in South-West Africa, 1903–07. During the brutal wars of pacification, German troops forced men, women, and children into the Kalahari desert where many perished.
48. The extraction of rubber from along the Putumayo River involved the horrific exploitation of native labourers.

exterminated whole strata of the population; not for a century have all the great and ancient cultural nations of Europe been attacked. Millions of human lives have been destroyed in the Vosges, the Ardennes, in Belgium, Poland, in the Carpathians, on the Save. Millions have been crippled. But of these millions, nine out of ten are working people from the city and the countryside.

It is our strength, our hope, that is mown down day after day like grass under the sickle. The best, most intelligent, most educated forces of international socialism, the bearers of the holiest traditions and the boldest heroes of the modern workers' movement, the vanguard of the entire world proletariat, the workers of England, France, Belgium, Germany, Russia – these are the ones now being hamstrung and led to the slaughter. These workers of the leading capitalist countries of Europe are exactly the ones who have the historical mission of carrying out the socialist transformation. Only from out of Europe, only from out of the oldest capitalist countries will the signal be given when the hour is ripe for the liberating social revolution. Only the English, French, Belgian, German, Russian, Italian workers together can lead the army of the exploited and enslaved of the five continents. When the time comes, only they can settle accounts with capitalism's work of global destruction, with its centuries of crime committed against primitive peoples.

But to push ahead to the victory of socialism we need a strong, activist, educated proletariat, and masses whose power lies in intellectual culture as well as numbers. These masses are being decimated by the world war. The flower of our mature and youthful strength, hundreds of thousands of whom were socialistically schooled in England, France, Belgium, Germany and Russia, the product of decades of educational and agitational training, and other hundreds of thousands who could be won for socialism tomorrow, fall and moulder on the miserable battlefields. The fruits of decades of sacrifice and the efforts of generations are destroyed in a few weeks. The key troops of the international proletariat are torn up by the roots.

The blood-letting of the June days [1848] paralysed the French workers' movement for a decade and a half. Then the blood-letting of the Commune massacres again retarded it for more than a decade. What is now occurring is an unprecedented mass slaughter that is reducing the adult working population of all the leading civilised countries to women, old people and cripples. This blood-letting threatens to bleed the European workers' movement to death. Another such world war and the outlook for socialism will be buried beneath the rubble heaped up by imperialist barbarism. This is more significant than the ruthless destruction of Liège and the Rheims cathedral. This is an assault, not on the bourgeois culture of the past, but on the socialist culture of the future, a lethal blow against that force which carries the future of humanity within itself and which alone can bear the precious treasures of the past into a better society. Here capitalism lays bare its death's head; here it betrays the fact that its historical rationale is used up; its continued domination is no longer reconcilable with the progress of humanity.

CHAPTER EIGHT

The world war today is demonstrably not only murder on a grand scale; it is also suicide of the working classes of Europe. The soldiers of socialism, the proletarians of England, France, Germany, Russia and Belgium have for months been killing one another at the behest of capital. They are driving the cold steel of murder into each other's hearts. Locked in the embrace of death, they tumble into a common grave.

"*Deutschland, Deutschland über Alles!* Long live democracy! Long live the Tsar and Slav-dom! Ten thousand tarpaulins guaranteed up to regulations! A hundred thousand kilos of bacon, coffee-substitute for immediate delivery!"... Dividends are rising, and the proletarians are falling. And with every one there sinks into the grave a fighter of the future, a soldier of the revolution, mankind's saviour from the yoke of capitalism.

The madness will cease and the bloody demons of hell will vanish only when workers in Germany and France, England and Russia finally awake from their stupor, extend to each other a brotherly hand, and drown out the bestial chorus of imperialist warmongers and the shrill cry of capitalist hyenas with labour's old and mighty battle cry:

"Proletarians of all lands, unite!"

Militarism and
Anti-Militarism

KARL LIEBKNECHT

Introduction

Published in 1907, *Militarism and Anti-militarism* was a polemical intervention aimed at shaking up the German Socialist Democratic Party (SPD). Karl Liebknecht was concerned that the SPD leadership and the party more broadly were not taking the need to confront militarism seriously. As he wrote in the book: "In the disruptive peace before the storm our Party life is becoming sluggish, and parliamentary work overcome by languor and paralysis".

The SPD from its earliest days had called for the replacement of the standing army by a popular militia and in parliament had voted against the military budget. However the SPD had never opposed the notion of German national self-defence from invasion. The SPD's 1891 Erfurt program called for:

> Training of all to be capable of bearing arms. Armed nation instead of standing army. Decisions of war and peace by the representatives of the people. Settlement of all international disputes by the method of arbitration.[1]

By the early 1900s party leader August Bebel was shifting his position, arguing that socialists sought to humanise and democratise the army in order to strengthen it. Bebel now claimed the SPD only voted against the military budget as it was financed by indirect taxation, which disproportionally impacted workers, rather than by direct taxes.

Liebknecht was, as it were, born into the SPD and the working-class movement. His father Wilhelm Liebknecht was a party founder, long-term leader and close associate of Karl Marx and Frederick Engels. And Karl (named naturally after Marx) spent years living in the household of the other party founder and long-term leader, August Bebel.

Right from his early years in the SPD Liebknecht had, along with his legal defence work for the party, addressed the question of militarism, both its domestic use (against strikes and political unrest) and its role in preparing for imperialist war. From around 1904 Liebknecht threw himself into building the newly emerging youth movement,

---
1. Steenson 1981, p.247.

which was strongly supportive of his anti-militarist message. His book is essentially an expanded version of a talk he had delivered in 1906 at a conference of the Young Workers' Union of Germany.

Previously, at the 1904 Bremen SPD conference, Liebknecht had moved a motion:

> The party should undertake a propaganda campaign in the most appropriate way among those called up for military service, before they actually enter the army, in order to win them over to socialism.[2]

The motion was defeated, but Liebknecht was not deterred and followed his cause up, again unsuccessfully, at subsequent conferences – Jena 1905, Mannheim 1906 and Essen 1907. Liebknecht's best chance of success had appeared to be at Mannheim, when, under the impact of the 1905 Revolution in Russia, leftish sentiment was strong in the SPD. Bebel had to use all his immense authority as long-term party leader to isolate Liebknecht and defeat his motion. Bebel demagogically turned it into a question of confidence in the leadership:

> The party executive wants nothing to do with anything of the sort...and if you do decide that, then please elect your own special bodies. We will not join in.[3]

Reflecting the fact that the SPD was increasingly attempting to integrate itself into the mainstream of German capitalism and wished to avoid any serious clash with the authorities, the party leaders hung Liebknecht out to dry after his arrest for high treason for publishing *Militarism and Anti-militarism*. Gustav Noske issued a declaration on behalf of the Reichstag fraction that the book did not represent the views of the party but merely those of a "single individual".[4]

The response of rank-and-file workers to Liebknecht's campaigning was, however, sharply different from that of the rightward-moving SPD leaders. His 1907 trial for high treason made him a hero to the mass of party members. The SPD paper *Vorwärts* described the Berlin "farewell celebration" for Liebknecht on his way to detention:

> Tumultuous cheers greeted him and were taken up immediately by the crowds that flooded the streets like a mighty torrent. The windows of the houses were crowded with people. In the streets the workers' *Marseillaise* was sung and in between cheers rang out over and over again.[5]

Berlin workers went on to elect the still imprisoned Liebknecht to the Prussian House of Deputies. In 1912 they elected him to the German federal parliament, the Reichstag.

In the pre-war years Liebknecht was something of a maverick politically. He was of a leftish bent, backing party radicals against right-wing union officials in the polarised mass strike debate of 1905. However he did not belong to the left, the right, or the centre factions of the party. In his anti-militarist and youth movement activity some of his allies, such as Ludwig Frank, were right-wing revisionists, conservative on class issues,

---

2. Trotnow 1984, p.55.
3. Trotnow 1984, pp.67–8.
4. Trotnow 1984, p.68.
5. Trotnow 1984, p.72.

but of a pacifist sentiment. Then in the 1912 Chemnitz Congress debate on imperialism Liebknecht backed the centrists Karl Kautsky and Hugo Haase (supported by the pro-imperialist right) against their left-wing opponents, Paul Lensch and Anton Pannekoek.[6] This reflects the major problem of lack of clarification between revolutionary and reformist politics in the SPD prior to the sharp test of world war.

As well, prior to the war Liebknecht did not have a political relationship with his war-time comrade and fellow founder of the Spartacus League and then the German Communist Party, Rosa Luxemburg. This added to the difficulties of creating a cohesive party leadership with experience of working together over a period of years.

The outbreak of World War I and the SPD's vote for war credits came as a profound shock to Liebknecht and to socialists all around the world, given the central role of the SPD in the Second Socialist International. The whole movement was rocked with debates on the issues of war, imperialism, the reasons for the SPD's reformist degeneration and the need for a new, genuinely revolutionary socialist international.[7]

The SPD leaders argued it was necessary to support German self-defence against barbaric Russia. Prior to 1914 Liebknecht had not questioned the duty of national defence even for an imperialist power like Germany. However he quickly recognised that World War I was a murderous imperialist war fought in the interests of the capitalists, not workers. Workers of every country had to fight, not just against the war but to challenge the whole capitalist order that inflicted such barbarism upon them.

Initially Liebknecht adhered to party discipline and voted for war credits on 4 August 1914. However on 2 December 1914 he made a decisive stance; alone among 110 SPD deputies, he voted against the war. It was a vital first step that helped stimulate the anti-war movement in Germany and internationally. He was reviled and denounced for his courage and defiance and punished by being conscripted into the army in February 1915.

He was jailed for his famous declaration: "Down with the government! Down with the war!" at the 1916 May Day demonstration in Berlin, organised by the Spartacist League. In a defiant statement to the judges at his military court martial he wrote:

> He who does not attack the enemy, imperialism, face to face, but instead attacks those far away, those outside his shooting range – and that with the help and approval of his own government (that is, of those very representatives of imperialism who directly oppose him) – he is no Socialist, but a miserable lackey of the ruling class.[8]

Liebknecht remained in jail from 1916 until October 1918, when he was freed by the outbreak of the German revolution. He immediately set out to drive the revolution forward to total victory for the working class. Along with Rosa Luxemburg he played a central role in the formation of the German Communist Party, dedicated to workers' power. But he had only a few short months of heroic activism left. The German capitalist class and their supporters in the reformist SPD were determined to eliminate this threat to

---

6. Salvadori 1990, pp.177–8.
7. See Armstrong 2023 for an analysis of these debates.
8. Quoted in Lock 1973, p.xxxvii.

their rule. On 15 January 1919 they had Liebknecht murdered alongside Rosa Luxemburg.

Mick Armstrong, January 2025

References

Armstrong, Mick 2023, "From Marx to Lenin: Debates that forged the socialist approach to war", *Marxist Left Review*, 26, Spring 2023.

Lock, Graham 1973, "Introduction", *Militarism and Anti-Militarism*, Rivers Press.

Salvadori, Massimo 1990, *Karl Kautsky and the Socialist Revolution 1880–1938*, Verso.

Steenson, Gary 1981, *"Not One Man! Not One Penny!" German Social Democracy, 1863–1914*, University of Pittsburgh Press.

Trotnow, Helmut 1984, *Karl Liebknecht. A Political Biography*, Archon Books.

Preface

A few weeks ago *Die Grenzboten* reported a conversation between Bismarck and Professor Dr Otto Kämmel which took place in October 1892, and in which Bismarck, the "Hero of the Century", himself tore off the mask of constitutionalism in his very own cynical style. Among other things, he said:

> In Rome, whoever put himself outside of the law was banished, *aqua et igne interdictus*; in the Middle Ages he was said to be outlawed. Social Democracy ought to be treated in a similar way: it should be deprived of its political rights, of its right to participate in elections. I would have gone that far. *The Social Democratic problem is in fact a military problem.* Social Democracy is being treated with an extraordinary lack of serious attention at present. It is now attempting – with success – to win over the non-commissioned officers. In Hamburg a large part of the troops already consists of Social Democrats, since the local people have the right to join only the local battalions. What if these troops should one day refuse to obey the Kaiser and to fire on their fathers and brothers? Would we then be forced to mobilise the Hanover and Mecklenburg regiments against Hamburg? In that case we should have something like the Paris Commune on our hands. The Kaiser then took fright. He told me that he did not want one day to be called the "Kartätschenprinz" – the shrapnel prince – like his grandfather, and did not want to *"wade up to his ankles in blood"* at the very beginning of his reign. At the time I told him: "Your Majesty will have to go in much deeper if you draw back now!"

"The Social Democratic problem is a military problem." This is the whole point; it says more and goes much deeper than von Massow's cry of distress: "Our only hope is the bayonets and cannons of our soldiers".[9] *"The Social Democratic problem is a military problem."* That is the keynote of all the tunes sung by the firebrands. Anyone who had not yet been convinced by the earlier indiscretions of Bismarck and Puttkamer, by the speech to the Alexander regiment,[10] by the *Hamburger Nachrichten* and the thoroughbred Junker, von

---
9. See Arendt's *Deutsches Wochenblatt*, middle of November 1896, and the *Sozialdemokratische Partei-Correspondenz*, year II, No.4.
10. This refers to a speech by Wilhelm II to the Kaiser Alexander Regiment on 28 March, 1901: "You are...so to speak the bodyguard of the King of Prussia, and you must always be ready, day and night, to put your life at risk,

Oldenburg-Januschau, would have had his eyes opened by the Hohenlohe-Delbruck revelations which were corroborated around the end of the year through the county court judge Kulemann, and by the cruel words of Bismarck cited above.

The Social Democratic problem – in so far as it is a political problem – is in the last resort a military problem. This should be a constant reminder to Social Democracy and a tactical principle of the first rank.

The enemy at home, Social Democracy, is "more dangerous than the enemy abroad, because it poisons the soul of our people and wrests the weapons from our hands before we have even lifted them". This is how the *Kreuz-Zeitung* of January 21, 1907, proclaimed the sovereignty of class interests over national interests in an electoral struggle which was waged "under the banner of nationalism"! And this electoral struggle was carried on in the face of an ever-increasing menace to electoral and trade-union rights, and of "Bonaparte's sword", which Prince Bülow waved around the heads of the German Social Democrats in his New Year's Eve letter in order to frighten them; it was carried on in the face of a class struggle raised to white heat.[11] Only someone who was blind and deaf could deny that these signs, as well as many others, indicate the approach of a storm or even of a hurricane.

The problem of the struggle against "militarism at home" has therefore taken on an importance of a most pressing kind.

The elections of 1907 were, however, also fought on the national question, on the colonial question, and over chauvinism and imperialism. And they showed how miserably weak, in spite of all this, was the resistance of the German people to the pseudo-patriotic rat-traps laid by these contemptible business patriots. They taught us what pompous demagogy can be pressed into use by the government, by the ruling classes and by the whole howling pack of "patriots" whenever "things most holy" are concerned. These elections provided the proletariat with some necessary enlightenment, causing it to question its own role and teaching it about the relation of social and political forces. They educated it, and freed it from the unfortunate "habit of victory"; and they excited a welcome force resulting in a deepening of the proletarian movement and of our understanding of the psychology of the masses with regard to national campaigns. Certainly the causes of our so-called setback, which was actually not a setback and puzzled the victors more than the vanquished, were manifold; but there is no doubt that precisely those sections of the proletariat which are contaminated and influenced by militarism, which are already at the mercy of government terrorism – for example, the state workers and junior officials – have formed an especially firm obstacle to the extension of Social Democratic influence.

This also raises sharply, as far as the German labour movement is concerned, the

---

to spill your blood for your king!... If it should happen that the city rises up against its rulers, the regiment must punish this improper conduct of the people towards its king with the bayonet".

11. On the evening of the second ballot (February 5, 1907) troops of the Berlin garrison were provided with live cartridges and held ready to march. On June 25, 1905, the last time the second ballot was held, the Pioneers appeared in Spandau in the Schönwalder Strasse in order to "bring to their senses" the workers excited by the election result.

question of anti-militarism and the question of the youth movement and of the education of young people, and ensures that these points will receive more attention in future.

The following work is the elaboration of a paper read by the author on September 30, 1906, to the first conference of the German Young Socialist League in Mannheim. It does not pretend to offer something new; it is simply intended to be a compilation of material which is already known or even commonplace. Nor does it claim to be exhaustive. The author has attempted, as far as he is able, to collect the disconnected material scattered throughout the newspapers and periodicals. Thanks above all to our Belgian comrade de Man, it has been possible to provide at least a brief account of the anti-militarist and youth movement in the most important countries.

If here and there errors have crept in, they should be excused on account of the difficulty of coping with the material, but also on account of the frequent unreliability of the sources, which are often even contradictory.

In the realm of militarism things are in constant flux at the present time, so that, for example, the information given below on the French and English military reforms will certainly soon be overtaken by events.

That is even more true of anti-militarism and the proletarian youth movement, the newest manifestations of the proletarian struggle for freedom, which are everywhere developing quickly, and making pleasing headway in spite of setbacks. Since this work was set up in type it has been learned that the Finnish Young Socialist Societies held their first congress in Tammerfors on December 8 and 9, 1906, where a Young Workers' League was founded which will be attached to the Finnish Labour Party and whose special task, apart from the education of the young workers in class consciousness, will be the struggle against militarism in all its aspects.

People will be inclined to complain that the theoretical basis of our work is too slight and the historical depth not sufficient. Against this it ought to be said that the pamphlet has a topical political task, that of promoting anti-militarist thought.

Many people again will be unhappy with the accumulation of countless, often apparently unimportant details, especially in connection with the history of the Young Socialist movement and of anti-militarism. This dissatisfaction may be justified. The author, however, started from the assumption that it is first of all through details that one is able to gain a living insight into the upward and downward movement in organisational development and into the invention and modification of tactical principles, and to put them to use in the desired manner – the more so since it is precisely details which present the main difficulty in anti-militarist agitation and organisation.

Dr Karl Liebknecht

Berlin, February 11, 1907

Part I – Militarism

CHAPTER ONE

General

1. On the essence and meaning of militarism

Militarism! Few slogans have been so frequently used in our time, and few denote a phenomenon so complicated, multiform, many-sided, and at the same time so interesting and significant in its origin and nature, its methods and *effects*. It is a phenomenon which is deeply rooted in the structure of class-divided social orders, yet can take on within the same type of social order, according to the special natural, political, social and economic circumstances of individual states and territories, an extraordinary variety of forms.

Militarism is one of the most important and powerful signs of life of most social orders, because it is the strongest, most concentrated and exclusive expression of the national, cultural and class instinct for self-preservation, the most elementary of all instincts.

A history of militarism in the deepest sense discloses the very essence of human development and of its motive force, and a dissection of capitalist militarism involves the disclosure of the most secret and least obvious roots of capitalism. The history of militarism is at the same time the history of the political, social, economic and, in general, the cultural relations of tension between states and nations, as well as the history of the class struggles within individual ante and national units.

There can of course be no question here of even attempting such a history, but we will indicate a few general aspects.

2. Origin and basis of social relations of power

In the last resort the basis of every social relation of power is the superiority of *physical force*,[12] which as a social phenomenon does not appear in the form of the greater

---

12. And also of course of intellectual force, which is the inseparable regulator of physical force in so far as it effects the best possible use of that force and makes the physical force of others serve its purpose, which it actually

physical strength of individuals, since as far as this relation is concerned, one human being is worth as much as any other, and a purely numerical majority is decisive. The relation of numbers with which we are concerned does not simply correspond to the numerical relation between groups of persons with contradictory interests, but is determined – since not everyone is conscious of his own real interests, especially not of his fundamental interests, and above all since not everyone recognises or acknowledges the interests of his class as his own interests – essentially by the level of intellectual and moral development of each class, by which is decided the extensive and intensive degree of class consciousness. This intellectual and moral level is itself determined by the economic position of the individual interest groups (classes), while the social and political position represents rather a consequence, though of course one which is very strongly retroactive, and an expression of the relation of power.

Purely economic superiority also contributes *directly* to the displacement and confusion of the numerical ratio, since economic pressure not only influences the height of the intellectual and moral level and thus the consciousness of class interest, but also produces a tendency to act in accordance with this more or less understood class interest. The fact that the political machinery of the class in control lends it increased means of power to "correct" the numerical relation in favour of the ruling interest group is taught us by all the well-known institutions: police, law courts, schools, together with the church, which must also be included here – institutions which are created by the political and legislative machinery and used as an executive, administrative instrument. The first two work chiefly by means of threats, intimidation and violence, the school chiefly by blocking up as far as possible all those channels through which class consciousness can travel to the brain and heart. The church on the other hand works most effectively by awakening a passion for the make-believe delights of heaven and a fear of the tortures of hell.

But even the numerical ratio so determined does not decide absolutely the relation of power. An armed man increases his physical strength by many times through his possession of a weapon. The degree of the increase depends upon the development of the technique of arms, including fortification and strategy (whose form is essentially a consequence of the technique of arms). The intellectual and economic superiority of one interest group over another is turned into a simple physical superiority through the possession of arms, or of better arms, on the part of the ruling class. The possibility is thus created of the complete domination of the class-conscious majority by a class-conscious minority.

Even when the division into classes is decided by the economic position, the political relation of power between the classes is determined by the economic position of individuals only in the first place; in the second place it is determined by the countless

does through the use of the physical force available to it and acquired. The extent to which this use of physical force exists as a social phenomenon, that is to say, the extent to which it contributes to the determination of the structure of the social relation of power in virtue of the scale and regularity of its occurrence in the relations between individual interest groups, depends as a rule essentially on the economic position of those groups. Some of the more important aspects of this question will be discussed later.

intellectual, moral and physical means of power at the disposal of the economically dominant class through its economic class position. The fact that these instruments of power exist cannot affect class divisions, since these are created by a quite independent set of conditions which, with a power like that of nature, forces certain classes, which may well represent a majority, into economic dependence on other classes, which may represent a tiny minority – a dependence which neither the class struggle nor any means of political power is capable of eliminating.[13] *The class struggle can therefore only be a struggle to develop class consciousness among class comrades – which embraces a readiness for the performance of revolutionary deeds and for sacrifice in the interest of one's class – and a struggle to capture those means of power which are of importance with regard either to the creation or to the suppression of class consciousness, as well as those physical and intellectual means of power whose possession means the multiplication of physical strength.*

This demonstrates what an important role the technique of arms plays in social struggles. It depends on this technique whether, in the case where it is no longer economically necessary, a minority remains in a position to dominate a majority *against its will* by military action, the "most concentrated form of political action" – at least for a certain length of time. Leaving aside the divisions between the classes, the development of the relations of power is in reality closely tied to the development of the technique of arms. As long as more or less everyone – even the person in the worst economic situation – can produce arms under essentially similar conditions of essentially similar efficacy, the majority principle, democracy, will be the normal political form of society. This must be true even in a situation of economic class division, in so far as the above condition holds. The natural process of development is of course that the division into classes, which is the consequence of economic-technical development, runs parallel with the cultivation of the technique of arms (including fortification and strategy). The production of arms therefore becomes to an ever greater degree a professional skill. Further, since class domination as a rule is constituted precisely by the economic superiority of one class over another, and since the improvement of the technique of arms leads to the production of arms[14] becoming ever more difficult and expensive, this production gradually becomes the monopoly of the economically dominant class. The physical basis of democracy is thus removed. The rule then is: whoever is in possession is in the right. A class which has once been in possession of the political means of power may be able temporarily to retain its *political* domination even when it loses its economic superiority.

After what has already been said, it ought not to need further demonstration that not only the form and character of the political relations of power but also the form and

---

13. "In the social production of their life, men enter into definite relations that are indispensable and independent of their will, relations of production which correspond to a definite stage of development of their material productive forces." – Karl Marx, Preface to *A Contribution to the Critique of Political Economy*.
14. To the category of arms proper belongs for example – apart from munitions and weapons of all kinds, including the system of searchlighting, and the fortresses and warships – the military communications system (horses, wagons, bicycles, the building of roads and bridges, ships in inland waters, railways, automobiles, telegraphs, wireless telegraphy, telephone, etc.). Nor should the telescope, airship, photography and spy dogs be forgotten.

character of the class struggles of a given period are determined by the technique of arms.

It is not enough that all citizens are equally armed and in possession of their weapons to safeguard permanently the rule of democracy. The equal distribution of arms in itself, as events in Switzerland have shown, does not rule out the possibility that this distribution may be done away with by a majority which is about to become a minority, or even by a minority which is better organised and ready to strike. The general and equal arming of the population can only become a permanent and irreversible characteristic when the production of arms itself is in the hands of the people.

The role of democratisation which the technique of arms can play has been very clearly depicted by Bulwer in one of his less known works, the remarkable utopia entitled *The Coming Race*. In this work he presupposes such a high technical development that every citizen can at any moment produce the most destructive results by the use of a small stick, easy to get hold of and loaded with a mysterious force similar to that of electricity. And indeed we can suppose that the time will come – even if it is far in the future – when technique and the easy domination by men of the most powerful forces of nature will reach a stage which makes the application of the technique of murder quite impossible, since it would mean the self-destruction of the human race. The exploitation of technical progress will then take on a new character; from a basically plutocratic activity it will to a certain extent become a democratic, general human possibility.

3. Some items from the history of militarism

In the lower cultures which know no division into classes, the weapon serves as a rule also as a tool for work. It is at the same time a means of acquiring food (by hunting, by cultivation, etc.) and a means of protection against wild beasts and of defence against hostile tribes, as well as a means of attacking them. The weapon has such a primitive character that anyone can easily acquire it at any time (stones and sticks, spears with stone tips, bows, etc.). This is also true of means of defence. Since no division of labour worthy of the name (if we except the most primitive of all such divisions, that between man and wife) yet exists, since all members of the community, at least within each division of sex, perform more or less the same function, and since there are as yet no relations of political or economic power, it follows that the weapon cannot be used inside the community to support such relations of power. It could not be used as a support in this way even if relations of power did exist, since only democratic relations are possible in conjunction with a primitive technique of arms.

If in this lowest form of culture the weapon is used inside the community at most to settle individual conflicts, the situation changes when a division between classes appears together with a higher development in the technique of arms. The primitive communism of the lower agricultural peoples in which women were dominant knows no social and therefore normally also no political relation of class domination. Generally speaking militarism does not appear. External complications compel these peoples to prepare themselves for war and even, for certain periods, produce military despotisms which are very commonly found among the nomadic peoples, owing to the constant threat of war and the division into classes which as a rule has already come into being.

Let us recall the organisation of the Greek and Roman armies, in which, in accordance with the division into classes, there existed a purely military hierarchy, organised according to the class position of the individual, which position determined the quality of his armament. Let us further think back to the feudal armies of knights, with their troops of squires mostly on foot and always much worse armed and equipped, who, according to Patrice Laroque, played rather the role of assistants to the combatants than that of combatants themselves. The fact that at this time the arming of the lower classes was permitted and even encouraged is to be explained not so much by the lack of general security offered by the state to the acknowledged interests of the individual, which in a sense made it necessary that everyone should be armed, as by the need for a possible mobilisation of the nation or state for attack on or defence against the external enemy. The differences in the armament of the different social classes always made it possible, however, that the technique of arms might be used to maintain or establish the relation of power. The Roman slave wars throw light in a most remarkable way on this side of the question.

The German Peasant War and the Wars of the German Towns are also important in this respect. Among the direct causes of the unfavourable outcome of the German Peasant War was above all the military-technical superiority of the feudal armies of the Church. But the fourteenth century Wars of the Towns directed against these very same armies turned out successfully, not only because at this time the technique of arms and especially that of firearms was exceptionally backward, the opposite of the position in the Peasant War of 1525, but above all in consequence of the great economic power of the towns. These, as localities in which social spheres of interest came into relation, brought together in close community the representatives of these spheres, without any notable admixture of contradictory elements. Further, owing to the manner in which they were built, the towns from the first held a tactical position of the same importance as that of the feudal lords and of the Church and Emperor in their castles and fortresses; this is similarly a military-technical element (fortification). Finally, it was important that the production of arms was in the hands of the towns; and as their citizens were quite superior in terms of technical preparedness, they overcame the army of the knights.[15]

As an examination of the Peasant and Town Wars in particular demonstrates, it is necessary to bear in mind the important role played by the different social classes, whether each class is united in one locality or mixed with other classes. When the class division coincides with the division of locality, it is simpler to wage the class struggle, not only because of the way in which class consciousness is thereby developed, but also

---

15. The development of Italy in the fifteenth century is of the greatest interest here, directly tempting one to make a more thorough investigation. It strengthens our fundamental thesis throughout. See Burckhardt, *Die Kultur der Renaissance in Italien*, ninth edition, Vol.I, pp.103ff.

because of the way in which, speaking from a purely technical point of view, the military organisational unity of the class comrades as well as the production and supply of arms is facilitated. This favourable local grouping of the classes has been of aid to all bourgeois revolutions,[16] but in the proletarian revolution is almost entirely lacking.[17]

Economic power is also found directly transformed into physical power in the mercenary armies of our day (just as it is where the distribution of armament in general is concerned), according to the Mephistophelian maxim: "If I can pay for six steeds, is their strength not mine? I drive away and am a real man, just as if I had twenty-four legs", and according to the maxim: *divide et impera!* – "divide and rule!" These two maxims are applied to the so-called *elite* troops. The Italian *condottieri* on the other hand show in a striking manner – as the Praetorians once did – what political power is conferred on those who possess weapons, military training and the art of strategy. The mercenary sought boldly for the crowns of princes, played ball with them, and became the natural heir to the supreme power of the state – a phenomenon which we see repeated down to our day in times of excitement and war when the mobilised military power rests in the hands of individuals: Napoleon and his generals are an example, Boulanger another![18]

The history of the German "Wars of Liberation" teaches us important lessons about the influence of the external political situation on the form of military organisation and of militarism in general. When in the disastrous Coalition Wars of 1806 against the French Revolution the feudal standing army of Frederick II was crushed as in a mortar by the citizen army of France, the helpless German governments were faced with the alternative: either to submit permanently to the pleasure or displeasure of the Corsican conqueror, or to defeat him with his own weapon, with a citizen army based on a general arming of the people. Their instinct for self-preservation and the spontaneous impulse of the people compelled them to take the latter course. The great period of the democratisation of Germany and especially of Prussia then began, impelled by external pressures which for a time alleviated the political, social and economic tension at home. Money and enthusiastic freedom fighters were required. The value of man increased. His social quality as a creator of wealth and a prospective taxpayer, together with his natural physical quality as a bearer of physical power, as a bearer of intelligence and enthusiasm, took on decisive significance and raised his rate of exchange, as always happens in times of general danger; but the influence of class distinction went down. The "Prussian people" had, to use the jargon of the military weeklies, "learned to suppress their quarrels during the long years of foreign rule." As so often is the case, financial and military questions played a revolutionising role. Various economic, social and political obstacles were removed. Industry and trade, which were financially of the first importance, were

---

16. Also to the [1905] Russian Revolution in its early stages. Especially characteristic, among the numerous other proofs, is the armed uprising in Moscow in December 1905, the astonishing tenacity of which is explained by the fact that the main body of the population of the town co-operated with the revolutionaries in the firing line, who were after all not very numerous. The tactics of urban guerrilla warfare, brilliantly developed in Moscow, will become epoch-making.
17. The fact of men working together in factories, etc., and living together in "working-class quarters" must, however, be taken into consideration.
18. See Burckhardt, *Die Kultur der Renaissance in Italien*, Vol.I, pp.22ff.

promoted as far as the petty-bureaucratic spirit of Prussia-Germany would allow it. Even political freedoms were introduced, or at least – promised. The people rose, the storm broke. The Scharnhorst-Gneisenau army based on universal military service drove the "hereditary enemy" back over the Rhine in the great Wars of Liberation, and set up a model to shame him who had shaken the world, who had undermined the France of the Great Revolution, though as an army it was not the kind of democratic organisation that Scharnhorst and Gneisenau had wanted to create. After the "moor" – the German people – had thus done his duty, he received suitable "thanks from the House of Hapsburg". The Karlsbad resolutions followed the Battle of the Nations at Leipzig; and one of the most important acts of the futile Metternich period of perfidious and accursed memory, when the external pressure had been removed and all the reactionary devils at home had been let loose again, was the abolition of the democratic army of the Wars of Liberation. The culturally developed areas of Germany might have been ready for such an army, but it was abruptly destroyed, together with all the glories of the great popular rising, under the dead weight of the East Elbean-Borussian lack of culture.

A superficial glance at the development of the military organisation finally demonstrates how closely dependent is the construction and size of the army not only on the social structure, but even more on the technique of arms. The revolutionising effect of the discovery of firearms is one of the most remarkable facts in the history of war.

CHAPTER TWO

Capitalist militarism

Preliminary remarks

Militarism is not specific to capitalism. It is moreover normal and necessary in every class-divided social order, of which the capitalist system is the last. Capitalism, of course, like every other class-divided social order, develops its own special variety of militarism;[19] for militarism is by its very essence a means to an end, or to several ends, which differ according to the kind of social order in question and which can be attained according to this difference in different ways. This comes out not only in military organisation, but also in the other features of militarism which manifest themselves when it carries out its tasks.

The capitalist stage of development is best met with an army based on universal military service, an army which, though it is based on the people, is not a people's army but an army hostile to the people, or at least one which is being built up in that direction.

Sometimes it appears as a standing army, sometimes as a militia force. The standing army, which is not peculiar to capitalism,[20] appears as its most developed, even as its normal form. This will be demonstrated below.

---

19. Bernstein wrongly says in *La Vie Socialiste* of June 5, 1905, that the present-day militarist institutions are only an inheritance from the more or less feudal monarchy.
20. See Russia, where quite special circumstances, which did not grow out of internal conditions, helped to bring about this result. The hired armies are for instance standing armies on a basis different from that of universal military service. The Italian towns of the fifteenth century also had a militia force. (Burckhardt, *Die Kultur der Renaissance*, Vol.I, p.327.)

1. "Militarism against the external enemy", navalism and colonial militarism. Possibilities of war and disarmament

The army of the capitalist social order, like the army of any other class-divided social order, fulfils a double role.

It is first of all a national institution, designed for external aggression or for protection against an external danger; in short designed for use in cases of international complication or, to use a military phrase, for use "against the external enemy".

This function of the army is in no sense eliminated by the latest developments. For capitalism war is in fact, to use the words of Moltke, "a link in God's world order".[21] In Europe itself there is admittedly something of a tendency for certain causes of war to be eliminated: the probability of war breaking out in Europe is decreasing, in spite of Alsace-Lorraine and the anxiety caused by the French trinity of Clemenceau, Pichon and Picquart, in spite of the Eastern question, in spite of Pan-Islamism and in spite of the revolution taking place in Russia. On the other hand new and highly dangerous sources of tension have arisen in consequence of the aims of commercial and political expansion[22] pursued by the so-called civilised states, sources which have been handed down to us by the Eastern question and Pan-Islamism in the first instance, and as a consequence of world policy, and especially colonial policy, which – as Bülow himself unreservedly acknowledged in the German Reichstag on November 14, 1906[23] – conceals countless possibilities of conflict.[24] This policy has at the same time pushed forward ever more energetically two other forms of militarism: naval militarism and colonial militarism. We Germans know a few things about this development!

Navalism, naval militarism, is the twin brother of militarism on land and bears all its repulsive and virulent features. It is at present, to a still higher degree than militarism on land, not only the consequence but also the cause of international dangers, of the danger of a world war.

If some people, whether honest or deceitful, want to make us believe for example that the tension between Germany and England[25] is due to misunderstandings, to the inflammatory words of malicious journalists, to the boastful expressions of bad musicians in the concert of diplomacy, we know different. We know that this tension is a necessary consequence of the sharpening economic competition between England

---

21. In his well-known letter to Bluntschli (December 1880) he writes: "Eternal peace is a dream, and not a nice one, and war is a link in God's world order. In war are expressed the noblest virtues of man: courage and renunciation, loyalty and willingness for sacrifice of life. Without war the world would sink into the morass of materialism". A few months earlier Moltke had written: "Every war is a national disaster" (*Gesammelte Schriften und Denkwürdigkeiten*, Berlin n.d., Vol.II, pp.195 and 200), and in 1841 he had written in an article in the *Augsburger Allgemeine Zeitung*: "We openly associate ourselves with the much derided idea of a general European peace".
22. The total value of the world's export trade, according to Hübner's tables, rose from 75,224 million marks in 1891 to almost 109,000 million in 1905.
23. "What today complicates our situation and makes it difficult are our overseas aims and interests."
24. Moltke's opinions on this subject were very unsettled. According to him the time of cabinet wars is past; but on the other hand he considers the party leaders as criminal and dangerous provokers of war. The party leaders and – the stock exchange! It is true that now and then he has more profound insight. (*Gesammelte Schriften und Denkwürdigkeiten*, Vol.III, pp.1ff., 126, 135, 138.)
25. Which is characterised after all by that fantastic abortion of English jingoism entitled "The Invasion of 1910".

and Germany on the world market, therefore a direct consequence of unrestrained capitalist development and international competition. The Spanish-American war over Cuba, Italy's Abyssinian war, England's war in the Transvaal, the Sino-Japanese war, the adventure of the Great Powers in China, the Russo-Japanese war: all, though their particular causes and conditions are manifold, possess one great common feature, that they are of expansion. And if we recall the Anglo-Russian tension in Tibet, Persia and Afghanistan, the Japanese-American disagreements of the winter of 1906, and finally the glorious and memorable Morocco conflict of December 1906 with its Franco-Spanish co-operation,[26] we recognise that the capitalist policy of expansion and its colonial policy have placed countless mines under the edifice of world peace. The fuses lie in the most varied hands, and the mines may easily and unexpectedly explode.[27] A time may of course come when the division of the world is so far advanced that one may expect the formation of a trust governing all possible colonial possessions by the colony-owning states, that is to say, the elimination of colonial competition between the states, just as has been achieved within certain limits through cartels and trusts in the field of private competition between capitalists. But that will take a good while, and may be postponed to the quite remote future by the economic and national rise of China alone.

Thus all the alleged *plans for disarmament* appear for the moment to be simple folly, empty talk, attempts to cheat. The stamp of the tsar as the author of the comedy of the Hague[28] can be found throughout.

Recently the soap bubble of England's alleged disarmament has burst in a ludicrous manner: Haldane, the minister of war, the alleged promoter of such intentions, has come out in the sharpest words against any reduction of the active armed forces, and has been revealed and shown up as a militaristic agitator,[29] while at the same time the Anglo-French military convention rises above the horizon. And at the very same hour at which the second "peace conference" is being prepared, Sweden is enlarging its navy, the military budget is growing ever larger in America[30] and Japan, and in France the Clemenceau ministry is stressing the need for a strong army and navy by demanding an increase in spending of 208 million marks.[31] The *Hamburger Nachrichten* meanwhile suggests that belief in military armament as the only salvation is the quintessence of the outlook of the ruling class of Germany, and the German people are favoured by the

---

26. France spent more than 100 millions in 1906, as a result of the Morocco dispute, to secure its eastern border from a military standpoint!
27. On the question of the alleged but never fully explained plan of Semler, the representative of the Hamburg shipping firms to capture Fernando Po *à la* Jameson, see the debates of the budget commission at the beginning (December 1906).
28. The peace conference held at The Hague in May–June 1899. It was inspired by tsarist Russia, which was unable to keep up with the other powers in the armaments race.
29. It is irrelevant that he remains opposed to universal military service – a fact which the *Kreuz-Zeitung* of 29 November 1906, regrets, on the ground that universal military service would educate the British people to a better appreciation of the seriousness of war! In Germany indeed, according to the wish of the knights of the *Kreuz-Zeitung*, the only purpose of universal military service is to force sacrifice of blood and property on the people, while the decision as to war and peace remains for those to gamble with who least understand the seriousness of war. They quite understand the value of democracy abroad, of course!
30. See chapter 4, "Another dilemma" and Roosevelt's message of December 4, 1906.
31. Mainly based on the Morocco conflict.

government with demands for further increases in the military budget,[32] for which even our Liberals stretch out their hands.[33] Thus we can judge the naivety of the French senator d'Estournelles de Constant, a member of court of the Hague, displayed in his latest essay on the limitation of armaments.[34] In fact, for this political dreamer it does not even take one swallow to make the summer of disarmament – a sparrow is enough for him. It is almost refreshing after this to see the honest brutality with which the Great Powers taking part in the conference let Stead's proposal fall, and even resisted the disarmament question being put on the agenda of the second conference.

The third offshoot of capitalism in the military field, *colonial militarism*, deserves a few words. The colonial army – that is to say, the standing colonial army, not the colonial militia force allegedly "planned" for German South-West Africa,[35] and even less the quite different militia of the almost independent British colonies – plays an extremely important role for Britain; its importance is also increasing for the other civilised states. For Britain such an army fulfils not only the task of the suppression or checking of the "internal colonial enemy" (that is, the natives of the colonies), but also that of providing a means of force against the external colonial enemy (Russia, for example). For the other states with colonies, especially America and Germany,[36] the first and almost exclusive task of the colonial army, often under the name of a "defensive formation or of a "foreign legion",[37] is to drive the luckless natives into slavery, to turn them into forced labourers for the capitalists, and – when they wish to defend their native land against the foreign robbers and blood-suckers – to shoot them down mercilessly, to cut them down with the sword and to starve them out. The colonial army, which is often made up of the scum of the European population,[38] is the most bestial, the most abominable of all the tools used by our capitalist states. There is hardly a crime which colonial militarism and the tropical frenzy bred of it has not committed.[39] Men like Tippelskirch, Woermann, Podbielski, Leist, Wehlan, Peters, Ahrenberg & Co. are evidence and proof of this for Germany. They are the fruits by which we recognise the essence of colonial policy,

---

32. 24¾ millions for the navy, 51 millions for the army, 7 millions interest – total: an increase of about 83 million marks as against the budget of 1906–7! Rosy prospects of further "limitless" naval armament expenditure are given in an obviously inspired article in the *Reichsboten* of 21 December 1906. There is also the vast colonial war expenditure (the China expedition: 454 million marks; the South-West African rising: 490 millions so far; the East African rising: 2 millions, etc.). The question of the ratification of all this expenditure has now, on 13 December 1906, caused a conflict and the dissolution of the Reichstag.
33. See for instance the *Berliner Tageblatt* of 27 October 1906, and above all the notorious bill introduced by Ablass on 13 December 1906, as well as the Liberal electoral slogan of 25 January 1907.
34. *La Revue* of October 1, 1906. The "results actually achieved" by the disarmament movement, prophesied by the editor of the *Revue*, remain his own deep secret.
35. Dernburg in the Reichstag sitting of 29 November 1906
36. Whose colonial expenditure, even according to Dernburg's memorandum of October 1906, is of an overwhelmingly military character, in spite of all attempts to conceal the fact in the balance sheet.
37. Since 31 December 1900, France has possessed a regular colonial army, with which the most evil experiments are being carried out. See the *Hamburgischer Correspondent*, No.621, 7 December 1906, note on p.49. In Germany the formation of such an army is being busily worked on, and the progress is rapid.
38. See Péroz, *France et Japon en Indochine*; Famin, *L'armée coloniale*; E. Reclus in *Patriotisme et colonisation*; Däumig, *Schlachtopfer des Militarismus*; *Die Neue Zeit*, year XVIII (1899–1900), Vol.2, p.365; on the *bataillons d'Afrique*, p.369. See also, for Germany, the Deputy Roeren in the Reichstag on 3 December 1906.
39. The disciplinary system also assumes an especially sharp form of brutality. On the question of the French Foreign Légion and the *bataillons d'Afrique*, see Däumig, *Schlachtopfer des Militarismus*; on the elimination of the *biribi*, see pp.27–8, 34.

of that colonial policy which – under the deceptive mask[40] of spreading Christianity and civilisation or of defending the national honour – profits and deceives with pious gaze in the service of the colonial interests of the capitalists, murders and assaults the defenceless, burns up their property, robs and plunders their goods and possessions, and scorns and shames Christianity and civilisation.[41] The events in India and Tonkin, in the Congo State, in German South-West Africa and in the Philippines eclipse even the stars of a Cortez or a Pisarro.

2. Proletariat and war

Even if the function of militarism against the external enemy is described as a national function, that does not mean that it is a function which conforms to the interests, welfare and will of the peoples ruled and exploited by capitalism. The proletariat of the whole world can expect no advantage from the policy which makes it necessary that militarism against the external enemy should exist; indeed, its interests are in the sharpest contradiction to militarism, which directly or indirectly serves the ruling classes of capitalism in their exploitation. It is a policy whose function is more or less skilfully to pave the way into the world for the disordered chaotic production and senseless murderous competition of capitalism, in the process of which it tramples underfoot all civilised duties towards the less developed peoples. And actually it attains nothing, except for the fact that it insanely endangers the whole framework of our civilisation by bringing into existence the threat of world war.

The proletariat too welcomes the mighty industrial progress of our time. But it knows that this economic progress could have come about without the armed hand, without militarism and naval militarism, without the trident in our fist, and without the bestialities of our colonial economic policy, if only it were served by sensibly directed communities working according to international agreement and in conformity with the duties and interests of civilisation. The proletariat knows that our world policy is to a large extent a policy of forcible and clumsy attempts to overcome and confuse the social and political difficulties which the ruling classes see themselves faced with at home; in short, a Bonapartist policy of attempts at deception and deceit. The proletariat

---

40. This hypocritical and shameful cloak is now thrown off with all the cynicism one could wish for. See the article of G.B. in the monthly journal *Die deutschen Kolonien* (October 1906), and the remarks of Strantz at the conference of the Pan-German Society (September 1906): "We do not want to make Christians of the people in the colonies, but to make them work for us. This dizzy talk about humaneness is quite ludicrous. German sentimentality has robbed us of a man like Peters". Further, Heinrich Hartert writes in *Der Tag* of 21 December 1906 that it is "the duty of the mission...to adjust itself to given conditions"; but it has "often made itself directly troublesome to the trader". This constitutes the main point of dispute in colonial policy between the Centre Party and the government, and only in this context can one understand the unrestrained and fierce attack made by the trader Dernburg against the so-called shadow government of the Centre. In this respect too the divine "answer of Alexander" applies to foreign countries. For America the *Kreuz-Zeitung* preaches the following (29 September 1906): "The simple extermination of whole tribes of Indians is so inhuman and un-Christian that it cannot under any circumstances be justified – especially since for the Americans it is in no way a question of to be or not to be". Where that is the question, therefore, according to the conception of the colony-owning Christians, he who professes love for his neighbours may even "exterminate whole tribes"!
41. See the memorable debates in the German Reichstag between 28 November and 4 December 1906, in which the abscess was lanced.

knows that the enemies of the workers prefer to cook their soup over the fire of narrow-minded chauvinism, that the fear of war carefully fostered by Bismarck in 1887 aided precisely the most dangerous forces of reaction, and that a recently exposed neat little plan of very important persons was intended to snatch away from the German people, in a confused period of war jingoism "after the return of a victorious army", its right to elect the Reichstag.[42] The proletariat knows that this policy is an attempt to exploit economic progress for its own ends, and especially that all the benefit from our colonial policy flows only into the capacious pockets of the class of employers, of capitalism, the sworn enemy of the proletariat itself. It knows that the wars waged by the ruling classes inflict on it the most scandalous sacrifices of property and blood,[43] for which, after its work is complete, it is rewarded with miserable disablement pensions, veterans' aid funds, barrel-organs and kicks of all kinds. It knows that in every war a volcano of hun-like brutality and baseness erupts among the peoples involved, and that for years civilisation is set back and barbarism reigns.[44] It knows that the fatherland, for which it must fight, is not its own fatherland, that the proletariat of every land has only one real enemy: the capitalist class which oppresses and exploits it; that because of its special interests the proletariat of every land is closely united with the proletariat of every other land; that all national interests recede before the common interests of the international proletariat; and that the international coalition of exploitation and slavery must be opposed by the international coalition of the exploited, the enslaved. It knows that, in so far as it is used in a war, it is led to fight against its own brothers and class comrades and so to fight against its own interests.

The class-conscious proletariat does not simply remain cool towards the international task of the army, as well as towards the whole capitalist policy of expansion, but takes up a serious and clear-sighted position of opposition to this task and policy. Faced with the important task of struggling against this aspect of militarism too, it is becoming ever more conscious of its mission. This is shown by the international congresses, and by the exchange of demonstrations of solidarity between German and French socialists at the time of the outbreak of the Franco-German war, between the Spanish and American socialists when the Cuban war broke out, and between the Russian and Japanese socialists when the East Asian war broke out in 1904. It is also shown by the decision of the Swedish Social Democrats in 1905 to call a general strike in the case of a war between Sweden and Norway, and by the parliamentary position taken up by the German Social Democrats with regard to war credits in 1870 as well as in the Morocco conflict; and it is shown by the attitude of the class-conscious proletariat towards intervention in Russia.

---

42. See the *Hamburger Nachrichten* of 3 November 1906.
43. The sacrifice of human life in war between 1799 and 1904 (excluding the Russo-Japanese war) is estimated at about 15 millions.
44. See Moltke, *Gesammelte Schriften und Denkwürdigkeiten*, Vol.II, p.288. Here war is supposed to raise the level of morality and efficiency, and especially to produce moral energy.

3. Characteristics of "militarism against the internal enemy" and its task

Militarism is, however, not only a means of defence and a weapon against the external enemy; it has a second task,[45] which comes more and more into prominence with the sharpening of class contradictions and the growth of proletarian class consciousness. Thus the outer form of militarism and its inner character are more and more precisely determined: it has the task of protecting the prevailing social order, of supporting capitalism and all reaction against the struggle of the working class for freedom. Here militarism manifests itself as a pure tool in the hands of the ruling classes, designed to hinder the development of class consciousness by its alliance with the police and the system of justice, with the school and church, and further to secure for a minority at any cost, even against the conscious will of the majority of the people, its dominant position in the state and its freedom to exploit.

This is how modern militarism stands before us. It wants neither more nor less than the squaring of the circle; it arms the people against the people itself; it is insolent enough to force the workers – by artificial but ruthless attempts to introduce into our social organisation a principle of division according to age – to become oppressors, enemies and murderers of their own class comrades and friends, of their parents, brothers, sisters and children, murderers of their own past and future. It wants to be at the same time democratic and despotic, enlightened and machine-like, at the same time to serve the nation and to be its enemy.

It must not, however, be forgotten that militarism is also directed against the nationalist and even the religious enemy[46] at home – in Germany for example against the Poles,[47] Alsatians and Danes – and even finds employment in conflicts between the non-proletarian classes; that it is a phenomenon which takes many forms and often changes its character; and that Prussian-German militarism has blossomed into a very special flower owing to the peculiar semi-absolutist, feudal-bureaucratic conditions in Germany. This Prussian-German militarism possesses all the evil and dangerous qualities of every form of capitalist militarism, so that it is well qualified to stand as a paradigm of contemporary militarism, in its forms, methods and effects. Just as it is said, to use the words of Bismarck, that no one has been able to imitate the Prussian lieutenant, so indeed no one has been able to imitate Prussian-German militarism, which has become not simply a state within the state, but actually a state above the state.

Let us next consider the way in which the army is constituted in other countries. Here we must take into account not only the army proper but also the *gendarmerie* and police, which often have the character of special military organisations designed for everyday service against the internal enemy, and in their rough and violent nature bear the mark of military origin.

---

45. The task of bolstering up the existing internal order falls to militarism not only in the capitalist system but in all class-divided social orders.
46. See the French "struggle for culture" during the conflict of December 1906.
47. See the electoral row in Upper Silesia in 1903.

4. The constitution of the army in some foreign countries

We find special forms of army constitution for example in Britain and America, in Switzerland and Belgium.

Great Britain has a hired army (a "regular army") and a militia force, together with the Yeomanry. It also has the so-called Volunteers, a mostly unpaid force which in 1905 numbered 245,000 men. The standing army, including the militia – in which substitution is permitted – numbered in the same year around 444,000 men, of which, however, only about 162,000 were stationed in England. Further, a militarily organised police corps has been prepared for Ireland (about 12,000 men). The standing army is for the most part used outside the home country, especially in India, where the army of about 230,000 men[48] is two-thirds composed of natives. The colonies as a rule have their own militia and volunteer corps. The relation between Britain's home and colonial militarism is marked by the military budget, which for example in 1897 amounted to about 360 million marks at home and about 500 millions for India. There is also the immense navy with a complement of around 200,000 men together with marine troops.

The constitution of the army in the United States of America is a mixture of standing army and militia. The standing army, based on conscription[49] and constitutionally limited to a maximum of 100,000 men, actually numbered in peace time according to an estimate of 1905 around 61,000 men (on October 15, 1906, including the Philippine Scouts, 67,253 men), of which 3,800 were officers, most of whom had passed through West Point Military Academy. In the same year the militia numbered about 111,000 men. It is organised in a fairly democratic way. In times of peace it is under the governor, and is not highly armed or trained. The often militarily organised police forces also play an important role. Quite peculiar is another organisation which, formally speaking, does not belong here, but which cannot be ignored because of the function it performs. In all capitalist countries we find "black hundreds", gangs organised by the bosses, even if only in the sense that the capitalists arm their strike-breakers (something which is not rare for example in Switzerland and France, and was seen in Germany in last year's shipyard strike in Hamburg and in the Nuremberg events of 1906). But in the armed Pinkerton detectives the American capitalists have a "black hundred" of first quality permanently at their disposal. If we finally take note of the roughly 30,000 men who formed the navy in 1905, we see that the United States offers good examples of the most important forms of armed state power.

In Switzerland there existed until recently a real popular army, a general arming of the people. Every Swiss citizen capable of bearing arms possessed a gun and ammunition permanently at home. This was the army of democracy, with which Gaston Moch deals in his well-known book. Since Switzerland has a multinational citizenry, as does Belgium,

---

48.   In 1905–6: 229,820; in the Native States in 1903: 136,837.
49.   Enlistment is becoming even more difficult, and the percentage of foreigners recruited is rising – a fact which is worrying the American government.

it was natural that "external militarism" could take on and preserve a particularly mild character here, to the success of which numerous other factors have contributed. But with the sharpening of class contradictions, "militarism at home" changed its character. The need of the capitalist section of the population to consolidate its power caused the possession of arms and ammunition in the hands of the proletariat to be felt as a hindrance to the freedom to exploit and oppress, even as a danger to the existence of the capitalist class. Thus in September 1899 the disarming of the people began with the withdrawal of ammunition, while at the same time there was an attempt to extend existing militaristic tendencies according to the pattern of the great military states. Thus even in the famous Swiss militia the frightening traits which have made every standing army into a disgrace to civilisation are more and more evident. The resolution of the National Council of December 21, 1906, concerning the law on military reorganisation, which dealt with the use of soldiers in strikes, changes nothing in this respect.

Belgium's need of soldiers for the standing army is, because of its neutrality, considerably less than the "supply" of soldiers (about half). The system of general military service is therefore complemented by the system of exemptions and finally by the system of buying oneself out, of substitution, which has cut deeply into the character of the army. Of course, only the wealthy are in a position to pay for someone to take their place, and equally naturally they make full use of the system. If this already well developed system of substitution was not in itself especially significant politically, it did lead – in a country which was heavily composed of proletarians and where a great percentage of workers were to be found among those liable for military service as well those excused from it – to an extremely dangerous situation for the ruling class. The army, proletarian through and through, was – in so far as it was not already composed in and for itself of class-conscious and determined proletarians – so rapidly convinced of the anti-militarist propaganda that for years the possibility of using it as a tool of the ruling class against the internal enemy has been ruled out, and it is no longer so used. But an answer was at hand.

For a long time there had existed the organisation of the so-called Civil Guard. To the Civil Guard belong those who have been lucky in the draw and those who have bought themselves out of the army; but only those can join who provide their own uniform and weapon, an arrangement (a kind of weeding-out system) whose effect is that the poorer part of the population more or less excludes itself. Earlier it was nothing more than a great masquerade, its members were mostly liberal and the organisation democratic. The Civil Guards kept their weapons at home, chose their officers themselves, etc. But with the increasing unreliability of the standing army a change came about. The administration and direction of the Civil Guard were taken out of the hands of the municipalities and put into those of the government, while the democratic arrangements were abolished, and the weapons taken away from individuals and locked up in the stores of the military administration. A rather tighter form of military duty was introduced and the training of the Civil Guards transferred to the worst of the ex-officers of the standing army. The age group between 20 and 30 must now exercise no fewer than three evenings in the week and half a Sunday every fortnight. And whereas previously in relation to the organisation of these exercises the old method – or lack of method – recalling the days of our "old-time town soldiers" was used, now everything is much more sharply controlled and punctuality enforced on pain of punishment. It is worth noting that this new organisation of the Civil Guard only took place in communities of over 20,000 inhabitants, while elsewhere the Civil Guard has remained an absurd shadow. This fact too brands the organisation with the mark of its true goal, which is to be a special defensive force of the government in the struggle against the "internal enemy". In 1905 the standing army, excluding the *gendarmerie*, numbered around 46,000 men, the active Civil Guard around 44,000, almost exactly as many!

Belgium thus possesses one army directed against the external enemy and one directed against the internal enemy, a very cunning arrangement which, as the use of the Civil Guard in the recent strikes and struggles over voting rights proves, has performed and will perform good service for the capitalist regime of Belgium.

The country also has a *gendarmerie*, which in strikes and disturbances as well as in war takes on a simple military role. It is very numerous and distributed over the whole country; of great mobility, it can at any time be concentrated, moved and mobilised. In Tervueren near Brussels it has a general barracks for its flying squad, from which in the case of strikes and the like it swarms out as if from a wasps' nest. It is made up for the most part of former non-commissioned officers, is excellently armed and well paid; in short, an elite force. The Civil Guard was created simply for its task in the class struggle, so that it represents nothing but a special military mobilisation of the capitalist class itself, which is quite conscious of its own interests; but the "watchdogs of capital" organised in the *gendarmerie* play their role no less well, according to the saying: "Whoever pays me, I'll sing to his tune".

Japan, which stands on about the same capitalist-feudal level of development as Germany, has also in recent years – in spite of its land position similar to that of Britain, and indeed in consequence of the tension in its external position – become a true counterpart of Germany in relation to militarism, apart perhaps from the better military training of its forces.

Conclusions

From all this it follows that the size and special organisational character of the army is essentially determined by the international situation, by the function of the army against the external enemy. International tension is as a rule very high today and – even in the non-capitalist states, because of competition with and the need for protection against the capitalist states – necessitates the use of all citizens capable of bearing arms, as well as of the toughest forms of organisation: the standing army and universal military service. This tension may, however, either through natural causes – for example, England's island position, and even in a sense that of the United States of America – or through cultural-political causes – for example, Switzerland's and the Netherlands' declaration of neutrality – be subject to a very considerable relaxation.

"Militarism at home", on the other hand, which faces the internal enemy, is a phenomenon which always necessarily accompanies capitalist development; Gaston Moch himself describes "the restoration of order" as "a legitimate function of a popular army". And if militarism exhibits very different forms in regard to this function, this is simply explained by the fact that its fulfilment does not depend so much on international competition, so that it can take on very different forms and many more national peculiarities.

Britain, incidentally, and also America (where for example from 1896 to 1906 the standing army was strengthened from about 27,000 to about 61,000 men, the number of naval personnel doubled, the budget of the department of war increased by two and a half times, and that of the department of the navy by more than three times, while for 1907 Taft has again demanded an extra 100 million) are driven more and more along the path of European-Continental militarism, a fact which is certainly determined in the first place by the change in the international situation and the requirements of jingoistic-imperialist world policy, but in the second place without doubt by the change in internal relations of tension, by the increase in the danger of class war. The militaristic attacks of the British War Minister Haldane in September 1906 are hardly coincidental with the energetic independent appearance of the organised British working class on the political stage.[50]

The tendency to introduce general conscription according to the Swiss model, which has still not been passed in England in spite of the important public agitation for it which has been carried on, but which has found significant expression in the United States in Roosevelt's message of December 4, 1906, is no symptom of progress. It means in spite of everything a strengthening of militarism in relation to the present position, and lies after all on the steep path to the standing army, about which the example of Switzerland can teach us something.

Militarism undoubtedly possesses, with respect to the manifold combination of factors determined by the extent and character of the special requirements of external and internal defence, a plurality of aspects and a flexibility which is most clearly seen in army organisation. This flexibility, however, comes into play everywhere within the boundaries which are set by that goal which is absolutely essential to militarism, the protection of capitalism.

The development of militarism can nevertheless take quite different paths. While for example France under Picquart was seriously engaged in shortening considerably

---

50. Haldane's own political position, sharply hostile to the Labour Party, is demonstrated by the facts reported by Rothstein in *Die Neue Zeit*, 25th year (1906–7), Vol.I, p.121. Whether the conflict over the school legislation between the Upper and Lower Houses in November–December 1906 is also a symptom of sharpening tension only the future can tell us. The recently reported rejection of general compulsory service by Haldane does not stand in contradiction to this, but accords with it.

the training time of the Reserve and Territorial forces,[51] in the reform of the *biribi* and in the abolition of the special military jurisdiction,[52] the President of the German military court of the Reich, von Massow, was resigning his post in autumn 1906, because the military command (the Prussian War Ministry) had by means of legal interpretations formally and directly interfered in the independence of the military courts (circular of spring 1905), an independence which of course had taken on a peculiar character in the action against the judges in the Bilse case.[53] These "French concessions" were almost exclusively based on anti-clericalism. Clericalism had important support in the army; the government needed the proletariat in the "struggle for culture". This combination is of course neither permanent, nor does it arise from an essential, lasting tendency of development. It depends, as far as its nature is concerned, on the passing conjuncture, and goes hand in hand with an energetic struggle against militarism, as we have shown.

Russia is interesting from this point of view. The high state of tension in its international position has forced it to introduce universal military service, while as an Asiatic-Despotic state it is faced with an unequalled internal conflict. The internal enemy of tsarism is not only the proletariat, but also the great mass of the peasantry and bourgeoisie, even indeed a large part of the nobility. Ninety-nine percent of Russian soldiers are by class position bitter enemies of tsarist despotism. A low level of culture, national and religious conflicts, and also contradictions in economic and social interests, together with the more or less subtle pressure exercised by the extensive bureaucratic apparatus as well as the unfavourable local organisation, the inadequately developed transport system and other things: all these represent an important check on the development of class consciousness. There exists a much attacked system of elite troops, who are provided with every facility: the *gendarmerie*, for example, and especially the Cossacks, which effectively constitute a special social class on account of their good pay and other material provision, of their extensive political privileges, and of the arrangement by which they live in a semi-socialist community; they are thus closely bound in an artificial way to the ruling classes. In this way tsarism tries to secure a sufficient number of loyal supporters to offset the ferment which has penetrated deep into the ranks of the army. And to all this, to these "watchdogs of tsarism", there must be added the Circassians,[54] and other barbarian peoples living in the empire of the fist, who were loosed over the land like a pack of wolves in the Baltic counter-revolution, together with all the other numberless parasites on tsarism, the police and their accomplices, and the hooligans and black hundreds.

But if in the bourgeois-capitalist states the army based on universal military service

---

51. Rejected by the Chamber for the time being in December 1906.
52. See especially Assistant State Secretary Chéron in the debate in the Chamber on 10 December 1906, and *L'Humanité* of 11 December 1906.
53. The court-martial of Lieutenant Bilse took place in Metz in November 1903. He had written a novel depicting the dissolute morals of the officer corps and was sentenced to six months' imprisonment. His judges were later reprimanded for having conducted the trial in public, for the facts which were brought to light discredited the military system.
54. In the *Dünazeitung* of 4 December (17) 1906, even the District Councillor von Sivers-Römershof speaks of the "bloodthirsty Circassians".

and designed as a weapon against the proletariat represents a frightful and bizarre contradiction, the army based on the same system under the despotic tsarist system of government is a weapon which is necessarily turned more and more with crushing weight against the tsarist despotism itself. The experiences of the anti-militarist movement in Russia can therefore only be applied to the bourgeois-capitalist states with the greatest of care. And if the efforts of the ruling classes of capitalism in the bourgeois-capitalist states to bribe the people to fight against itself – to a great extent indeed with money actually taken from the people – are finally doomed to failure, we already see before our very eyes how the desperate and pitiable attempts of tsarism to buy off the revolution by bribery are suffering a rapid and wretched fiasco in the tragic world of Russian finance, in spite of all the attempts of unscrupulous international capital to save the regime. The question of financial loans is certainly an important one, at least for the tempo of the revolution. But if the revolutions cannot easily be made, it is even less easy to buy them off,[55] even with the means available to the big capitalists of the world.

---

55. Not even in the recently prominent modern form of cheap trade and discount in concessions and natural riches to American trusts, the "*dernier cri*" in the double sense of tsarist foreign policy.

CHAPTER THREE

Methods and effects of militarism

1. The immediate object

We now move on to a special examination of the methods and effects of militarism, and in doing so direct our attention to a paradigm case of militarism, the Prussian-German bureaucratic-feudal-capitalist form – that very worst form of capitalist militarism, that state above the state.

Even if it is true that contemporary militarism is nothing more than a manifestation of our capitalist society, it is nevertheless a manifestation which has become almost independent and very nearly an end in itself.

Militarism, in order to attain its ends, must transform the army into a manageable, flexible and effective instrument. It must raise it to the highest possible level on the military-technical side; in addition, since it consists of men and not of machines and is therefore a living mechanism, it must be filled with the right "spirit".

The first aspect of the matter finally resolves itself into a financial question; this will be dealt with later. Here we shall go into the second aspect.

Its content has three facets. Militarism seeks to produce and foster the military spirit first off in the active army; then in those groups which become important when, like the reserve and militia, they are used to supplement the army in the case of mobilisation; and finally in all the other groups of the population which serve as a base and support for those strata which are to be employed for militarist or anti-militarist purposes.

2. Military pedagogy

The education of the soldier

The true "military spirit", also called "patriotic spirit" and in Prussia-Germany "spirit of loyalty to the king", means in brief a readiness at any time when so ordered to strike at the external and internal enemy. In order to produce this spirit the most perfect stupidity is needed, or at least the lowest possible level of intelligence. This makes it possible to drive on the masses like a herd of cattle in whatever direction is dictated by the interests of the "existing order". The confession of the war minister, von Einem, that he preferred a soldier loyal to the king, even if he were a bad shot, to one who was less submissive, even if he were a good shot, surely sprang from the depths of the heart of this representative of German militarism.

But here militarism finds itself in an unfortunate predicament. The technique of arms, strategy and tactics now make a significant demand on the intelligence,[56] and make the intelligent soldier, other things being equal, the more proficient.[57] For this reason alone militarism in the present day could no longer do anything simply with a crowd of fools. But neither can capitalism make use of such a crowd, because of the economic tasks which have to be performed by the masses and especially by the proletariat. Capitalism is therefore forced by a tragic fate, in order to be able to exploit, in order to be able to extract the highest possible profits – this is its inevitable task in life – to produce systematically on a vast scale among its slaves the very intelligence which, it knows quite well, must bring its own death and destruction. All attempts, through skilful manoeuvring and artful co-operation with church and school, to steer the ship of capitalism between the Scylla of an intelligence so low that it makes exploitation altogether too difficult, and lowers the proletarian to the level of a useless beast of burden, and the Charybdis of an education which revolutionises the heads of the exploited, which everywhere opens the gates of class consciousness, which is necessarily destructive of capitalism – such attempts are desperate and hopeless. Only the agricultural workers of the region east of the Elbe – who, according to the famous words of Kröcher, are actually the most stupid of labourers, though, it should be noted, they can still provide the Junker with his best workers – now supply militarism on a large scale with material which allows itself to be led like a horde of slaves simply on a word of command. This material, however, can be put to use only cautiously and within definite limits, for its level of intelligence is too low even for militarism.

It is often said that our best soldiers are Social Democrats. Here is registered the difficulty of the task of providing the army, based on universal conscription, with the

---

56. See Caprivi's remarks in the Reichstag on February 27, 1891; likewise those of the War Minister von Kaltenborn-Stachau: "The demands made on the non-commissioned officers have become greater as a consequence of the new armament, the new regulations on training, etc."
57. See the remarks of the Bavarian General von Sauer made at the end of October 1898 before the National Economic Society in Munich (in Bebel, *Nicht stehendes Heer sondern Volkswehr*, Stuttgart 1898, p.77).

METHODS AND EFFECTS OF MILITARISM

correct military spirit.[58] Since mere slavish and abject obedience does not suffice, and is anyway no longer possible, militarism has to use a roundabout way of strengthening the will of its troops in order to create for itself "shooting automatons".[59] It must bend the will by moral and psychological influence or by force; it must entice or compel it. The principle of the carrot and the stick is applicable here. The true "spirit" required by militarism, in respect first of all of its function against the external enemy, is chauvinistic pig-headedness, narrow-mindedness and arrogance; second, in respect of its function against the internal enemy, it is a lack of understanding and even hatred of all progress, of every undertaking and endeavour which might in any way threaten the power of the class dominant at the time. This is the direction in which militarism must guide the thoughts and feelings of the soldiers, in so far as it wants to lure with the carrot those whose class interests are opposed to all chauvinism and for whom progress should appear as the only reasonable goal until the time when the existing social order is overthrown. It must also not be forgotten that the proletarian whose age makes him liable for military service, although as a rule he is more independent and capable of political insight than the bourgeois of the same age, is not so firm in his class consciousness.

The system of influencing the troops from the moral and psychological standpoint is a most daring and cunning one, whereby, instead of being separated according to their social class, the soldiers are divided according to their age, in order to create a special class of proletarians of 20 to 22 years of age whose thoughts and feelings will be completely opposite to those of the proletarians in the other, "older" classes.

First of all, the proletarian in uniform is sharply and ruthlessly cut off from his class comrades and his family. This is done by taking him away from his home, which is systematically done in Germany, and especially by shutting him up in barracks.[60] One might almost speak of a repetition of the Jesuit method of education, a counterpart of monastic organisation.

Next it is necessary to extend this isolation for as long as possible, a tendency which is only checked by financial difficulties when it cannot find a military-technical justification. This circumstance is for example essentially the reason for the introduction in 1893 of the two-year period of military service in Germany.[61]

Finally it is necessary to make the best possible use of the time available to capture the minds of the trainees. Different means are used to this end. Just as in the case of the

---

58. See in this connection the moving complaint of Caprivi in the Reichstag sitting of February 27, 1891.
59. These "shooting automatons" (cf. also Corporal Lück) can however become very dangerous, because of course it may be that one day the mechanism is set in motion by an unauthorised person. Then the bourgeoisie will set up a cry, afraid not only of its own capitalist resemblance to God, but also of its feudal relations, and like the hunter in *Struwwelpeter* who is himself pursued will cry out in fear: "Please help me, people!", and complain about the "discipline of the German army being raised to a point where the soldier can no longer use his critical reason", as the *Leipziger Tageblatt* and other papers did in the Köpenick case – which of course does not hinder the bourgeoisie, in the perplexity of its position, from keeping itself always ready to offer sacrifices to the Moloch of this militaristic madness, with "discipline raised to a point where the soldier can no longer use his critical reason". Another tragic contradiction!
60. From the standpoint of health this is very serious, and has for example led in France to the people being infected to a high degree with tuberculosis and syphilis. In the French army five to seven times as many cases of tuberculosis are recorded as in the German. In a few decades, so a French warning has it, France will be decimated unless the system of barracks is abolished.
61. See Schippel, *Sozialdemokratisches Reichstag-Handbuch*, Berlin 1902, p.929.

Church, all human weaknesses and the senses are put to use in the service of this military pedagogy. Ambition and vanity are encouraged, the military uniform is proclaimed as the most noble dress, the soldier's honour glorified as especially distinguished, and the rank of soldier trumpeted as the most important and respected; and indeed, it is endowed with many privileges.[62] The authorities speculate on men's love of finery: in contradiction to their purely military purpose, uniforms are trimmed with colourful tinsel like carnival costumes and cut according to the coarse taste of the lower classes, whom these authorities want to capture. All kinds of petty glittering distinctions, decorations, stripes for good shooting, etc., serve the same base instinct – for showing off and being looked up to. And how much of the suffering of soldiers has been soothed by military music, which, along with the glittering trimmings of the uniform and the pompous military ostentation, is to be thanked for that extensive popularity which our "wonderful army of war" can boast of among children, fools, servant girls and the lumpenproletariat? Whoever has once examined the dubious public which watches parades and the throng which follows the processions of the Berlin palace guard will understand this perfectly well. It is well known in fact that this attraction to the military uniform which is found in certain civilian circles constitutes an important aspect of temptation for the uneducated elements in the army.

All these means are that much more effective the lower the intellectual level of the soldiers, the lower their social position. For such elements are easier to deceive, not only on account of their slight capacity for critical judgment, but also because for them there is a difference between the level of their former civilian life and that of their military position – one need only imagine an American Negro[63] or an East Prussian serf suddenly dressed in the "most distinguished" uniform! In this way a tragic contradiction arises: that the effect of these means on the intelligent industrial proletariat, for whom they were first designed, is less than on those elements whom it seems hardly necessary to influence in this direction, at least for the time being, since they already constitute an adequately pliable material for militarism. But the same methods may also contribute to the preservation of the "spirit" acceptable to militarism. The same end is served by the regimental feasts, the celebrations of the Kaiser's birthday and the like.

When everything has been done to place the soldier to a degree in a state of intoxication, to drug his mind, to fire his feelings and imagination, it is necessary systematically to work upon his powers of reasoning. A system of instruction attempts to cram him with a childish, distorted picture of the world, designed to suit the purpose of militarism. Of course this instruction, mostly given by uneducated men incapable of proper teaching, does not have any effect at all on the intelligent industrial workers who are

---

62. See the state of helplessness of the police in relation to the military, and especially to officers, when they commit excesses. One might also note the privilege accorded to the army of marching frequently in closed ranks through the towns, often in processions of endless length, thus completely holding up traffic without sense or reason: parades whose only basis is military aesthetics. The most absurd example of the social danger and ludicrous pomposity of such pampered madness was seen some years ago in Berlin, when a detachment of the fire brigade in a great hurry was simply halted by a marching military column, which would not disturb its beautiful and majestic order by giving way. This action was, it is true, later censured.

63. See the essay "Der amerikanische Neger als Soldat", in No.638 of the *Berliner Lokal-Anzeiger*, 1906.

often more intelligent than their instructors. It is an attempt to attain an impossible object, resembling an arrow which rebounds on the one who shot it. This was recently made clear to General Liebert by *Die Post* and by Max Lorenz (whose understanding has been quickened by competition for profit) in regard to the anti-Social Democratic "instruction" of soldiers.

Hard drilling and the discipline of the barracks, the canonisation of the uniform of the officers[64] and non-commissioned officers,[65] which in many fields really seems to be *legibus solutus* and sacrosanct – in short, the discipline and control which clasp the soldier in an iron bond in everything he does or thinks, on or off duty – serve to produce the necessary flexibility and obedience of will. Each individual is so ruthlessly bent, pulled and twisted that the strongest spine is in danger of breaking, and either bends or breaks.[66]

The zealous fostering of the "religious" spirit, which was demanded by a motion of the budget committee of the Reichstag in February 1892 as a special goal of military education, though rejected without prejudice, is also designed to complete the work of military oppression and enslavement.

Instruction and religious propaganda constitute at the same time the carrot and the stick, the latter being used for the most part carefully and in a disguised form.

The most attractive carrot, successfully used as a means of enticement for the formation and placing of the important permanent cadres of the army, is the system of "capitulation", with the prospect of premiums for the non-commissioned officers[67] and of the "certificate of maintenance in civilian life",[68] which is a very cunning and

---

64. Curious saints, it is true! One might recall the Bilse case of November 1903* and the many "little garrisons" *à la* Forbach, the regulations concerning gambling and the drinking of champagne, duelling by officers – that *fine fleur* of the honour of officers – the Brüsewitz stabbing (October 1896) and the Hüssen shooting (*Prinz Arenberg und die Arenberge*, Berlin 1904, pp.13ff.), the Harmlos and Ruhstrat affairs, the photographic novels of Bilse and Beyerlein, Schlicht's (Count Baudissin) *Erstklassige Menschen*, Jesco von Puttkamer, and last but not least the Prince Arenberg scandal, which also belongs here. The French "small garrison town" of Verdun made quite a stir in the autumn of 1906. Naturally, those who worship the uniform consider these things as a "likeable, piquant weakness" in those they worship, who nevertheless adhere firmly to the Christian faith. Here of course we see once again the international solidarity of the noblest and best! An interesting case is the disclosure early in 1903 of the mutual flagellation by officers of the British Grenadier Guards (*La Jeunesse Socialiste*, March 1903).
65. The non-commissioned officer is – "God's representative on earth!"
66. The statistics of suicide among soldiers provides the most striking evidence of this. Even this phenomenon is international. According to official statistics there was one suicide in every 3,700 men in Germany in 1901, in Austria one in about every 920. In the Austrian Tenth Army corps 80 soldiers and 12 officers committed suicide in 1901, a further 127 became insane and were invalided out in consequence of self-mutilation and maltreatment. In the same period 400 men deserted and 725 were condemned to hard labour or rigorous confinement! In these matters the struggle between nationalities certainly makes things much worse.
67. Introduced into Germany in 1891 (maximum 1,000 marks). It had already been in existence in Saxony and Württemberg, and a precedent had also been set in the Reich by the granting of "non-recurrent allowances". It is also found elsewhere; in France for example – though admittedly it meets with little success – the amounts are much larger (up to 4,000 francs). The schools for non-commissioned officers also belong in this category – see the speech of Vogel von Falckenstein in the Reichstag on March 2, 1891.
68. Caprivi's speech in the Reichstag on February 27, 1891, is the classical confession of a beautiful capitalist-militarist soul, together with its fears and needs, with its hopes and aims, and with its methods of attaining those aims. It opens wide a window permitting us a close examination of the innermost secrets of the soul. It begins with the statement that "only on one condition would the reintroduction of the (anti-)socialist law be renounced: on the condition that all measures be taken to pull the ground from under the feet of Social Democracy or to take up the struggle against it"; one of these measures (thus a substitute for the anti-socialist law) being the payment of premiums Lion-commissioned officers in conjunction with the certificate of maintenance in civilian life. Caprivi continued:

"The demands made upon the non-commissioned officers are increasing, in consequence of the increasing level of national education. The senior officer can fill his post only if he feels superior to those he commands.

"If it is now difficult to enforce discipline, it will become even more difficult if we have to take up the struggle against Social Democracy; by a struggle I do not mean in this context shooting and stabbing. My recollections go back to the year 1848. Conditions at that time were very much better, since current ideas had not arisen out

dangerous arrangement. As we shall demonstrate below, it contaminates our whole public life with militarism.

The whip used by militarism is, however, above all the system of discipline,[69] the military law with its rigorous threat to even the slightest opposition to the so-called military spirit, and military justice with its semi-mediaeval procedure, which deals out inhuman, barbarous punishment in the face of the slightest insubordination. Excesses committed by superiors against their subordinates meet, however, with light punishment, while the men's right of self-defence has been almost completely taken away. Nothing makes one more angry with militarism and nothing at the same time is more instructive than simply reading the military articles and reports of military criminal trials.

To this category belong also the examples of the ill-treatment of soldiers, of which more will be said later. This ill-treatment is not legal, but is nevertheless probably the most effective of all coercive means of discipline used by militarism.

There is an attempt to tame men in the way in which beasts are tamed. Recruits are drugged, confused, flattered, bribed, pressed, locked up, disciplined and beaten. Thus grain upon grain is mixed and kneaded to serve as mortar for the great edifice of the army, stone added to stone, calculated to form a fortress against revolution.[70]

The fact that all these means of enticement, discipline and punishment are weapons in the class struggle becomes obvious if we examine the "Institute for one-year volunteers". The one-year volunteer, the son of a bourgeois and intended as an officer of the

---

of long years of schooling but had suddenly come to the fore, and the old non-commissioned officers had a much easier task when facing the men than they do now when faced with Social Democracy. *("Hear, hear!" from the Right.)* To mention an extreme case: we need far better non-commissioned officers for street fighting against Social Democracy than we need for fighting the enemy. In the face of the enemy the troops can be inspired with patriotism and other lofty sentiments, and be stirred to self-sacrifice. But street fighting and all that is associated with it is not a factor which can raise the feeling of dignity of the troops; they always feel that they are up against their own countrymen... The non-commissioned officers can only retain their superiority if we seek to raise them higher. The allied governments want to raise the level of the non-commissioned officer class."

It was necessary, he continued, to make the non-commissioned officers a "class of men whose very existence would be bound to the state".

This at the same time is a fine psychological description of the élite troops.

69. Arrest, together with deprivation of food, bed and light; fatigue drill and the like; in the field also the barbarous *Anbinden* or "binding on". The Austrian *Krummschliessen* "looking in a crooked position" and "binding on", the Belgian *cachots* and the internationally used "cat-o'-nine-tails" and the like are well known. Not so well remembered perhaps are the dreadful methods of torture used in the French disciplinary detachments and also applied to "politicals": the *poucettes*, the *menottes* and the *crapaudine* (see the illustrated brochure published by the Fédération socialiste autonome du Cher in 1902, entitled *Les Bagnes Militaires* – Breton's speech in the Chamber; Georges Darien, *biribi* [which is the collective name for all the military disciplinary institutions in North Africa], Dubois-Desaulle, *Sous la Casque*, Paris 1899). On the *compagnies de discipline*, the *pénitenciers* and the *travaux forcés* (disciplinary companies, penitentiaries, hard labour) in the French Foreign Legion and its victims, see Däumig, *Schlachtopfer des Militarismus*. There are now energetic attempts to suppress the *biribi* (see the Chamber discussions on December 8 and 10, 1906). The disciplinary beatings which the officers of the British Grenadier Guards inflict on one another with praiseworthy democratic zeal deserve to be mentioned here as a curiosity (*La Jeunesse Socialiste*, March 1903).

70. The result of all these educational methods from the military standpoint has been discussed elsewhere. Here we will only point to the moral result, which brings the bourgeois as well as the anarchist and half-anarchist opponents of the army to utter especially passionate and widespread cries of pathos and indignation. "The army is the school for crime" (Anatole France); "drunkenness, misbehaviour and hypocrisy are what barrack life teaches" (Professor Richet). According to the *Manuel du soldat*, the term of service is "an apprenticeship in brutality and vulgarity"; "a school of immorality"; it leads to "moral cowardice, servility and slavish fear". Certain military festivals can indeed hardly be conceived without that patriotic drunkenness which of course helps to uphold the state. On what Pastor César calls the "drunken and rowdy feasts" of the military clubs, see the *Leipziger Volkszeitung* of December 1, 1906. The result in terms of health is also less than pleasing. The sanitary state of the standing armies of England and America, those democratic countries, is quite horrifying. The death rate was much higher than in Germany: 7.13 and 6.18 per thousand in 1906–7. According to the report of HM O'Reilly, Surgeon-General of the Army, dysentery and alcoholism are worse in the American army than anywhere else in the world.

reserve, is generally considered above suspicion where anti-capitalist and anti-militarist, and especially revolutionary leanings are concerned. He is therefore spared being sent away from his home, being shut up in barracks, being instructed and forced to attend church, and even spared a large part of the hard drilling. It is of course only in exceptional cases that he falls into the snares of discipline and military law, and even then mostly without incurring severe punishment. And those who exploit the ordinary soldiers rarely dare, in spite of their great instinctive hatred for everything "cultured", to attack these volunteers. The training of the officers provides another striking proof of our thesis.

It is of great importance for military discipline that men work together in a mass, within which the independence of the individual is to a great extent abolished. Each individual in the army, like a criminal in a galley, is chained to all the others, and practically incapable of free action. The strength of the others, which is a hundred thousand times greater, prevents him by its overwhelming power from making any independent move. All the members of this mighty machine are subjected, not only to the hypnotic suggestion of those in command, but also to a special kind of hypnotism, mass hypnotism – which, however, is bound to be without effect on an army made up of educated and dedicated opponents of militarism.

In the field of the education of the soldier, the twin tasks of militarism are obviously by no means always satisfied together, but often come into conflict. This applies both to training and equipment. Military training demands ever more imperiously a constant increase in the level of independence of the soldier. But as a "watchdog of capital" he requires no independence; indeed, he must have none (his qualification for suicide must not be denied). In short, war against the external enemy demands men, war against the internal enemy demands slaves, machines. As far as training and equipment are concerned, it is impossible to dispense with the bright uniforms, the glittering buttons and helmets, the flags, parade drills, cavalry attacks and all the other rubbish needed to create the spirit required in the struggle against the internal enemy – but in war against the external enemy these may become quite fatal or simply impossible.[71] This tragic conflict, whose manifold implications cannot be thoroughly dealt with here, has not been grasped by all the well-intentioned critics of our militarism,[72] who in their innocence want simply to lay down the criterion for military training.

This conflict of interests within militarism, this self-contradiction from which it suffers, tends to take on a continually sharper form. It depends at any moment upon the relation between political tension abroad and at home as to which of the two contradictory interests gains the upper hand. It should not be forgotten that here lies the germ of the self-destruction of militarism.

When the war against the internal enemy in the case of an armed revolution makes

---

71. In the struggle against the internal enemy we naturally include here the struggle against the spirit of international proletarian solidarity, a spirit to which "militarism against the external enemy" is so averse.
72. See *Die Sozialdemokratie im Heere, Reform des deutschen Heeresdienstes zur Abwehr des Sozialismus*, by an Officer, published by Costenoble in Jena, 1901. Also the material in Bebel's *Nicht stehendes Heer sondern Volkswehr*, pp.46ff., and *Handbuch für sozialdemokratische Wahler. Der Reichstag 1848–1903*, Berlin 1903, pp.23ff.

such requirements of a military-technical kind that the dressed-up slaves and machines are no longer able to put down the revolt, then the last hour of coercive rule by the minority, the capitalist oligarchy, will strike.

It is important enough that this military spirit in general means disorder and confusion in proletarian class consciousness, and that militarism serves capitalism by contaminating our public life with this spirit in every direction simultaneously – leaving aside the purely militaristic contamination of which it is the cause. It does this for example by creating and furthering a feeling of servility in the proletarian in relation to the economic, social and political exploitation to which he is subject, thus retarding as far as possible the proletarian struggle for freedom. We shall have to come back to this point.

Bureaucratic and semi-military organisation of the civil population

Militarism seeks neither more nor less than to exert the most lasting and effective influence possible on those who belong to the active army. Next it attempts to arrogate to itself as much power as it possibly can over these persons, for example by a system of control, by a far-reaching extension of military jurisdiction and of the system of military courts of honour, which is even applied to officers in the reserve[73] and to those in positions of command. Especially characteristic in this respect is the subjection to military jurisdiction of men called up before the control committee, something which is claimed by the military authorities for the whole time during which a control committee is sitting. This is a quite open breach of the law. Not the slightest basis exists for the establishment of such a right, and it constitutes nothing less than usurpation. Here must also be mentioned the so-called young men's defence organisations and military clubs, with their official or semi-military management and their aping of the military dress, fooling and feasting. A most important role is played in the field of military activity by the officers of the reserve, who bring the spirit of the military caste into civilian life and immortalise it. Still more important is the subjection almost without exception of the higher officials of the state and communal administration, as well as of justice and the education system,[74] to military discipline, the militaristic spirit and the whole militarist conception of life. Every opposition movement which proves awkward and is not absolutely impossible to suppress is thus eliminated in advance. In this way – in conjunction with the system of military qualification for civilian life, which plays the same role for the subalterns and lower officials – the submissiveness of the civil executive is assured. Care is thus taken that the trees of class justice and the system of class education grow high into the sky of militarism, while the trees of self-government[75] are well pruned. It should also be mentioned here that officers on active service and those in the reserve

---

73. See in this connection the well known case of Gädke, in which the Prussian Court of Appeal gave legal approval to the unheard of aspirations of militarism.
74. Also many members of the medical profession; as to the results, see for instance the note in *Vorwärts* of 17 January 1894. It is not only the military doctors of the reserve who are subject to military pressure; it is brought to bear on the professional medical organisations and thus on the non-military doctors.
75. The daring adventure of Voigt, the "Captain" of Köpenick, the gifted cobbler and convict, has been characterised by the Liberals in this connection as a warning.

are forbidden to write publicly. Together with the highly instructive Gädke case, all this is the best evidence that militarism is striving ruthlessly for the spiritual subjugation and centralised control of all those who come within its reach, and is also evidence of its tendency continuously to extend its sphere of influence, whether by legal or illegal means, and of its limitless and insatiable craving for power.

Other military influences on the civil population

A still more important fruit of militarism's desire for expansion than the nuisance caused by the officers of the reserve is the troublesome system of military qualification for civilian life, which apart from its purely military aim also serves the purpose of sending out a following of loyal and enthusiastic representatives and advocates of the military spirit to all branches of the state and communal administration. At the same time the reliability and readiness of the bureaucratic apparatus which serves capitalism to strike[76] is supposed to be secured, and the "correct" way of thinking, that which "upholds the state", to be spread among the masses of the population who are especially "in need of education". This "educational" aim of the certificate of maintenance in civilian life was acknowledged with splendid unanimity and frankness in February 1891 in the German Reichstag by Caprivi, the Imperial Chancellor, and the representatives of the ruling classes. This is therefore the ideal – based on upholding the state – of our popular education, which by chance, after the corporal had to leave the desk, has been embodied in a roundabout way in the non-commissioned officer.

The results of this education are, however, not very great. The poor devil who is "militarily qualified for civilian life" is very badly paid as a lower official. And in the end it may not even be possible to get hold of a German non-commissioned officer *pour le roi de Prusse*.[77] The eternal problem of buying out the revolution!

In this connection it must be further mentioned that the same means by which the military enthusiasm of the soldiers is produced and maintained – all the tinsel and splendour, for example – are at the same time used to influence in favour of militarism the population outside of the army, including the circles from which the army is recruited, which provide it with its glitter, which have to bear its costs and stand in "danger" of falling to the enemy at home. Haldane, the British minister of war, was intelligent enough to recognise this during his visit to Prussia in the autumn of 1906. He said that a valuable "phenomenon which accompanies militarism is that through coming into closer touch with the army and with war preparations the nation is educated in prudence and loyalty".[78]

A quite different means used by militarism to spread its spirit lies in its capacity *as consumer and producer* as well as in the influence it carries over great state economic concerns of strategic importance. A whole army of manufacturers, artisans and merchants, together with their employees, lives on military work, in that it takes part in the

---
76. In the figurative and the literal sense of the word! See Part I, chapter 4, Preliminary remarks.
77. In Germany there exists a kind of union of these officials, the *Bund deutscher Militäranwarter*.
78. See the *Lokal-Anzeiger*, No.496, 1906.

production and transportation of articles necessary for equipping, lodging and maintaining the army, as well as of all other articles used by the soldiers. These parasites on the army sometimes, especially in the smaller garrison towns, impress themselves upon the whole of public life; indeed, the more powerful of them rule like princes over great communities and play first fiddle in the state and in the empire. The influence which they wield, thanks to militarism, enables them at the same time to exploit it with astonishing patience and to box its ears. They repay it – one hand washes the other – by becoming its keenest agitators, driven on, it is true, by their capitalist interest. Who does not know their names: Krupp, Stumm, Ehrhardt, Loewe, Woermann, Tippelskirch, Nobel, the Powder Ring, etc.? Who does not know of the profits taken by Krupp from armour plate, those pocketed by Tippelskirch and the corruption that goes with them, the inflated freight and demurrage charges of Woermann, and the net profits of the Powder Ring, amounting to 100 and 150 percent, which have lightened the German treasury to the tune of many millions?[79] In Austria especially the suppliers' swindling caused a great sensation.[80] And every campaign means a golden harvest for the swindlers, for the pack of parasites – not only in Russia.[81] These great men reward militarism, as we have said, in the most Christian way, simply by robbing it, or rather the people. They pour the holy ghost of militarism over "their" workers and everything that depends on them, and wage a ruthless war against revolution. Of course neither these workers nor the great mass of the small army suppliers have a real material interest in the army. In countries which lack a standing army the prosperity and well-being of trade and industry is certainly in no worse a condition than in states which do possess such an army, and those persons employed in military production would be no worse off economically if no army existed. But meanwhile they do not for the most part see beyond the ends of their noses, and humble themselves obligingly to the energetic influence of militarism, so that counter-agitation meets with great difficulties.

As an employer in the great economic concerns (in the supply depots, the preserve factories, the clothing depots, repair depots, arms and munition factories, dockyards, etc.), militarism willingly and without exception delivers up its employees – there were 54,723 of them employed in state concerns by the German army and navy administration on October 31, 1904[82] – to every kind of reactionary-patriotic demagogy, like that of the Imperial League against Social Democracy. It also attempts systematically and in the most ruthless manner to further the patriotic-militaristic spirit by means of enticements like titles, decorations, festivals like those organised by the military clubs and – impossible pensions, slandering of the trade unions, and real barracks discipline.[83] The military

---

79. See G. Feuchter, *Der Deutsche Pulver-Ring und das Militär-Pulvergeschäft*, Göppingen 1896, pp.25 and 30.
80. Details in *Lustig ist's Soldatenleben*, Wien 1896, p.51.
81. Where the last stragglers of the swarm of vultures involved in the East Asian war, the Gurko-Lidvalls, caused a great stir toward the end of 1906.
82. Naval administration: 18,939; Prussian army administration, excluding the Ordnance department: 11,119; Prussian Ordnance department: 16,825; Bavarian army administration: 4,632; Saxon army administration: 2,754; Württemberg army administration: 374 (see the printed documents of the Reichstag, 1905–6, No.144).
83. In the Posen arms theft case of the winter of 1906, the accused, a factory worker at Spandau, repeatedly stated that he had to obey Lieutenant Poppe, the thief, who "as an officer" was "to a certain extent his superior"; that was what they had been taught. Poppe was not employed in the concern to which the accused belonged. His

workshops, more than any other state workshops, constitute the most difficult field for the education of the proletariat.

Of course, the anti-labour influence has its limits, and the military administration has no illusions in view of the successes achieved by the Social Democrats, especially among the "imperial" dock workers. All the threats – even the most childish, to close down the military workshops if the Social Democratic vote among the workers should continue to increase, threats which were used in the election of 1903 in Spandau – are incapable of hindering the development of class consciousness as long as militarism pays such niggardly wages to its workers and thus pushes them into the arms of social democracy. One need only recall the frequent movements for higher wages among the workers in the "royal" factories, and the countless conflicts which these workers come into with the military administration, which often take on a lively character[84] for one's pessimism to disappear.

The railways, post and telegraph are institutions of outstanding strategic importance, no less in the war against the internal enemy than in that against the external enemy. These indispensable strategic factors may, however, be rendered useless for capitalism by a strike, which can lead to a complete paralysis of the military organism. That is why militarism tries so hard to instil its spirit into the organisations of officials and workers in the transport concerns and productive concerns allied to them (railway workshops, coach factories, etc.). And how unscrupulously this aim is pursued (even leaving aside the system of military qualification for civilian life) is shown by the fact that in many states the employees are subjected to military law. It will also be made clear by a brief glance at the political position of these employees in the militarist states, where they are deprived of the right to form trade unions, either by administrative order, as in Germany and France,[85] or by special laws, as for example in Italy, Holland and Russia.[86] We must not of course forget that the capitalist state, apart from these militarist interests, has a quite general interest in preventing the employees of the transport organisations from succumbing to aspirations "antagonistic to the state". But this aim must remain unfulfilled in the long run, however many difficulties it presents in the meanwhile to the labour movement. It is shattered by the low pay and effective proletarian position of the employees of the transport concerns.

---

genuine officer's uniform assisted him in his manipulations among the civilian population just as the fake uniform had assisted the Captain of Köpenick.

84. The struggles in the workshops at Spandau which come up every year in the Reichstag are well known. On the Berlin corps clothing department, see the *Fachzeitung der Schneider* of August 25, 1906. On the French naval arsenals of Brest, Lorient, Cherbourg, Rochefort and Toulon, see *Les Temps Nouveaux* of November 11, 1905. At present (December 1906) a strong movement is under way among the arsenal workers of Toulon, of which the outcome cannot be foreseen.

85. The French government has attempted explicitly to justify these measures by drawing attention to anti-militarist propaganda. See *Les Temps Nouveaux* of November 11, 1906.

86. Law of December 2, 1905; see in this connection the *Leipziger Volkszeitung* of December 14, 1906.

Militarism as Machiavellianism and as a political regulator

Militarism makes its appearance first as the army itself then as a system which projects itself beyond the army and clasps the whole society in a network of militaristic and semi-militaristic institutions – the system of control, the courts of honour, the ban on public writing, the reserve officer system, the certificate of maintenance in civilian life, the militarisation of the whole bureaucratic apparatus (which in the first place is due to the trouble caused by the reserve officers and to the system of military qualification for civilian life), the young men's defence organisations, the military clubs and so on. Militarism also makes its appearance as a system which *saturates the whole public and private life of the people with the militaristic spirit*. The Church, the school, and a certain tendency to cheapness in art, together with the press, a wretched, venal rabble of *littérateurs*, and the social nimbus which surrounds "our glorious war army" like a halo – all these work together in a tenacious and cunning manner. Militarism, together with the Catholic Church, is the most highly developed Machiavellianism in the history of the world, and the most Machiavellian of all the Machiavellianisms of capitalism.

The frequently mentioned coup of the cobbler Captain of Köpenick[87] presents us with the catechism of militarist methods of education and their results. The most sublime point in the catechism is the sacred manner in which the whole of bourgeois society regards the officer's uniform. In the six-hour examination by which this convict put our army, our bureaucratic apparatus and our subjection to Prussia to the test, those under examination passed so brilliantly that even their teachers' hair stood on end in the face of this quintessence of their pedagogy. No hat of Gessler has ever met with such obliging servility and self-humiliation as the hat of the immortal Captain of Köpenick, no sacred cloak of Trier has found so much credulous devotion as his uniform. This classical satire, whose great effect lies in the fact that it has killed by ridicule the principles of military pedagogy, would similarly have killed off militarism itself to the strains of the world's laughter, were it not for the fact that militarism – which suddenly finds itself in the strange role of a sorcerer's apprentice – is as necessary to bourgeois society as our daily bread and the air we breathe. The old and tragic conflict! Capitalism and its mighty servant militarism by no means love each other; rather they fear and hate one another, and have good reason to do so. They regard each other – so independent has this servant become – as a necessary evil, and again there are reasons for this. Thus the lesson of Köpenick, which bourgeois society cannot follow, will remain simply a powerful means of agitation for anti-militarism and for social democracy,[88] whose prospects

---

87. Friedrich Wilhelm Voigt (1849–1922) was a German fraudster with convictions for theft, burglary and forgery. In 1906, masquerading as a Prussian military officer, he "confiscated" more than 4,000 marks from a municipal treasury, an escapade that made him a folk hero as "the Captain of Köpenick". He was jailed for two years, but was pardoned by Kaiser Wilhelm II.
88. It is delightful to see the *Kreuz-Zeitung* writhing in this painful trap. It seeks in its great embarrassment to turn the spear and make out that social democracy is in fatal difficulties, that the Köpenick affair had disclosed to all the world its plans for the event of a revolution, which had thus been frustrated. An especially absurd aspect of this silly frightened talk is the illusion that such plans could ever be frustrated in the capitalist order and that the knights of the *Kreuz-Zeitung* would even move a finger in such a hopeless attempt. "Thank God, we can

are the better the more militarism brings things to a head.

What the Captain of Köpenick did for militarism in the field of practice by his swindles was done by the invaluable Gustav Tuch at the end of the eighties in the field of honest theory. In his thick and dusty volume entitled *The Extended Military State in its Social Significance*, he sketched out a picture of the society of the future of which militarism was the heart and soul, the central sun which lighted, warmed and directed everything, the one true "national and civilised socialism". The whole state was turned into a single barracks, which was the elementary school, the college and the factory for manufacturing patriotic feeling, while the army was an all-embracing organisation of strike-breakers. This delightful hallucination of a thousand-year rule of militarism was in fact only methodical madness, but the fact that it was *methodical* in the way it worked out militaristic goals and methods, free from every restraint in conception, gives it a symptomatic meaning.[89]

Militarism has in fact already become the central sun in one dominant field, as we shall show in more detail below. Around it revolves the solar system of class legislation, bureaucratism, police administration, class justice, and clericalism of all kinds. It is the final regulator, sometimes secret and sometimes open, of all the tactics of the class struggle – not only of the capitalist classes but also of the proletariat, in its trade union organisation no less than in its political organisation.

---

still depend on the military!" – this was after all the most honest heart-cry of our bourgeois philistines after the Köpenick affair.
89. See K. Kautsky, *Die Neue Zeit*, year V (1887), p.331.

CHAPTER FOUR

Particulars of some of the main sins of militarism

1. The ill-treatment of soldiers, or militarism as a penitent but incorrigible sinner

Two dilemmas

The militarists are not stupid. This is clear from the nature of the education system, which has been most cunningly worked out. They are remarkably skilful in their speculations on mass psychology. Although the standing army of Frederick, composed as it was of mercenaries and the dregs of the population, could be held together by the discipline of drill and by physical violence for the performance of its more mechanical tasks, this no longer applies to our army which is drawn from the whole population with its higher level of intelligence and morality, which is built on the principle of citizen duty and which makes great demands on the individual. This was immediately and clearly seen by Scharnhorst and Gneisenau, whose army reorganisation was inaugurated with the announcement of the abolition of capital punishment.[90] Nevertheless assaults, abuse, blows and all kinds of refined and horrible methods of ill-treatment belong to the stock-in-trade of the present-day military education system, as we have already pointed out.

The attitude taken on the militarist side towards the ill-treatment of soldiers is of course not determined by considerations of ethics, civilisation, humane feelings, justice, Christianity and similar fine things, but by purely Jesuitical considerations of expediency. The fact that this constitutes a hidden underground menace to discipline and even to

---

90. See the very interesting but quite illusory *Regulations on Military Discipline*.

the "spirit" of the army[91] is far from being generally understood.[92] The ridicule by the old hands of the recruits and soldiers who make trouble, the vulgar barracks jokes and coarse abuse of all kinds, as well as a considerable amount of pushing around, of beating, etc., of men being tossed in the air or dragged along the ground – all this is approved even in our day by the majority of the non-commissioned officers and even of the officers, who have become cut off from and hostile to the people and who have been trained to be narrow-minded politicians in miniature. In their hearts they approve of these things, and even regard them as necessary. The struggle against these excesses meets a resolute passive resistance from the very beginning. One can hear every day – not openly, but on the quiet – how the superiors characterise the demand that "the fellows" should be treated according to human dignity as stupid humanitarian drivel. Army service is harsh. But even when the underground menace of secret disciplinary ill-treatment has been recognised, one again finds oneself in one of those dilemmas into which a coercive system, which goes against the path of natural development, must land at every step. We have already brought some of these dilemmas to light. The method of ill-treatment, as we shall show later in more detail, is an indispensable auxiliary to the normal drill method. Capitalist militarism, for which a disciplinary structure based on free will is impossible, cannot avoid the use of such treatment. In spite of all doubts and regrets, this system serves – not officially, we repeat, but through official channels – as an illegal but necessary method of military education.

But apart from these general doubts, the militarists have had a bad conscience since the time when they began to get caught, that is, since the time when ruthless Social Democratic criticism began to be levelled at the military organisation and when even wide strata of the middle class began to recoil in the face of this militaristic morality. Militarism had to bear with set teeth the fact that it was not being run and commanded simply by the Supreme War Lord, but that materially it was dependent above all on the representatives of the people, upon whom it looked with scorn and contempt, that is, on the Reichstag, in which sit even representatives of the "common people" – in short, it was dependent on the "rabble", who, under the protection of their Reichstag immunity, could lay bare the essence of the militarist system. It therefore found itself obliged, suppressing its rage, to keep this rabble, the "Reichstag fellows", as well as the despised public opinion, in a good mood. It was a case of not putting the military piety of the bourgeoisie to too severe a test, for the bourgeoisie, though it was ordinarily ready to pay for every possible military requirement, quite often and especially in times of financial difficulty tried to kick against the pricks. It was also a question of easing its position in relation to the electors, who, as far as their position in life is concerned, belong to the

---

91. The perceptive order made by Manteuffel and dated April 14, 1885, says among other things: "Abuse injures and destroys the sense of honour, and the officer who abuses his subordinates is digging his own grave; for one cannot rely on the loyalty or bravery of someone who allows himself to be abused... In a word, subordinates are what they are treated as by their superiors, from the general down to the lieutenant".
92. The mass of deserters and those liable for service but who evade it serves among other things as a rough guide. 15,000 German deserters lost their lives during the first thirty years of the glorious Empire in the French Colonial Army alone. The bloody battle of Vionville in comparison only resulted in 16,000 dead and wounded. See Däumig, *Schlachtopfer des Militarismus.*

anti-militarist classes and who, on recognising their true class position, would go over to the side of Social Democracy. It was therefore finally a question of depriving Social Democracy of its most effective weapons, so that the next tactic adopted was that of keeping quiet and hushing things up. The proceedings of the military courts were kept secret; "no ray of light fell in the darkness of their heart". And if any ray of light did manage to get in, they lied, disputed the evidence and embellished the matter with all their might. But the torch of Social Democracy shed more and more light even behind the barracks walls and through the bars of military prisons and fortresses.

The military debates in the German Reichstag in the '80s and '90s of the last century represent a hard and passionate struggle for the recognition of the fact that the horrors of the barracks were not a rare and isolated phenomenon, but a regular, very frequent and to a certain extent organic, constitutional manifestation of militarism. Good service was rendered in this struggle by the fact that in other states the proceedings of the military courts were carried out in public, which made it easier to prove without doubt that military ill-treatment was a normal property of militarism, even of the republican militarism of France, even of Belgian militarism and even, to an increasing extent, of the militarism of the Swiss militia. Social Democratic criticism scored a victory essentially because of the impression created by the decrees of Prince George of Saxony (of June 8, 1891)[93] and of the Bavarian Ministry of War (of December 13, 1891), published in *Vorwärts* early in 1892, as well as by the Reichstag debates of February 15 to 17, 1892. After the usual "considerations" and wrangling, a reform of our military criminal procedure was, with great difficulty, finally achieved in 1898. It was nevertheless still quite possible to hang the cloak of Christian love over the frightful secrets of the barracks, and on a wide scale, by excluding publicity. But in spite of all the decrees effectively ruling out such publicity, in spite of the action taken against the judges in the Bilse case, the reform soon brought into the open such a cloudburst of horrifying cases of ill-treatment that all the objections to the criticism made by the Social Democrats were brushed aside without any trouble, and the torturing of soldiers was recognised almost everywhere, if unwillingly, to be a standing institution of militarism in its support for the state.

There were attempts, not always of an honest nature, to come to grips with this frightening institution which provided so much opportunity for Social Democratic "agitation". Even if these attempts were not genuine, in that their promoters did not believe in their success, the point was to create an impression that there was dissatisfaction with the phenomenon and a desire to attempt to get rid of it. The torturers began to be prosecuted in a relatively thorough way. But for militarism the fight against the ill-treatment of soldiers is of course less important than its interest in military discipline and in preparing the people to bear arms in the fight against what are in fact, their own international and national interests. One only has to compare the sentences passed

---

93. They speak of "very serious conditions", of "refined torture", of the "efflux of brutality and degeneracy" which, given the officers in charge, is "hardly credible", and was thought to have been rendered "practically impossible by the system of supervision. On February 8, 1895, *Vorwärts* published an imperial decree, also applicable in this context, and addressed to the generals in command. The decrees of Scharnhorst and Gneisenau (after Jena) and of Manteuffel (April 18, 1885) are relevant in another connection, as is the decree of the Prince of Saxe-Meiningen.

on torturers of the commonest kind with those which are often passed on soldiers for quite minor offences, and offences committed in a state of excitement or of drunkenness – such actions, directed against officers, take place almost every day. In this case the slightest misdemeanours against the holy ghost of militarism are punished with bloodthirsty and draconian measures. But where it is the soldiers who are ill-treated, comparative indulgence is shown to their torturers, in a spirit of understanding. It is therefore quite natural that the struggle of military justice against such ill-treatment, and against the merciless strangling of every trace of an awakening demand for independence and equal rights among the lower ranks, meets with little success. The case of the Prince of Saxe-Meiningen is relevant here. He had the courage to appeal to the men to support the struggle against ill-treatment, in fact to make it their duty to support it in order to get to the root of the evil with more determination than usual. But because of this bold step the prince was forced to retire from the service.[94] This case throws a somewhat lurid light upon the feeble and hopeless character of the official struggle against ill-treatment in the army.

The pamphlet written by our comrade Rudolf Kraff, a former Bavarian officer, entitled *Opfer der Kaserne* (Victims of the Barracks), puts together valuable material with a skill which only someone with personal experience could possess. The regular compilation by our party press of details of trials concerning the ill-treatment of soldiers – and of sailors[95] – news of which has come up from time to time, provides an overwhelming mass of material. But this material has unfortunately not yet been worked over.[96] This is an important and profitable task which ought to be put in hand.

Because of our fundamental standpoint we cherish no illusions about militarism. The Scharnhorst decree on military punishment says: "Experience teaches us that recruits can be taught to drill without the use of blows. An officer who thinks this impossible lacks either the necessary ability to teach or a clear understanding of what really constitutes the teaching of drill..." – and this is theoretically true, but too far in advance of its time to be possible in practice. The ill-treatment of soldiers springs from the very essence of capitalist militarism. The human material is for the most part, as far as the mind is concerned, and to an even greater extent as far as the body is concerned, not fitted for the demands made upon it by military life, especially those of the parade drill. More and more young men enter the army whose outlook is hostile and dangerous to the military spirit. It is necessary to tear out a part of the soul of these "fellows", and instil a new spirit of patriotism and loyalty to the crown. All these tasks cannot be solved by even the cleverest instructors, let alone the kind of instructors at the disposal of militarism.

---

94. See for example the case of the unfortunate Rückenbrodt. In this case a terrible part was played by the use of a rope-like packing of asbestos with wire twisted round it. The torturers, with biting irony, called it the "military educator". (*Vorwärts*, September 25, 1906.)

95. See the *Frankfurter Zeitung* of April 6, 1903, the *Verhandlungen des Reichstages* of March 4 and 8, 1904, especially the speeches of the deputies Bebel, Ledebour and Müller-Meiningen, and *Vorwärts* of May 6, 13, 14 and 21, 1903. Also the cabinet order reprinted in the *Armee-Verordnungsblatt* of April 29, 1903, which stresses that it is not the duty of soldiers to make complaints, but only their right. See in addition the *Militär-Wochenblatt* of May 29, 1903, according to which the fact that the Prince of Saxe-Meiningen had been reprimanded and sacked had caused a "most embarrassing sensation". In what circles?

96. There is something in *Prinz Arenberg und die Arenberge*, pp.15ff., about "aristocrats who ill-treat soldiers".

PARTICULARS OF SOME OF THE MAIN SINS OF MILITARISM

Here again, therefore, militarism must be more economical than it would like to be.[97]

And the existence of these military instructors is by no means assured. They are entirely dependent on the goodwill, on the whim of their superiors. They may expect to be sacked at any moment if they cease to perform their main task – that of fashioning the soldiers after the image of militarism. This is an excellent means of ensuring the pliability of the whole apparatus of military officers (commissioned and non-commissioned) in the hands of the authority in command. One can easily understand that such superiors drill the men with a nervous ruthlessness which soon comes to no more than the statement: "If you do not obey orders I will use violence". And this violence is finally employed in the form of ill-treatment by the superior ranks, who have absolute power of life and death over their subordinates, themselves in a position of unconditional subjection. But it is a natural and humanly necessary consequence, and even the newly baked Japanese militarism quickly found itself involved in the same methods.[98] Militarism finds itself therefore, in this dilemma too.

The causes of such "pleasures of military life" are of course varied. The degree of education of the people, above all, exercises a strong moderating influence.[99] And it is not surprising that even French colonial militarism contrasts favourably with the militarism of the Prusso-German fatherland.[100]

But this method of using violence as a disciplinary measure, which is due to a necessity inherent in the system, provides us with excellent means of fighting militarism at its roots and of achieving success, of stirring up ever greater masses of the people and of spreading consciousness among strata which it would otherwise be impossible, or at least much more difficult, to reach. Ill-treatment of soldiers, together with military class justice, is one of the manifestations of the uncivilised character of capitalism which makes people most angry. Since it is at the same time an underground menace to military discipline, it is the most powerful weapon in the hands of the proletariat in its struggle for freedom. This sin of capitalism is turned back with double force against itself. However penitent the sinner, whether in genuine contrition or in the manner of the fox in a children's story, we must not allow these weapons to be snatched from us, for in spite of his sackcloth and ashes this sinner is incorrigible.

---

97. On February 27, 1891, Caprivi explained in connection with the ill-treatment of soldiers that "the educated non-commissioned officer is of more use to us than the common one, because the former more seldom allows himself to be carried away by his temperament, even when he is angry". But where are educated NCOs to be found, unless they are kidnapped?
98. See for instance the *Brandenburger Zeitung* of December 8, 1906.
99. The river Main forms no demarcation line here. In the domain of the ill-treatment of the soldier, at least, German unity and solidarity have been realised.
100. See Däumig, *Schlachtopfer des Militarismus*, p.370.

2. The cost of militarism, or *La douloureuse*

Another dilemma

Historical materialism, the theory of dialectical development, is the doctrine of the essential necessity of retribution. Every class society is doomed to self-destruction. Every class society is a force which wants to do evil and does what is good, as it wants to do good but must do evil. It is doomed to destruction by the inherited sin of its class character, for, whether it likes it or not, it must eventually produce the Oedipus which will strike it down – but unlike the legendary Theban, in full consciousness of parricide. This applies in any case to the capitalist social order and to the proletariat.

The ruling class of capitalism would of course like to look after its financial interests without being disturbed. But the peace which it would like is neither permitted by capitalist competition, national or international, nor does it suit for any length of time the taste of those from whose skin capitalism cuts its thongs. It is therefore necessary for capitalism to build a terrible fortress of domination, bristling with weapons, in order to protect the system of wage slavery and the divine right of profit. But even though capitalism requires militarism, it by no means finds the cost of militarism agreeable; on the contrary, it finds it very disagreeable. Yet since in our day it is no longer possible, according to the old prescription of Cadmus, to sow teeth and to see armed soldiers spring up out of the ground, there is nothing to be done but to put up with the greed of militarism and to feed its insatiable hunger. The budget discussions which take place every year in the parliaments show how much pain this financial question causes to the ruling classes. Capitalism, which is addicted to surplus value, is once again hit in its weak spot – finance. The fact that it costs so much is the only thing which keeps militarism within some kind of limit, at least in so far as the cost has to be borne by the bourgeoisie itself. But of course the morality of profit seeks and finds a convenient and miserly way out, by piling the greatest part or at least a large part of the burden on the shoulders of those strata of the population which are not only the weakest, but are also the very groups whose suppression and exploitation is the chief purpose of militarism. Like other ruling classes in other societies, the capitalist classes make use of their position of domination, which is based essentially on the exploitation of the proletariat, to force the oppressed and exploited classes not only to forge their own chains but also to help pay for them. It is not enough that the sons of the people are made into torturers of the people – even the pay of these torturers is wrung to the utmost from the sweat and blood of the people itself. And even if the provocative and bloody nature of this robbery sometimes comes to the surface, capitalism still remains true unto death to its faith – faith in the golden calf.

It is true that by throwing the military burden onto the shoulders of the poorer classes one lowers the degree to which these classes can be exploited. But this is inevitable, and

PARTICULARS OF SOME OF THE MAIN SINS OF MILITARISM

also helps to place capitalism, greedy for profit, in further financial difficulties.

Militarism weighs like lead on our whole life. But it is especially an *economic* weight, a pressure under which our economic life groans, a vampire which constantly, year after year, sucks the blood of the economy by drawing the strength of the nation away from productive and cultural work, as well as by the direct effect of its insane cost. Thus in Germany at present about 655,000[101] of the strongest and most capable workers, mostly aged between 20 and 22, are withdrawn from work in this way. In Germany too the swelling military and naval expenditure amounts for example (including colonial[102] but not supplementary expenditure) to over 1,300 million marks for 1906–7, that is, to roughly 1 milliards. The expenditure of the other military states is, relatively speaking, no less heavy,[103] and even the military expenditure of the richer states, such as the USA,[104] Britain (which spent 1,321 million marks on the army and navy in 1904–5!), Belgium and Switzerland, is so enormous that it constitutes the chief item in the state budget. There is a tendency everywhere for costs to increase to the very boundaries of possibility.

The following compilation of the *Manuel du Soldat* is very revealing:

In 1899 Europe had a military budget of 7,184,321,093 francs. There were 4,169,321 men employed in a military capacity. If they were working they could produce daily (at the rate of three francs per man) to the value of 12,507,963 francs. Further, 710,342 horses were required for military purposes, which, at a rate of 2 francs per day per horse, could produce daily to the value of 1,420,684 francs. This makes a total of 13,928,647 francs. If we multiply this number by 300 it makes, when added to the budget, a loss in productive value of 11,362,915,313 francs.

But from 1899 to 1906–7 the military budget of Germany alone has grown from about 920 million marks to about 1,300 millions, or by more than 40 percent. Total European military expenditure, without counting the cost of the Russo-Japanese war, would now come to about 13,000,000,000 marks a year, or about 13 percent of all world trade. Such a policy must surely end in bankruptcy.

Just as in the Russian Baltic provinces the military suppression of the revolutionary movement was for a long time delegated to the barons, who had been particularly affected by the movement, so in America the possibility has been created of entrusting to the bourgeoisie, even in times of peace, a certain element of the task of maintaining capitalist order. This is the role of the Pinkertons, who have straightway become a legal institution directly employed in the class struggle; This institution, like the Belgian form of the Civil Guard, has at any rate the advantage that it moderates the phenomena which accompany militarism (ill-treatment of soldiers, the cost, etc.)[105] and is disliked by the bourgeoisie itself. The enemy of capitalist society is thereby partially deprived of highly

---
101. In 1906–7 there were 614,362 men in the standing army, and in 1905–6 there were 40,672 men in the navy.
102. Each soldier fighting in German South-West Africa cost the German Reich 9,500 marks in 1906.
103. In France, for example, a total of 1,101,260,000 francs in 1905! Since 1870 France has spent nearly 40 milliard francs for military purposes (excluding the colonies!).
104. See Part 1, chapter 2.5.
105. But even in the USA the Departments of War and of the Navy alone in 1904–5 took $240 million out of a total budget of 720 millions.

effective propaganda matter. But this way of avoiding the problem, which is also more acceptable to the proletariat, is normally ruled out for the capitalist states, as we have already pointed out. As far as one can see ahead, they are unable to adopt the much less costly militia system because of the political task which must be performed by the army at home, because of the function it performs in the class struggle. This function in fact accords with the striking tendency to do away with the existing militia system.

By comparing the total expenditure of the German Reich for 1906–7, which came to 2,397,324,000 marks, with the portion which falls to the share of the army and navy, it can be seen that all the other items are simply peripheral in comparison with this great sum, and that the whole taxation system and financial policy centre round the military budget, "like the host of stars around the sun".

Militarism therefore becomes a dangerous impediment, often even the gravedigger of that cultural progress which in itself might be in the interest of the social order of our day. The school, art and science, public hygiene, the communications system: all these are treated in the most shabby fashion because, to use a popular expression, the greed of Moloch leaves nothing over for culture. The words of the minister, that cultural requirements are not to suffer, were endorsed with genuine approval only by the East Elbean Junkers who have some cultural pretensions. They could only cause ironic smiles among the other representatives of capitalist culture.

The figures are conclusive. It is enough to compare the German military expenditure of 1 milliards for 1906 with the 171 millions which Prussia spent in the same year for education of every kind, or the 420 millions which Austria-Hungary spent for military purposes in 1900 with the 5½ millions which it spent on primary schools. The most recent Prussian law on the maintenance of schools, with its petty rules on the question of teachers' pay, as well as Studt's notorious decree against raising teachers' pay in the towns, speak volumes.

Germany could, with the funds at its disposal, solve all its cultural problems. And the more these problems were solved, the easier it would be to pay the cost. But militarism blocks the way.

The manner in which military costs are met in Germany – but the situation is not much different elsewhere, for example in France – is especially pernicious. It is militarism, one might almost say, which creates and supports our oppressive and unjust system of indirect taxation. The whole imperial customs and taxation policy, which tends to exploit the great masses of people, that to say the poor sections of the population, is essentially the cause of the fact that, in 1906 for example, the cost of living for the bulk of the people rose by between 10 and 15 percent in comparison with the average for the years 1900–4. This policy, apart from serving Junkerdom, that class of parasites (and the loving care from which they benefit is for the most part based on the militarist system) serves, above all, the aims of militarism.

It is also militarism which is mainly to be thanked for the fact that our communications system, whose extension and perfection should after all be in the best interests of a capitalism which was intelligent and perceptive of its own needs, nevertheless fails by a long way to satisfy the demands made by traffic and technical developments. The system is instead employed as a milk cow, to impose a special indirect tax upon the people. The story of the last imperial finance bill introduced by Stengel would open even the eyes of the blind. One can calculate almost to the penny that this bill was only called forth by the need to fill up a 200-million Mark hole which militarism has again torn out of the state treasury. And the system of taxation laws, which puts heavy duty on items of mass consumption like beer and tobacco, and even on traffic, on which the vitality of capitalism depends, constitutes an excellent illustration of the point made above.

There is no doubt that militarism is in many respects a burden on capitalism, that this burden attaches itself as firmly to the neck of capitalism as the old man of the seas to that of Sinbad the Sailor. Capitalism needs militarism just as spies are needed in wartime and executioners and torturers in peacetime. It may hate militarism, but it cannot do without it, just as the civilised Christian abhors sins against the gospel yet cannot live without sin. Militarism is an inherited sin of capitalism, a sin which is of course open to rectification here and there,[106] but which will be eliminated only in the purgatory of socialism.

3. The army as a tool against the proletariat in the economic struggle

Preliminary remark

We have already seen how militarism has actually become the axis around which our political, social and economic life more and more revolves, how it pulls the wires which make the puppets of the capitalist puppet theatre dance on their strings. We have seen what goal militarism serves, how it seeks to attain this goal, and how in the pursuit of this goal it is forced by physical necessity to produce the very poison which will bring about its death. We have also discussed the important role which it plays – rather unsuccessfully – as a school for the inculcation of militarist ideas among those in uniform and among civilians. But militarism is not satisfied with all this. Even now, in peacetime, it exerts its influence in various directions in order to uphold the state and to prepare for the great day when, having served its time as apprentice and journeyman, it must deliver its masterpiece, for the day when the people will dare to rise in rebellion against its masters, the day of the great cataclysm.

On this day – and its bodyguard would prefer to see it come now rather than tomorrow, since it could be more sure of its ability to turn it into a massacre of Social Democracy – on that day it will shoot and kill, murder to its heart's content in order (with God's aid) to save King and Fatherland. As its ideal, its model, it will take January

---
106. See Part 1, chapter 2.5.

22, 1905, and the bloody May Week of 1871. Schönfeldt, the commander of the Vienna corps, made the following pledge to the bourgeoisie at a banquet in April 1904: "You may rest assured that you will find us behind you when the existence of society and the enjoyment of hard-earned property are threatened. When the bourgeois stands in the front line, the soldier will hurry to his aid!"

The iron fist is thus always raised to strike a crushing blow. There are hypocrites who talk of "safeguarding law and order", of "protecting the freedom to work", but what they mean is "safeguarding oppression" and "protecting exploitation". If the proletariat makes its presence felt with undue liveliness and power, militarism immediately rattles its sabres to try and frighten it back into its place. The omnipresent and almighty force of militarism – which stands behind every action taken by the state power against the workers and in the last instance lends it insuperable power – far from remaining in the background, behind the vanguard of the police and gendarmerie, is quite prepared to carry out everyday work, to strengthen the pillars of the capitalist order in the hand-to-hand struggle. It is precisely this multiplicity of activity which characterises the scheming nature of capitalist militarism.

Soldiers as competitors of free labourers

Militarism is well aware, as a functionary of capitalism, that its highest and most sacred duty is to protect the employers' profits. So it considers itself quite free, even bound, officially or unofficially, to place the soldiers like beasts of burden at the disposal of the exploiting classes and especially of Junkerdom. This is meant to solve the problem of the shortage of agricultural workers, a shortage brought about by the inhuman exploitation and brutality to which they are subject.

Soldiers are also given leave to gather in the harvest – another practice detrimental to the interests of labour, like the system of orderlies. It also makes it clear, even to the monomaniacs of the goose step and parade drill, that to present the system of long-term service as a military necessity is an unscrupulous and clumsy swindle. And it calls up memories, which are not at all flattering, of the company system as it existed before Jena. One should bear in mind, for example, the much discussed decrees of the general command to the Ist,[107] IVth, Xth[108] and XVIIth Prussian army corps in 1906. The very many instances in which the post and railways draw upon soldiers for help in cases of heavy traffic should also be mentioned here, though their significance is more complex.

The army and strike-breaking

Militarism interferes directly with the struggles of the labour movement for freedom by employing soldiers as blacklegs under military command. In this connection

---

[107]. The editor of the *Königsberger Volkszeitung* was condemned to a heavy fine in the autumn of 1906 for alleged libel, in that he criticised the decree concerning the granting of leave during the harvest.
[108]. See the reply of the general in command in *Vorwärts*, November 3, 1906.

we might recall the case, recently brought to the fore again, of Lieutenant-General von Liebert, the present commander of the "Imperial Union to Oppose Slander by Social Democracy", who as a simple colonel in 1896 had already grasped the fact that a strike is a public calamity like a fire or a water famine. That is to say, it is calamity for the employers' class, whose guardian angel and executor von Liebert considered himself to be.

Specially notorious in Germany is the method employed in the Nuremberg strike of 1906, a method which consisted in pushing the men who were leaving their jobs back into the ranks of the blacklegs, by the use of a little gentle pressure.

Three events which took place outside of Germany are of much greater importance. First, there was the mass military blacklegging in the general strike of the railways in Holland in January 1903. The result of this episode was that the railwaymen were deprived of the right to form trade unions.[109] Second was the general strike of the Hungarian railway workers in 1904, where the military administration went even further. On the one hand it formed a blackleg column out of men on active service, who, contrary to the law, were kept under military command when their period of service had finished. On the other hand it went so far as to call up the reservists and men of the *Landwehr* who were to be found among the railwaymen, as well as non-railwaymen in the same groups who were technically suitable, and forced them to work as blacklegs on the railways. Third was the Bulgarian railway strike declared on January 2,1907.

No less important is the struggle inaugurated by the ministers of agriculture and war in Hungary at the beginning of December 1906 against the right of the agricultural workers to form trade unions and go on strike. The careful training of soldiers to take part in blackleg columns for the harvest is very important here.

In France too blacklegging by soldiers is a well-known phenomenon.[110]

The fact that military education systematically encourages blacklegging, and the danger caused to the fighting proletariat by those workers who have just come out of the army and are quite ready to stab their class comrades in the back – these things also contribute to the gains made by international militarism.[111]

4. The rule of the sword and rifle against strikes

Preliminary remarks

The military authorities have for a long time been convinced of the capitalist truth of the proposition that behind every strike lurks the hydra of revolution. The army is therefore always ready, if the fists, swords and revolvers of the police are not sufficient to curb the so-called strike excesses, to force the unruly slaves of the employers into

---

109. The strike began on January 30, 1903, and ended victoriously on February 1. On March 10 the anti-strike law came before the chamber, on April 6 the general strike was declared, on April 9 the anti-strike law was voted through, on April 13 the general strike collapsed. The mills of capitalism grind quickly when "Holland is in danger".
110. See the *Manuel du Soldat*, p.9.
111. Ibid., p.8.

submission with its swords and rifles.

This is true of all capitalist countries and also, even especially, of Russia, though it is not yet completely capitalist and cannot be regarded as typical because of its peculiar political and cultural conditions. And even if Italy and Austria march at the head of the column in this respect, it is very important for the historical understanding of the republican state form structured by a capitalist political economy to point out again and again that, apart from England, soldiers have nowhere been such willing tools in the hands of the bourgeoisie for crushing strikes, nowhere behaved in such a bloodthirsty and ruthless manner as in the semi-republican and republican states, such as Belgium and France. With these, moreover, the freest states in the world – Switzerland and America – can well hold their own. Russia of course, here as in every other respect, cannot be beaten. Barbarism, or rather brutish ferocity, constitutes the general cultural situation of its ruling classes. It is the natural moving force behind its militarism, which since the time of the first harmless stirrings of the proletariat, has literally drowned in blood those peaceful workers who in their desperate need were asking for relief. No single event need be named here, for that would mean arbitrarily tearing one link out of a chain endless in time and space. For every drop of proletarian blood shed in all the other European countries put together, a proletarian life has been taken by tsarism in its struggle to suppress the most modest demands of the labour movement.

Essentially related to this use of military force is the activity of the colonial armies and defence detachments against the natives of the colonies who do not allow themselves to be pressed into the yoke of the vilest exploitation and greed. But we cannot go into this question in more detail here.

Often it is not possible to draw a sharp line of demarcation between the army, properly speaking, and the *gendarmerie* and police. They work hand in hand, replace and supplement one another, and are linked closely together, precisely because the characteristics which come into play here – the violent aggression, the willingness and readiness ruthlessly and recklessly to make armed attacks on the people – these characteristics exist among the police and *gendarmerie* too. These qualities are in the main a genuine product of the barracks, the fruit of militarist pedagogy and training.

Italy

Ottavio Dinale has published two related articles[112] on the question of the massacres of workers in Italy. He deals not only with the actual street massacres, but also with those which had been planned in connection with workers' demonstrations in the economic struggle apart from strikes. The articles show in a striking manner how quickly the Italian army is on hand on such occasions, what petty reasons justify its attacks, and what extreme violence it uses against defenceless crowds. Even when crowds have been broken up and are fleeing, they have been attacked and fired on. In summing up, Dinale points

---
112. *Le Mouvement Socialiste*, May–June and August–September 1906, *Les massacres de classe en Italie*.

out that in Italy the "king's bullets" have smashed the bones of Italian workers five, six or even ten times a year. He points out that the Italian bourgeoisie, the originator of the massacres, is one of the most reactionary and backward in the world, and that in its eyes socialism is not a political conception but only a kind of criminal thinking, of criminality pure and simple, which presents the greatest danger to law and order. He quotes the words of the Milan newspaper *L'idea liberale* on the day following the Grammichele massacre: "The dead and the wounded—these people have been overtaken by the fate they deserve – *shrapnel is the most precious element of civilisation and order!*".

After such a standard has been set, one can hardly be astonished that even a so-called democratic government like that of Giolitti never tried to call the army to order for its bloody barbarities. On the contrary, the military was officially praised for having "done its duty". It seems even more natural that a motion of the Socialist parliamentary fraction on limiting the use of the army in conflicts with the masses was not carried.

The shootings of May 1898 made the situation in regard to the class struggle clear even for the blind and the shortsighted optimists. The following is an almost complete record of blood-letting in recent years:

		Dead	Wounded
Berra	June 27, 1901	2	10
Patugnano	May 4, 1902	1	7
Cassano	August 5, 1902	1	3
Candela	September 8, 1902	5	11
Giarratana	October 13, 1902	2	12
Galatina	April 20, 1903	2	1
Piere	May 21, 1903	3	1
Torre Annunziata	August 31, 1903	7	10
Cerignola	May 17, 1904	3	40
Buggera	September 4, 1904	3	10
Castelluzo	September 11, 1904	1	12
Sestri Ponente	September 15, 1904	2	2
Foggia	April 15, 1905	7	20
St. Elpidio	May 15, 1905	4	2
Grammichele	August 16, 1905	8	20
Scarano	March 21, 1906	1	9
Muro	March 23, 1906	2	4
Turin	April 4, 1906	1	6
Calimera	April 30, 1906	2	3
Cagliari	May 12, 1906	2	7
Nebida	May 21, 1906	1	1
Sonneza	May 21, 1906	6	6
Benventare	May 24, 1906	2	2

That makes a total of 23 massacres, 78 dead and 199 wounded! A good harvest!

There have also been countless cases in Italy which did not end in bloodshed but in which the military has mobilised against strikers or against workers and "peasants" in general who were demonstrating for economic demands. These army "exercises" are a part of everyday life on the other side of the Alps.[113]

We might also point out here what is commonly known: that according to Hervé's testimony,[114] there are as many massacres of workers and peasants in Spain – on whose dominions the sun once never set, but now no longer seems to want to rise – as there are in Italy.

Austria-Hungary

As everyone knows, things are not much better here, in the dual monarchy under the black and yellow flag. The Socialist delegate Daszynski quite justifiably exclaimed in the Austrian parliament on September 25, 1903: "In strikes, in demonstrations of the people as well as in cases where national feelings are inflamed, it is always the army which turns the bayonet against the people, against the workers, against the peasants". To show the link with the realm of politics, he pointed out that "we are living in a state in which, even in times of peace, the army is the only cement binding such disparate elements", and referred to the Graz events of 1897 and to the bloodshed in Graslitz. It is well known that the military made a bloody intervention in Vienna, Graz and Budapest when Badeni was overthrown in November 1897. The frequent massacres of workers, especially in Galicia, are in everyone's memory (here we will only mention that the blood of the agricultural workers was shed in 1902 in Burowicki and in Ubinie in Kamionka), as are the bloody events in Palkenau, Nürschau and Ostrau. For these last events, however, the responsibility rests with the *gendarmerie*, a special force subject to purely military discipline and designed to maintain law and order. It is partly under the command of the military authorities and partly under that of the civil administration. During the general strike in Trieste in 1902 there were also clashes with the army. Ten people were killed or wounded. The events in Lemberg in 1902 during the masons' strike also deserve mention. During political demonstrations connected with the strike, hussars rode into the crowd and fired, killing five people. The riot at Innsbrück in 1905, which was based on a purely nationalist quarrel, lies however outside of the scope of this work.

Excesses of the most serious kind committed by the military authorities against the people have been frequent in Hungary, and continue up to the present day. The *gendarmerie* of course did its "duty" in a "thorough" way, as in the disturbance at Tamasi on the Puszta when without any reason it shot at a peaceful crowd of agricultural workers. It is enough to bear in mind one recent event, namely the battle which was fought in the Hunyad province on September 2, 1906, in which the military brutally attacked the

---
113. See for example *Les Temps Nouveaux* of December 16, 1905 (Ancona, Taurisano).
114. *Leur Patrie*, Paris n.d., p.99.

strikers of the Petroseny coal mine. Many people were seriously wounded, of which two died, and 150 were slightly wounded.

The skirmishes and battles between the army and the proletariat, in addition to the political struggles which have taken place in the dual monarchy of the Habsburgs – all these will be dealt with later.

Daszynski, in the speech already quoted, made the claim that *"bayonets should not be mixed up with politics"*. But as everyone knows they have since that time been put to political use with even more force and violence.

Belgium

In Belgium there is a long history of massacres of workers. The events of the years 1867 and 1868 are important, especially because of the intervention of the International. The whole thing was set in motion by the so-called hunger revolt of Marchienne in 1867, when processions of unarmed workers were attacked and cut down by a company of soldiers. In March 1868 there followed the massacre of Charleroi, and in 1869 the infamous massacres of Seraing and Borinage.

The Charleroi massacre was set up by the military and *gendarmerie*, and directed against striking miners who had been driven to desperation by cut-backs and wage reductions. At the same time it made it possible for the International to carry on vigorous agitation in Belgium, and this in turn, after the General Council had issued a proclamation, helped the International to improve its organisation to a considerable degree.[115]

During the so-called hunger revolts of 1886, in which the demand for a general franchise, though it was not clearly stated, played a role alongside the economic questions, the scenes of the '60s were repeated. On April 3, 1886, General Baron Van der Smissen issued his notorious circular, later repudiated by the Chamber itself. The circular stated, rather cynically: "*L'usage des armes est fait sans aucune sommation*", i.e. weapons are to be used without warning being given. The human sacrifice was great beyond measure. Sixteen workers were killed at Roux by a single volley. And on top of all this class justice puts its stamp of approval by the heavy sentences it passes on the workers. From 1886 to 1902 scarcely a strike took place in Belgium without military intervention. During these years alone about 80 people were killed. In the general strike of 1893 (we mention it although it was of a political character) there were many dead left upon the battlefield. The names of Verviers, Roux, La Louvière, Jemappes, Ostende, Borgerhout, Mont are burned in letters of fire into the minds of the class-conscious workers of Belgium. They are blood-stained pages in the thick book of sins of Belgian capitalism. The standing army was mobilised for the last time in 1902 during the general strike, when the reservists were called up. The unfavourable reports which the ministry received as to the soldiers' mood and opinions were soon confirmed. The soldiers manifested their revolutionary ideas in a quite unashamed manner by singing the *Marseillaise*, hissing the officers, etc.

---
115. In this connection see G. Jaeckh, *Die Internationale*, Leipzig 1904, pp.69ff.

The result was the usual one: the Flemish soldiers were sent to the Walloon districts and *vice versa*. But the final outcome was that the standing army was no longer brought into use. Since 1902 the proletarian soldiers of Belgium have relinquished their honourable role of watch-dog of capitalism, of being a "flying squad watching over the employers' stores of gold", at least as far as militarism at home is concerned. The *gendarmerie* and civil guard now do the job. To protect its sacred right to exploitation the bourgeoisie must now act for itself, it must risk its own skin – if one can talk of such a risk when the opposition consists of the unarmed masses. It is shown elsewhere that the civil guard performs its function quite adequately in the struggle against the enemy at home.

France

In France the history of the class struggle is written in letters of blood. We will not go over the massacre of July 1830, a battle which lasted three days; or the 10,000 killed in the street-fighting of June 23 to 26, 1848 – the executioner's work of Cavaignac; or that of the "little Napoleon" on December 1, 1851; or the murder of the 28,000 heroes of the Commune, the sea of blood in which the French bourgeoisie, in its desire to avenge capitalism, tried to drown the rising of its slaves in the red week of May 1871 – *Père Lachaise* and the *mur des fédérés*, the tragic symbols of a heroism without comparison. All these events – revolutionary in the highest degree – in which militarism did its gruesome work are beyond the scope of our historical investigation.

The heroic deeds of militarism, its attacks upon defenceless strikers, began at an early date. The so-called revolt of the silk workers at Lyons, whose banner bore the famous and touching words "*Vivre en travaillant ou mourir en combattant*" (To live working or to die fighting) began in November 1831 when the military fired on a peaceful demonstration. The angry workers captured the town in a struggle lasting two days. The National Guard fraternised with them, but the military soon took over the town again without having to draw their swords. La Ricamerie, Saint-Aubin and Decazeville are names made famous under the Empire as early examples. At this time the bourgeois republicans fought as hard as they could against soldiers being sent to the strike areas. But scarcely had these republicans captured political power than they themselves began to practise the Bonapartist method they had just been fighting against, and very soon they went even further. Only when the guilty party was a cleric or monarchist did they find words of censure, based on political rancour. The new regime had its baptism of blood in Fourmies on May 1, 1891, when a shot from a Lebel rifle pierced the body of a young girl, Maria Blondeau. The day's toll, for which responsibility lies with the 145th regiment of the line, was 10 dead and 35 wounded. But Constant, the butcher of Fourmies, and his right-hand man Captain Chapuis are not isolated cases. Fourmies was followed in 1899 by Chalons-sur-Saône, in 1900 by La Martinique and then by Longwy, when the officers sealed and celebrated the Franco-Russian alliance by the use of the knout, and finally in May and June of 1905 by Villefranche-sur-Saône[116] and especially by the cavalry attacks and shootings in Limoges on April 17, 1905.[117] In December 1905 the tragedy of Combrée was played out,[118] and on January 20, 1907, force was used to throw people, demonstrating for a Sunday rest from work, off the streets of Paris.

We must not forget to mention Dunkirk, Le Creusot and Montceau-les-Mines where, according to the report of the Confédération Générale du Travail to the international conference in Dublin, the soldiers declared their solidarity with the strikers.[119]

Meslier's exclamation at the recent great trial of anti-militarists is quite true: "Since the murder of little Maria Blondeau at Fourmies the working class in France has lived through a long martyrdom and counted many victims". Nothing better reduces *ad absurdum* the illusions of the "new" – in fact quite ancient – method of peaceful development than the fact that the great rise in the level of anti-clerical and republican opinions and activity so conspicuous in recent years in France, the France of Millerandism, has produced no decrease in the numbers of military "punitive expeditions" against strikes; on the contrary, there has been an increase. Nor will the recently established radical-democratic ministry of Clemenceau, with its two Socialist members, bring about any change in the situation. Lafargue's caustic remark that "in so far as modern armies are not engaged in colonial robbery they are employed exclusively in protecting capitalist property"[120] also hits the nail on the head with regard to France.

United States of America

It is easy to understand what little importance is to be attached to the talk about equal rights to which the United States is accustomed,[121] and to see that, in cases of necessity, capitalism has its own way of talking – the cannon, the rifle, the sword are proof enough. In this manner capitalism, even in America, still manifests its superiority over the proletariat. The following facts are very instructive with regard to the crucial importance of the method of military recruitment, posting and training, designed to prepare the troops to be used against the "enemy at home". This method often takes on a peculiar character owing to the fact, which is a consequence of the special American conditions, that the workers are frequently well armed.

In the "New World", as in Belgium, the period of the massacres of workers begins with the unemployed workers' movement. On January 13, 1874, in New York a strong troop of police, without any provocation, attacked a procession of the unemployed.

---

116. See *Mouvement Socialiste* of September 1 and 15, 1905.
117. See the detailed descriptions in *Mouvement Socialiste*, Nos.155 and 156, and in *La Vie Socialiste*, 1st year, Nos.15–18. The National Congress at Chalons-sur-Saône (October–November 1905), having rejected the motion of the Socialist fraction in the Chamber for a parliamentary inquiry, dealt in a comprehensive resolution with Limoges and Konstantin's report on it.
118. *Les Temps Nouveaux*, December 16, 1905.
119. A great sensation was caused a few years ago by the pamphlet *L'armée aux grèves* (The Army in Strikes) by Lieutenant Z.
120. *L'Humanité*, October 9, 1906.
121. See Sombart, *Warum gibt es in den Vereinigten Staaten keinen Sozialismus?*, Tübingen 1906, p.129.

PARTICULARS OF SOME OF THE MAIN SINS OF MILITARISM

Hundreds of badly wounded workers were left on the battlefield of Tompkins Square.

Then followed the dramatic events of the railwaymen's strike of July 1877. The governor sent several companies of the state militia against the strikers of the Baltimore and Ohio railway, but this proved not to be enough. President Hayes sent 250 regular troops to help, but they fared no better. In Maryland ten of the militiamen called out were killed by rifle fire, and many more wounded. In Pittsburgh the local militia, called out by the sheriff, refused to intervene. The old trick of sending in troops from another district was tried. Six hundred militiamen sent from Philadelphia engaged the strikers in a short but violent battle. The troops were beaten, and fled the next morning. The militia called out against the strikers in Reading (Pennsylvania) was composed mostly of workers; they fraternised with the strikers, shared their ammunition with them and threatened to turn their weapons against any hostile militiamen. But one company, recruited almost exclusively from among the possessing classes and led by a headstrong officer, opened fire against the crowd, killing 13 and wounding 22. The company did not have to rejoice in its heroic act; it was soon in disarray and had to beat a retreat. St Louis, which for a time was completely in the hands of the strikers, was finally won back for "law and order" by the whole police force together with several companies of militia after they had laid a regular siege to the headquarters of the executive.[122]

For the horrors which swept over Chicago in May 1886 the responsibility must lie with Pinkerton and the police. MacCormick, the sewing-machine manufacturer, let loose his 300 armed Pinkertons against the strikers – allegedly in order to protect "those willing to work" – and thus gave impetus to the bloody attacks of the police, who struck out indiscriminately at men, women and children, killing six people and wounding many others. This was on May 3. On May 4 followed the famous dynamite bomb. This was the occasion for a fierce street fight in which four workers were killed and about fifty wounded. The results of the gruesome judicial sequel of May 4, 1886, in which democratic American class justice gave such a clear illustration of how far it will go, are known throughout the world.

The events of the years 1892–4 deserve closer examination. First, there were fierce fights between armed Pinkertons, enrolled by the employers, and the strikers during the strike at the Carnegie Iron and Steel Works at Homestead in July, 1892. Twelve people were killed and twenty badly wounded. The Pinkertons were overcome, but in the end the strikers were defeated after the occupation of the town by government troops and the declaration of martial law. Almost simultaneously a miners' strike broke out in Coeur d'Alène (Idaho). The militia, numbering only about a hundred men, was not in a position to intervene against the strikers, who were well-armed, in their struggle with the strike-breakers. Only the federal troops demanded by the governor managed to disperse the strikers.

The switchmen came out on strike in Buffalo in August 1892. The local militia, which

---
122. See Hillquit, *Geschichte des Sozialismus in den Vereinigten Staaten*, Stuttgart 1906, p.211. This is the work which has mostly been used here for information on North America.

was called out at the beginning of the strike, did not seem disposed to prevent picketing. Finally the sheriff was induced to ask the governor for troops. Within 48 hours almost the whole state militia appeared, outnumbering the strikers twenty times, and restored "peace".

During the same month the strikes at the Inman iron mines and at the Oliver Springs and Coal Creek coal mines gave the state governor the opportunity to bring out the whole of the state militia, after several isolated detachments of militia had been disarmed and sent home by the strikers. Here again, after the strike bad been broken, class justice took its merciless course.

Finally, let us recall the Chicago Pullman strike of 1894, during which the president of the United States, in spite of a protest by Altgeld, the governor of Illinois,[123] sent in federal troops which, together with the state militia, broke the strike. Twelve people were killed. It is clear that in this case, more than in any previous case, the system of justice worked hand in hand with militarism. So effective were the notorious injunctions and mass arrests in defeating the workers that the leader of the strike, Debs, said: "We were not beaten by the railroads, nor by the army, but by the power of the courts of the United States".[124]

What remains true, however, in spite of the fact that the militia frequently refused to act and that the workers were often armed, is that military force was decisive in the defeat of the workers in all the cases cited above. In the subsequent period, too, strikes in America were "in the majority of cases crushed with the help of the local police, the state militia or the federal troops", and of course also with the help of the government, "by means of injunctions". The strikes ended almost without exception in defeat for the workers, according to Hillquit's rather pessimistic account.[125]

Canada

Canada's "free" soil was stained with workers' blood at Hamilton on November 24, 1906. In a clash with striking railwaymen the militia wounded 50 people, some seriously.

Switzerland

Switzerland's book of sins in this field is truly long enough. As long ago as 1869 the government of the canton of Geneva set both police and militia against striking workers. In the same year the government of the canton of Vaud recalled by telegraph a battalion which had set out on a march, provided it with live ammunition and made it march with fixed bayonets into the town where the workers were on strike. In 1869 too the government of the canton of Basle made troops do picket duty when the silk-weavers went on strike to improve their pitiful condition. In the same year a strike broke out at

---

123. The same Altgeld who, on June 26, 1890, pardoned the Chicago anarchists.
124. See Hillquit, *Geschichte des Sozialismus in den Vereinigten Staaten*, pp.190, 209ff., 236ff., 306ff.
125. Ibid., p.314.

La Chaux-de-Fonds, and the new bourgeois government hurried to provide itself with arms and ammunition, anticipating that it might be necessary to mobilise the militia.

In 1875 it came to bloodshed. Two thousand workers on the St Gotthard tunnel had struck to protect themselves against the shameless truck system. The government of the canton of Uri, which, it is said, had been provided with 20,000 francs for the purpose by the contractors, mobilised the militia. The vigorous attack claimed its victims: several dead and fifteen wounded were left on this battlefield of the class struggle. Blood was also shed in 1901 by two companies called out by the government of the canton of Vallais to crush the strike of the workers on the Simplon tunnel. A number of workers were badly wounded as a result. In the same year two companies were put on picket duty in Ticino against a strike of Italian masons. In October 1902 the well-known Geneva events took place. In the course of a strike against a firm of American exploiters the workers were chased and beaten by order of the government of Geneva, and when the soldiers refused to carry out police duty they were thrown into prison and deprived of their civil rights. We will mention in passing that on this occasion members of the bourgeoisie who were not even called out armed themselves on a large scale against the workers. At about the same time the militia was mobilised at Basle against a strike. In 1904 the building contractors of La Chaux-de-Fonds called on the government for military aid against a strike of building workers. To their dismay, the strike progressed in a quite orderly manner in spite of all provocations and therefore, from their point of view, seemed hopeless. The cavalry and a battalion of infantry were on the scene at once, and by intimidation drove the workers, who had conducted their struggle in a lawful manner, back to their lives of factory slavery. The military were mobilised in 1904 during a strike on the Ricken in the canton of St Gall, allegedly in order to protect the fruit and vegetable crops which in fact were in no danger at all. In the same way St Gall sent its militia to Rorschach, where during a wage dispute an angry crowd had smashed a few window panes at a French-owned foundry.

The events which took place in Zurich in the summer of 1906 were of a very serious character. The great rise in the cost of living had led to the outbreak of a number of strikes, the aim of which was to raise wages. The building workers came out too for the same goal. Without any cause the militia made a bloody intervention. They attacked and beat the workers in the most brutal manner, they dragged strikers, especially foreign ones, to their barracks and there lashed them with riding whips – at the officers' command! And that was not enough: strike pickets and demonstrations were forbidden. An intervention in the Grand Council referring to the shameful events was first put off indefinitely and then strangled without discussion by the bourgeois majority. And to crown it all, six strike leaders were brought before the courts. Five of them were acquitted on August 24, 1906, but Sigg was condemned to eight months imprisonment and the loss of civil rights for one year for alleged incitement to mutiny by means of an anti-militarist leaflet addressed to the militia.

One can ask no more of a bourgeois republic or of a militia.

A special light is thrown on these data by the fact, already mentioned in another connection, that in 1899 those Swiss citizens not on active service were deprived of their ammunition. This, one can see, was carried out just in time to facilitate the employment of the militia in the interest of the bourgeoisie in a period when the class struggle was becoming more intense.

On December 21, 1906, the National Council adopted by 65 votes to 55 an amendment to the law on military organisation. According to this amendment, when conflicts of an economic mature "disturb or menace peace at home", the mobilisation of troops "thereby necessitated" may only take place for the purpose of "maintaining public order". (The law in its totality was passed by 105 votes to 4.) But it is clear that the amendment expresses precisely what was already the criterion for military intervention; it is therefore useless, absolutely useless, and the fact that a large minority voted *against* the amendment gives rise to thought.

Norway

Free Norway, which in the summer of 1905 passed through the most placid revolution in world history and then, to satisfy a primitive desire, crowned it by setting up a monarchy, follows the capitalist states exactly, in spite of the peasant romance which is attached to it.

The use of military force against strikers is not a rare occurrence in this land of democracy. An article in the *Tyvende Aarhundrede* of May 1, 1903, p.53, gives details of this. We learn here that in 1902 alone there were two such cases, in Dunderlands Dal and in Tromsö.

Germany

There remains Germany. It is precisely in Germany that the use of the military in economic struggles is not usual. There are at least very few cases to record in which the army made an active intervention, the following being exceptions. In the weavers' riots of 1844 the Prussian infantry killed 11 and wounded 24 of those miserable proletarians who had been almost tortured to death. Class justice sealed the defeat by passing an enormous number of sentences of hard labour. There was also the miners' strike of 1889, when on May 10 the troops called for by the provincial president, von Hagemeister, left three dead and four wounded in front of the Moltke mine, and two dead and five wounded on the battlefield in Bochum.[126] In the disturbances of February 1892 involving the Berlin unemployed the army did not intervene, but according to reliable sources the

---

126. On May 19, 1889, the German Kaiser said to a deputation waiting on him: "If I perceive that the movement betrays Social Democratic tendencies and that people are incited to unlawful resistance, I shall intervene with ruthless severity and make use of all the power at my disposal – which is considerable". According to the *Freisinnige-Zeitung* he added that if the least resistance were shown to the authorities he would have the trouble-makers shot.

Berlin military were held ready in their barracks on January 18, 1894, on the basis of a mere rumour that the unemployed had planned a demonstration in front of the palace.

This military "moderation" does not, however, have its base in some specially kindly and correct way of thinking on the part of the authorities which take the decisions. On the contrary! Germany has a strong force of police and *gendarmerie*, excellently organised as far as the ruling class is concerned. It is not in vain that Germany is a police state *kat'exochen* (archetypal, preeminently). The well-armed police and the well-armed *gendarmerie* here fulfil a role which elsewhere is played by the army. Moreover, they carry out their task more easily and with more adaptability, in regard to the complex situations which may arise at any moment, than the military machine, which works in a slower and more clumsy way.

The number of bloody conflicts between strikers and police or *gendarmerie* is big enough in Germany. The Berlin tramway strike of 1900 and the so-called Breslau riot of 1906 are no exceptions. Biewald's severed hand is only an especially revolting mark of the bloodthirsty progress made by the police, another product of military culture. This hand in fact finds itself in good company with countless cracked skulls, severed ears, noses, fingers and other members, and this good company is rapidly growing.

The number of victims cut down by the armed state power during strikes must be hardly smaller in Germany than in other states. Even an approximate estimate of the number is impossible, however, because full records are not kept of those wounded in conflicts with the police, nor are such things really taken note of. If there are fewer of these victims in Germany than elsewhere, it is not the goodwill and humane nature of the capitalist class and its state which are to be thanked. That becomes very clear when one considers the fact that here it is almost a rule that, whenever big strikes take place, the troops are assembled and held ready in the barracks. The most serious instance of this kind concerns the Ruhr miners' strike, which lasted from January 8 to February 10, 1905.[127] The bloodless outcome here is to be ascribed exclusively to the presence of mind, moderation, strict self-discipline, training and education of the German workers. We need have no doubt that the Prussian and Saxon governments would take up the side of the capitalist class in the economic struggle – with drums and trumpets, swords and guns – without thinking twice, if the occasion arose.

5. Military societies and strikes

Militarism attempts to maintain and extend militarist tendencies in men who have already finished their active service, through the use of military societies. It is therefore quite understandable that these societies intervene in strikes. They are not of course able to use violence in suppressing the economic struggles of the workers, but they may be characterised as organisations designed for blacklegging. Certain quarters, at least, would be only too ready to use them for this purpose. Only the fact that, in spite of all

127. See what took place in Landau-Kaiserslautern in September 1906.

precautions, a considerable proportion of opposition and even of Social Democratic elements is to be found in them prevents the fullest use being made of these military societies, together with the fact that in the conflicts between employers and workers, it is precisely those workers who lack social understanding and who are normally as mild as lambs who are the first to get enraged, so that they get an understanding of the class struggle and of their own class position driven into their heads. Moreover, excesses on the part of the employers annoy even the Christians and liberal workers' organisations.

In spite of these qualifications, the discussion which took place in June 1906 in Ostheim at a conference of the Federation of Military Societies of the Grand Duchy of Saxe-Weimar is very interesting. The discussion developed out of a principle adopted at a delegate conference, according to which it is a duty of the members to expel anyone who proves to belong to a party antagonistic to the state, and especially to the Social Democratic Party. It turned out that participation in any strike, or at least in those strikes which are contrary to one's duty of "loyalty to the Emperor, Prince and Fatherland", was to be considered as confirming the fact that someone held revolutionary views dangerous to the state. Since it depends on the very same high personages who play first fiddle in the military societies to declare where and when this loyalty is put into question in a strike, and since these gentlemen, like our police and our courts, tend to consider every strike – which often, directly or indirectly, puts their own closest interests at risk – as a Social Democratic machination, one can reckon on some productive work being done here by these societies. But it will not be as useful to the capitalist class as to Social Democracy, which thrives on such clumsy repression, since it only serves to enlighten the workers and weaken the military societies. These societies are expelling, in an ever more systematic way, not only Social Democrats but also the members of all the trade unions based on the principles of the modern labour movement. There is no doubt that, for the moment, this practice is putting certain difficulties in the way of the trade unions in the smaller towns, because the members are often bound to them by material advantages, for which they have paid quite high contributions.[128] This apart from the usual "pomp and panoply".[129]

The military societies find strong support in their aims from the practice of class justice. The administration has the impudence to treat them as non-political organisations, though their political-agitational character oozes through every pore. It is a helping hand which the organs of the capitalist state are bound to hold out to militarism, on the grounds of solidarity and in the interest of their common higher aim, the protection of the capitalist social order.

---

128. See the appeal of the Saxon Sharpshooters' and Riflemen's Military Society in the *Leipziger Volkszeitung*, December 1, 1906.
129. On the "drinking parties and brawls", to use the words of the pastor César, see the *Sozialdemokratische Partei-Correspondenz*, No.21, December 8, 1906.

6. The army as a tool against the proletariat in the political struggle, or the right of the cannon

Since the development of the class struggle, its most concentrated form, is the political struggle, it is natural that in the class struggle too militarism appears in its sharpest form in direct and indirect intervention in the political struggle. Militarism acts first of all as an economic power, as a producer and consumer. The ruthless exclusion of all Social Democrats, or those suspected of being such, from the military workshops, from those at Spandau for example; the unconditional surrender of the workers, who are under the influence of militarism, to the reactionary parties, and especially to the Imperial League against Social Democracy, Germany's black hundreds, at the same time as all contact with Social Democracy is prevented; these facts show how splendidly militarism has grasped its main task, protection of the interests of the employers, and with what military efficiency it carries out this task. No Krupp or Stumm, no capitalist can compete with militarism here, in the energy with which it defends capitalist interests. The Imperial League against Social Democracy, for example, controls the military workshops at Spandau in such a way that it almost plays the role of a vigilante, watching over the thoughts of every worker in the royal service. Its word and will decide which workers are to be sacked. This situation has been very strikingly shown up by the events in connection with the sacking of the executive committee of a harmless union of unskilled workmen in the military workshops in the summer of 1906.

A considerable influence is also exerted – though it is on the decline – by the military boycott of public houses which are used by the workers' associations or any other organisations which, in even a remote way, savour of Social Democracy. This boycott kills two birds with one stone. On the one hand it protects the soldiers from possible contamination by the revolutionary poison – this aspect really belongs to the field of military education discussed above. On the other hand it makes it difficult for the workers to get hold of rooms and halls for meetings, since they are often unable to hire a proper public meeting place. In Berlin for example this boycott has turned out to be impossible to apply and has been given up, but our comrades in the smaller towns suffer greatly from this plague, which of course is directed against the economic struggle of the proletariat.[130]

But these are only "the smallest of its sins". Militarism is not satisfied with endlessly interfering in the petty, everyday political struggle, though in this it never lets up. It has infinitely greater ambitions. It is the noblest and mightiest support of the throne and altar in all the greatest and most serious conflicts of capitalist reaction with the revolution. It threw its weight into the scales in the same way against the earlier revolutionary movements. This need only be briefly related.

---

130. To this category belongs also the threat of a military boycott – made for example during the 1903 Reichstag election campaign against those publicans at Spandau on whose premises the Social Democrats had displayed lists of electors in order to facilitate the checking of the lists. They had to be taken down (see *Denkschrift des Reichstages*, No.618, 1905–7).

We have already dealt with the gruesome laurel wreaths with which capitalist militarism crowned itself in the struggle against the proletariat of Paris in July 1830, in June 1848 and in May 1871, as well as in the riots provoked by "Napoleon the Little" on December 2, 1852. Of special interest here, because they took place in England, are the Chartist massacres of Newport and Birmingham in 1839, in which 10 people were killed and 50 wounded – *et tu, Brute!*

The whole of Russia has been under martial law at various degrees for the last two years to aid the cruel barbarities of tsarism, and to crush without mercy the liberation movement by means of the fist, whip, sword, rifle and gun, with which the army is turning this unhappy land into a great cemetery. Only the progress of the revolution and the disintegration of the army, which necessarily corresponds to the energy of the revolutionary forces, are reliable guarantees that this "Christian" but also suicidal plan will not be realised. As we have already pointed out, Russia has to be treated with many reservations when an examination of the capitalist states is being made.

The role played by the standing army in the first great Belgian electoral struggle is very important, as well as the role played in the second such struggle in 1902 by the national guard, the special militarist organisation used by the bourgeoisie in the class struggle.

Austria saw the mobilisation of the military against a workers' demonstration in the Vienna Prater on May 1, 1896, and we have already mentioned the events in Prague, Vienna and Glatz (1897), in Lemberg and Trieste (1902). But it provided a second brilliant example of militarist-political action on the large scale in the election fight of 1905. Bohemia especially was on the point of becoming the scene of civil war.[131] On November 5 and 28, 1905, the day on which election demonstrations were to be held, Prague, where the miners were also on strike, was filled with and surrounded by the army. The heights around were occupied by the artillery, ready to fire, and about eighty people were eventually wounded, though in fact by the police.

The events in Italy which belong to this section have already been mentioned.

Now we come to Germany, to that Germany whose supreme warlord, in a world-renowned speech – which has become a powerful weapon in the standing arsenal of anti-militarist propaganda in every country – gave the soldiers a curious interpretation of the fourth commandment. Not only did he make the well-known Sedan day speech against the "mob" in 1895, but also the famous appeal to the Alexander regiment on March 28, 1901. It was the proletariat as such, the only sound pillar of the "constitution", for which the military armament and Wrangel's manoeuvres were meant, which in 1848–9 shamelessly crushed the German revolution, more or less betrayed and abandoned by the German bourgeoisie, and robbed it of its birthright. One might also recall the Boyen-Lotzen affair of the shackles in September 1870, and the bloody fantasies of Bismarck-Puttkamer memory. At the time of the infamous anti-socialist law, these "heroes of the 19th century" looked forward, longed to see the workers forced into the streets and cut

---

131. See also the paper *Der Jugendliche Arbeiter*, December 1905 (on the shooting of 16-year-old Johann Hubac).

down with the sword, rifle and shrapnel in the most artistic and sportsmanlike way.[132] The fact that the army was held ready in the barracks in the case of May Day festivals[133] and Reichstag elections is still well remembered,[134] as are the events of 1896 during the process by which electoral rights were stolen from the people of Saxony, and the events of 1905–6, when the army participated in the "pacification" of the Saxon population.[135] When election demonstrations were held in Hamburg on January 17, 1906, "bloody Wednesday", police guns and swords sufficed to do the necessary work. The two corpses which adorned the pavements of the free Hansa town were their responsibility. The army, consisting of local people, was kept in the background.

On January 21, 1906, however, the defenders of capitalism showed themselves in their full glory. Whoever heard the guns rattle down the paved streets of Berlin on that "holy" Sunday has glimpsed the heart and soul of militarism. The sound of those guns still resounds in our ears today, and spurs us on in our struggle against militarism with untiring, relentless, ruthless determination.

On January 21, 1906, it was simply a question of a demonstration against the infamous Prussian three-class electoral system. But we know that our militarism would be at least as eager to reach for the sword and rifle if it were necessary to make some reactionary changes to the state constitution by means of a *coup d'état*. And the latest Hohenlohe and Delbruck revelations have shown how Bismarck in 1890 was on the point of dispersing the Reichstag, of abolishing the electoral system, of driving the proletarian masses onto the streets to face the guns and cannons, of crushing Social Democracy by shattering the defenceless ranks of the workers, and so of building a fortress of blood and iron on the broken proletarian bodies in order to protect Bismarckian-Junker reaction.[136] We have also heard that the German Kaiser would not endorse this plan because he first wished "to satisfy the legitimate complaints of the workers", "to meet their legitimate demands". We know, moreover, that the workers hold an opinion quite different from that of the ruling classes as to which of their demands are legitimate, and we know that the antagonism towards the Reichstag found among the most influential circles in northern Germany (especially marked in the ex-Communist Miquel, as the Hohenlohe memoirs have shown) is continually on the increase.[137] We also know that the danger of a "military solution of the social question by means of small calibre rifles and large

---

132. Ludwigshafen in the Palatinate was practically occupied by troops on the Sunday before the 1887 election, and only the presence of mind of the Social Democrats prevented an outbreak of shooting (see the description in the *Festschrift zur Mannheimer Parteitag*, 1906, pp.9ff.). The statement by the Kaiser recorded in the Hohenlohe memoirs for December 12, 1889, is interesting in this connection. He says that when the Social Democrats are in a majority on the Berlin town council they will set about robbing the citizens. But that will not worry him, he adds. He will have embrasures made in the palace and watch the looting going on. Then the citizens will have to implore him to come to their assistance.
133. This applied especially to the first May Day celebration (1890), which the military firebrands, the "military party" (Hohenlohe's memoirs, September 14, 1893) would have liked to use as the opportunity to settle the account in blood with the hated and dangerous Social Democrats.
134. For example the electoral riots at Laurahütte and Zabrze in Upper Silesia in 1903.
135. See the order concerning shooting made for January 21, 1906, published by the *Leipziger Volkszeitung* on April 3, 1906
136. This was of course brought to light by the *Hamburger Nachrichten* in March 1892.
137. See the *Handbuch für sozialdemokratische Wähler*, 1903, *Der Preussische Landtag, Handbuch für sozialdemokratische Wähler*, Berlin 1903, and above all the *Hamburger Nachrichten*, the *Kreuz-Zeitung*, the *Deutsche Tageszeitung* and *Die Post*, in connection with the project to dissolve the Reichstag on December 13, 1906, if the election result should be unfavourable.

calibre cannons appears today closer than ever.[138] Should the chief of the General Staff, Helmut von Moltke, become the Imperial Chancellor, as has been recently predicted, it would mean to all appearances a victory for the notorious military party at court.[139]

There has never been a shortage of "shrapnel princes", shrapnel Junkers and shrapnel generals in world history. One must be ready for everything. There is no time to lose.[140]

7. Military societies in the political struggle

The military societies of course manifest a very intensive political activity, which German justice naturally cannot see through its blindfold. Everyone knows how these societies are mobilised during elections, and how they force their members to leave the political organisations of the opposition. It is worth noting the way in which, to show their "loyalty to the king", they deprive the class-conscious workers of meeting-places. There are only two new facts to be brought forward. First, the decision of the Society of Old Soldiers of the XVIth Army Corps in Duisburg-Beeck to boycott the Kaiserhof Hotel in Duisburg because it had been let for a miners' meeting. Second, the expulsion from the military societies of Saxony of those publicans who allow their premises to be used by the workers for meetings.[141] It is not easy to take on these methods of struggle in the smaller towns, though when the workers are organised it simply means blows in the air.

The material which belongs to this section deserves to be systematically collected for use in the day-to-day struggle.

8. Militarism, a danger to peace

Nationalist contradictions – the need for national expansion as a consequence of the increase in population, the need for the annexation of territories possessing natural riches in order to increase the national wealth (which means the wealth of the ruling classes) and the need to make the state independent by constituting it as far as possible as a self-sufficient economic unit with regard to production (a natural tendency to promote and extend a policy of protectionism, a tendency which can, however, only

---

138. The appeal to the Prussian bayonets made by the thoroughbred Junker von Oldenburg-Januschau to the Reichstag in May 1905 and at the Provincial Conference of the Agrarian Federation in Konitz in December 1906 echoed the feelings in the hearts of, at least, a very influential camarilla.
139. The *Berliner Tageblatt* describes this up-and-coming character in the following terms: "Helmut von Moltke is said to be an outspoken reactionary, tempered by a certain soldierly frankness and a happy disposition, though he is also said to have spiritualist tendencies. He is not at all a man of theory, but a go-ahead man of action, cool but ready to make politics with the sword and rifle". There we have all the qualities so earnestly desired by our firebrands concentrated in one man.
140. So that the element of satire in the tragedy shall not be lacking, we will refer here to the farce played out in 1904 in the little Thuringian town of Hildburghausen. The students of the Technical Institute were angry with the police because not enough leniency had been shown towards the young bourgeois elements who had a habit of causing disturbances. One night they stormed the police station, and could only be forced back by a company of infantry – though without bloodshed. The sequel, before the Meiningen County Court, also deserves to be remembered. The accused "rebels" were not, as with workers in similar cases, sentenced to imprisonment or hard labour, but acquitted or given light fines. But the unfortunate lieutenant who intervened, and who may perhaps not kept strictly to the rules, was severely reprimanded.
141. See the declaration made by the President of the Federation of Saxon Military Societies, published in the *Leipziger Volkszeitung* on December 1, 1906.

PARTICULARS OF SOME OF THE MAIN SINS OF MILITARISM

diminish in the face of the ever expanding international division of labour), the need for facilitating communication at home and abroad (for example through the acquisition of navigable channels and of harbours, etc.), which is the means through which trade, the metabolism of the economic body, is effected – these contradictions, together with contradictions in the general cultural level, especially in the stage of political development, can easily, even in the present day, produce international political tensions. The most important political tensions which today can lead to world war arise, as has already been shown above, from the competition of individual states within the world economy, from world trade, from international politics with all its complications, and especially from colonial politics. Those who bear the main responsibility for these tensions are the powerful figures interested in the expansion of industry and trade. They may be said to be interested in a *successful* war.

We must not shut our eyes to the fact that the existence of the standing armies in which militarism has entrenched itself in the *most striking manner* in itself threatens world peace, and constitutes an autonomous danger of war. Apart from all this is the fact that the increase in military spending, that "endless screw", can lead to the inclination to let no favourable moment elapse without using one's temporary military superiority, or without starting a military conflict once it is thought necessary in order to prevent a further unfavourable shift in the balance of military power. This tendency, which as everyone knows was not without influence in France in the recent Morocco conflict,[142] determines rather the time of the outbreak of war than the fact of its outbreak.

But the standing army produces, as does the militia to a much smaller degree, a modern caste of warriors, a caste of persons who, so to speak, are trained for war from childhood, a privileged class of conquistadores who seek adventure and advancement in war. To this group belong also those strata who have something special to gain from war, those who supply arms, munitions, battleships, horses, material for fitting out and for clothing, catering and transport requirements; in short: the army contractors, who of course are also present but to a lesser degree in states where there exists a militia. Both these groups with war interests, that is, those interested in war, even simply in the waging of war (the most adventurous of the officers and those of the army contractors who are quite independent of military success) are, to use a popular expression, "on the inside". They have connections with the highest state offices and possess a great influence over those powers whose job it is to make the formal decision on war and peace. They miss no favourable opportunity of attempting to turn this influence, which they have for the most part gained through their exploitation of militarism, into pure gold, and to sacrifice countless numbers of proletarians on the altar of profit. They agitate for colonial expansion, forcing the "dear Fatherland" into dangerous and costly adventures which are, however, profitable to themselves, in order then to be able to agitate for a navy to save the same Fatherland in another way, which of course is again very

---
142. See the article by Major-General von Zeppelin in the *Kreuz-Zeitung*, December 23, 1906.

profitable for them.¹⁴³

The struggle against the standing army and the chauvinistic-militaristic spirit means struggle against a threat to peace between nations. The old saying, *si vis pacem para bellum* (if you want peace, prepare for war), may still apply to some individual state surrounded by militarist states, but by no means applies to the totality of the capitalist states against which Social Democracy directs its international agitation. And even less does this saying imply the need to prepare for war by means of a standing army. On the contrary, the saying in its inverted form, *si vis bellum para pacem*, applies to such an army – there is no more sure method of provoking war than such a method of securing peace! In the case of the aggressive economic-political imperialism of our day the standing army is indeed the adequate form of preparation for war.

Just as it is true that peace between nations is in the interest of the international proletariat, and beyond that in the interest of the whole of human civilisation, so it is true that the struggle against militarism – which, all in all, comes to a struggle against the sum and extract of all the tendencies of capitalism which disturb peace, stirring up nation against nation; in short, threatening a world war – this struggle is a struggle for civilisation which the proletariat is proud to wage, which it must wage in its very own interest, and in the waging of which no other class as such (a few well-meaning enthusiasts here only prove the rule) has anything like as great an interest.

Militarism also disturbs *peace at home*, not only by its brutalisation of the people and by the heavy economic burdens which it lays on them through taxes and duties, not only by the corruption which goes hand in hand with it (*vide* men like Woermann, Fischer, von Tippelskirch, Podbielski & Co.),¹⁴⁴ not only by the division of the people, already suffering enough from class division, into two castes, not only by military ill-treatment and military justice, but above all by the fact that it is a powerfully effective brake on every sort of progress, that it is an ingenious and very efficient instrument for keeping the valve of the social boiler firmly shut. For the person who considers the further development of the human race as necessary, the existence of militarism is the most important obstacle to the peaceful and steady character of such a development; for him untamed militarism is synonymous with the necessity of a blood-red twilight for the idols of capitalism.

9. The difficulties of the proletarian revolution

To abolish militarism or weaken it as much as possible is therefore a question of life or death for the political struggle for emancipation, a struggle whose form and mode militarism in a certain sense debases, and therefore decisively influences. It becomes even more a life or death question as the superiority of the army over the unarmed

---

143. See the *Rheinisch-Westfälische Zeitung* of December 5, 1906.
144. Tippelskirch & Co. were army contractors who secured a highly profitable monopoly in the supply of clothes and equipment to the colonial forces. In 1906 the firm was involved in a corruption scandal along with the Prussian minister von Podbielski, who was a partner in the firm, and the shipping firm Woermann & Co.

people, over the proletariat, increases in consequence of the highly developed technique and strategy, in consequence of the gigantic size of the armies, in consequence of the unfavourable way in which the classes are divided with regard to locality, and in consequence of the especially unfavourable relation of economic power in which the proletariat stands to the bourgeoisie. For all these reasons it will be far more difficult to make every coming proletarian revolution than it was to make all past revolutions. It is important always to remember that in the bourgeois revolution the leading force, the revolutionary bourgeoisie, had long held economic power in its hands before the revolution in the narrow sense broke out, and that there was a large class, economically subject to the bourgeoisie and exposed to its political influence, which the bourgeoisie could put to work to pull the chestnuts out of the fire. It is important to remember that the bourgeoisie had first of all to a certain degree picked up the old rubbish of feudalism before it broke it up and threw it in the lumber-room, while the members of the proletariat must conquer everything that was taken from them with the help of riches while themselves still going hungry and even at the risk of their lives.

Part II - Anti-Militarism

CHAPTER ONE

Anti-militarism of the Old and the New International

The *Communist Manifesto*, the most prophetic work in world literature, does not deal specifically with militarism or adequately with its accessory significance. It does, it is true, speak of the uprising "brought about sporadically by the proletarian struggle", and thus effectively indicates the role played by capitalist militarism *vis-à-vis* the struggle of the proletariat for freedom. It discusses at greater length the question of international – or rather inter-state – conflicts, and the capitalist policy of expansion (including colonial policy). The latter is regarded as a necessary consequence of capitalist development. It is predicted that national isolation and national contradictions would tend more and more to disappear *even under the domination of the bourgeoisie*, and that the domination of the proletariat would reduce them still further. One might almost say that the program of measures to be taken under the dictatorship of the proletariat contains nothing specifically about militarism. The conquest of political power which is supposed to have already been brought about embraces the "conquest", that is to say, the overthrow of militarism.

Special declarations about militarism began to appear with the congresses of the International. These declarations however refer exclusively to "militarism against the enemy abroad", to the position to be taken up with regard to war. The Lausanne Congress of 1867 contained this point on the agenda: "The Peace Congress in Geneva in 1868". It was decided to work together with the Peace Congress on the either naïve or ironical supposition that this congress would adopt the program of the International. War was characterised as a consequence of the class struggle.

At the third congress of the International held in Brussels in 1868 a resolution moved by Longuet in the name of a commission was unanimously adopted. It designated the lack of economic balance as the chief and lasting cause of war, stressing that a change can only be brought about by social reform. The labour movement is said to be able to reduce the number of wars by means of agitation and education of the people, and tireless work to this end is laid down as a duty. In case of war a general strike is advised, and the congress expresses its belief that the international solidarity of workers of all lands is strong enough to secure their aid in the war of the peoples against war.

Now the "new" International!

The resolution of the Paris Congress of 1899 is of the greatest interest in this connection. It deals with the standing armies, which it brands as the "negation of every democratic and republican regime", as the "military expression of the monarchical or oligarchic-capitalist regime", as a "tool for reactionary *coups d'état* and social oppression". It characterises these armies, together with the aggressive political positions whose tool they are, as the cause and consequence of the system of offensive wars and of the present danger of international conflicts. It repudiates these, both from a military-technical point of view and because of their direct disorganising and demoralising properties, hostile to all cultural progress, and also because of the unbearable military burdens which the armies impose on the peoples. It demands the abolition of the standing armies and the introduction of a universal citizen army, while regarding war as an inevitable consequence of capitalism.

This resolution is more thorough than any previous one in its characterisation of militarism.

The proceedings of the Brussels Congress in 1891 were also important. Here the question of war, of international militarism, was dealt with exclusively. The Nieuwenhuis resolution, which described war as the result of the international will of capitalism and as a means of smashing the power of the revolutionary movement, and which demanded that socialists of every land should answer every war with a general strike, was voted down. The Vaillant-Liebknecht resolution, which regards militarism as a necessary consequence of capitalism and peace between peoples as attainable only through the establishment of an international socialist system, was adopted. It calls on the workers to protest, by tireless agitation, against the barbarity of war and against alliances which promote it, and to speed the triumph of socialism by the development of the international organisations of the proletariat. This method of fighting was declared to be the only one capable of preventing the catastrophe of a world war.

The Zurich Congress of 1893 confirmed the Brussels resolution and indicated these ways of fighting against militarism: refusal to vote military credits, incessant protests against the standing armies, tireless agitation in favour of disarmament, support of all organisations which strive after world peace.

The London Congress of 1896 again discussed the two sides of militarism. It indicated as the chief causes of war the economic contradictions into which the ruling classes of the different countries have been forced by the capitalist mode of production.[145] Wars were considered to be acts of the ruling classes in their own interest at the cost of the

---

[145]. And not class contradictions! This question is specially dealt with here for the first time.

workers. The struggle against military oppression was seen as a part of the struggle against exploitation, and as a duty of the working class. The conquest of political power, the abolition of the capitalist mode of production, the seizure from the governments of the means of power of the capitalist class, the tools for maintaining the established order[146] – this was fixed as the objective. The standing armies were considered to increase the danger of war and to facilitate the brutal oppression of labour. The immediate demands were: abolition of the standing armies and introduction of a citizen force, together with international courts of arbitration, with the people to decide on questions of peace and war. The resolution concluded that the people could achieve its goal in this connection only after it had secured a *decisive influence on legislation*, and joined in a system of international socialism.

The Paris Congress of 1900 passed a comprehensive resolution on colonial expansionist politics, and the possibilities of international conflict inherent in the capitalist system. It also condemned the policy of national oppression, bringing together a few especially barbaric examples, and gave special attention to the struggle against militarism. It referred to the decisions of 1889, 1891 and 1896, pointed out the international and national danger of imperialist world politics, called upon the proletariat to redouble its efforts in the international struggle against militarism and its world politics, and proposed these practical means: international protest movements, refusal of all military, naval and colonial expenditure, and *"the education and organisation of the youth with the aim of fighting militarism"*.

A survey of these decisions shows a steady growth of practical political insight into militarism abroad, and an ever deeper and more specialised recognition of the causes and dangers of war, as well as the significance of "militarism at home". As far as the means of fighting militarism are concerned, however, the idea of a general strike against war brought forward in 1868 was far in advance of its time. In the same way, strikes of soldiers as a regular method of fighting against war were rejected by all later congresses – justifiably, in the circumstances. The recognised means of struggle, however, are progressing slowly. The refusal of military expenditure recommended to the proletariat is the only direct political manifestation of power against militarism, but it remains without significant immediate effect. All other proposals remain within the domain of propaganda in favour of changes in the legal position and in favour of future actions. This, of course, as is shown elsewhere, is the only domain more or less open to the proletariat for the moment. Even the refusal of military credits, as a rule, will have to be considered as a means of propaganda of this kind.

The chief difficulty for the moment, especially in Germany, lies in determining the form and method of anti-militarist propaganda. The fact that these have not been more carefully fixed in the congress decisions is due to the different external and internal position of the various countries, and from this point of view it may appear useful and even

---

146. This is not really the object of the conquest of political power, but the essence of the conquest itself – to safeguard by means of organisation what has been taken by the proletariat is of course one of the tasks of the dictatorship of the proletariat.

necessary. We should not, however, forget that the tendency of the decisions is to lay greater and greater weight on anti-militarist propaganda and to make this propaganda more specialised. The Paris decision shows this perfectly clearly. It reflects both the growing self-consciousness of the international proletariat and the growing conviction that it is necessary to set about gaining partial advances against militarism abroad and at home by the use of the class-conscious power of the proletariat.

In conclusion we should mention the circular sent out by the International Socialist Bureau in November 1905 at the suggestion of the French section of the International in connection with the Morocco conflict. It makes no positive proposals for action against the war, but simply states what is self-evident and elementary – that the parties which are affiliated to the Bureau should, in the event of a threatened war, immediately make contact in order to work out and vote upon the means of avoiding or hindering the war.

CHAPTER TWO
Anti-militarism abroad

The anti-militarist movement in capitalist countries other than Germany is for the most part strong and lively. This is especially true of the Latin countries such as Belgium, France and Italy, but also applies, though more recently, to Austria, Switzerland and the Scandinavian countries, and even to Holland, though anti-militarism is only just beginning to show itself there.

Belgium

Special anti-militarist propaganda was started in Belgium in 1886, when the army made large-scale interventions in strikes, as we have already seen. After leaflets had been distributed to remind the soldiers of their duty towards their working-class brothers,[147] two anti-militarist newspapers were founded: *Le Conscrit* and *La Caserne* (The Conscript and The Barracks).[148] The first always appears in January (before the drawing of lots in February), the second in September (before the recruits are called up on October 1). Both appear in Flemish as well as French (*De Loteling* and *De Kazerne*[149]). In 1896 the Party handed over both newspapers to the National Federation of Young Guards, founded in 1894.[150] But they remain under the control of the Party centre, to which the National Federation of Young Guards has sent delegates since 1896–7. The Young Guards were founded in 1893–4, though there were individuals in Brussels as early as the 1880s, mainly engaged in election work and in special anti-militarist propaganda. Since 1902 this has changed. The disappointments of the second general strike have caused the workers to go more carefully and slowly, and to pay great care to maintaining the

---
147. We have before us one of the leaflets issued by the Antwerp branch of the Socialist Labour Party in 1886.
 It goes straight to the essential point, calling on the soldiers to refuse to obey an order to fire on the people.
148. In regard to this activity see *La procès de la caserne*, Volksdrukkerij, Ghent 1905.
149. *De Loteling* and *De Kazerne* since 1887, *Le Caserne* since 1893, *La Conscrit* since 1899.
150. The Flemish papers were placed under the control of the Flemish Federation of the Socialist Young Guards in Ghent.

roots of organisation and propaganda. The aims of the Young Socialist organisations were broadened, and the development of education given first place – undoubtedly the more solid method of anti-militarist propaganda, or rather that which best prepares the ground for it. As far as these organisations are concerned, it is impossible to deal fully with their history here, tempting as this may be, though they are also closely linked with the anti-militarist struggle.[151]

A few words only, then: since 1896 the monthly journal *Avant Garde*, organ of the students and Young Guards, has been appearing in Brussels. Since 1900 the *Antimilitariste*, monthly organ of the National Federation of Young Guards, has also been appearing. Since 1903 this federation has also published the illustrated monthly *La Jeunesse Socialiste*. This will be replaced in 1907 by the monthly journal *La Jeunesse c'est l'Avenir* (Youth is the Future),[152] now controlled by the Walloon Federation of Hainaut and Namur. It has already been appearing since 1906 in Charleroi. Both journals were and are full of anti-militarist material. The same is true of the Flemish *De Zaaier* (The Sower), an illustrated monthly which has been published since 1903 on behalf of the Antwerp Federation of the *Jonge Wacht* (Young Guard). It was amalgamated in 1906 with the general Flemish-language Party paper *De Waarheid* (The Truth, published since 1902 at Ghent), but forms a special part of this journal with its own title. *De Waarheid* has a circulation of 3,000, *La Jeunesse c' est l'Avenir* of 5,000.

Some local organisations of the Young Guards – especially the Antwerp and Ghent Jonge Wachten – are engaged in vigorous anti-militarist activity of a literary kind, etc. The Antwerp group for instance published the paper *De Bloedwet* (Rule of Blood) in 1900, in order to agitate among conscripts (it has the same aim as *La Caserne*). It has also published the bi-monthly *Ontwapening* (Disarmament) since May 1, 1901, and finally, since 1905, *De Vrijheid* (Freedom). These papers all spread the anti-militarist word with great skill and enthusiasm. Hectographed bulletins are also produced. The Young Guards also do good work of course with leaflets and posters, mostly illustrated.[153] These are sometimes addressed to young workers and sometimes to conscripts and soldiers. Much useful literature in pamphlet form is also produced. Cheap postcards with an anti-militarist message, mostly illustrated, are sold in large numbers.

In Belgium more than half the young men liable to bear arms escape through the system of drawing lots. About 13,000 are called up every year. Around 60,00 copies of *Le Conscrit* and *La Caserne* are published altogether in the two languages.[154] They are normally specially posted to the recruits, whose addresses can easily be obtained. Then personal contact can be made with those recruits who have been singled out.

---

151. See Housiaux in *Die Neue Zeit*, April 23, 1904, Vol.2, pp.110ff., and the scattered congress reports. Three provincial federations exist: the Flemish (about 1,000 members), the Brabant (about 500 members) and the Walloon (about 8,000 members). The last was founded in September 1905. The Liège Congress of 1905 dissolved the National Council, which was reconstituted in rather different form in 1906 – the Flemish and Walloon Federations each elect a representative, and the National Congress elects the third (the National Secretary).
152. Its predecessor was the journal *Contre le militarisme, pour le socialisme* (Against Militarism, For Socialism).
153. During the process of the drawing of lots in 1906 the streets were plastered with some 20,000 explanatory posters and 80,000 illustrated posters.
154. In 1906 the print run of *La Conscrit* was over 68,000, that of *De Loteling* about 30,000, *La Caserne* slightly less. In 1905 100,000 copies of *La Caserne* were distributed for special purposes.

Meetings of recruits regularly take place in January and September, as well as fêtes, street demonstrations and other actions.

Contact is not lost with proletarians who have entered the army. In some Guards' groups a system of aid is organised, and an allowance made to members of the Guards who have been called up during the time of their service. This allowance varies with the amount of time for which a member has belonged to the group and with the amount he has subscribed. Such members have to provide regular reports on their experiences in the barracks, and remain in personal touch with the Guards. If such a member serves in a different locality from that of his organisation, he is put in touch with the local group. We cannot go into more detail for obvious reasons.

The agitation carried out in the barracks plays an important role in Belgium. There are about 15 soldiers' organisations (soldiers' unions) at present, which work closely together. An effort is of course made to eliminate these dangerous organisations. But although they are often suppressed, they always reappear, for their roots are too strong to be pulled up. Up to two-thirds of the men in a single regiment have been recruited. Some of the unions are closely connected with the Social Democratic Party.

Propaganda literature is brought into the barracks in large quantities, and is also distributed to soldiers in the streets and other public places. Meetings of soldiers take place. Many anti-militarist songs have been widely circulated.

The Party itself of course carries on strenuous anti-militarist agitation, and the women and girls take an active part too, in particular by helping the Young Guards in their agitation in the barracks. These efforts have met with great success. The pamphlet *Le catéchisme du conscrit* (The Conscript's Catechism), which appeared in several editions in 1896, is worthy of note. It resembles the French *Manuel du soldat*, and has been similarly subjected to fierce criminal prosecution.

Anti-militarist propaganda, indeed, comes up against severe persecution. This point can of course only be supported by an examination of the generally advanced political conditions in Belgium. In 1886 Anseele was condemned to six months' imprisonment for an appeal to mothers published in the *Vooruit* (Forward) to bring up their sons in such a way that they would never turn their guns against the people. *Le Conscrit* and *La Caserne* are constantly brought before the courts. Since their foundation heavy sentences have been pronounced every year in connection with their publication, and the same thing of course has happened since the publication has been taken over by the Young Guards. The first case was that against *Le Conscrit* in 1897, when two comrades were sentenced to six months' imprisonment. In 1904 Coenen, secretary of the National Federation of Young Guards, was called with five others before the jury in Brabant in connection with the appearance of posters appealing to recruits. The same thing was soon repeated, this time involving Coenen alone, because of an article which had appeared in *La Caserne*. But he was acquitted.[155] The sentences passed on Troclet in the middle of the 1890s on account of *Le catéchisme du conscrit* are also noteworthy.

---

155. See *La procès de la caserne*.

The chief crimes for which penalties are imposed are the following: calls to disobey orders, insulting the army (six months' imprisonment is the minimum punishment!), and the infamous *atteinte à la force obligatoire des lois* – attack on the principle that the law is binding. Where more than five people are shown to have conspired together the punishment is doubled. Every year sentences of imprisonment averaging from two to three years are passed. In 1903 the secretary of the National Federation was sentenced to three years in prison. It is true, however, that half of the accused are acquitted. The system under which the prisoners live is harsh. No distinction is made, on principle, between political and non-political prisoners.

Treatment accorded to anti-militarist soldiers is cruel, at least by Belgian standards. Those opposing militarism are threatened with three to five years' prison in the harsh correctional system. For the slightest offence the barbarous medieval punishment called the *cachot* is inflicted. The prisoners must lie in irons in an unheated cell, and are fed on bread and water. The cells are built over water, are damp, and in winter a spell in them can be dangerous to life. This goes together with the ill-treatment dealt out by the NCOs, who are themselves given this job as a disciplinary punishment.

The extent of the growth of Belgian anti-militarism, in spite of its struggle against fire and sword, has been shown elsewhere, and can be said to be an almost complete success. In the critical year 1902 the whole population took such an interest in the propaganda that officers attempting to stop the agitation which was carried on openly in the streets among the soldiers were often attacked.

We must also mention the Groupes des Anciens Militaires (ex-soldiers' groups). They were formerly organised as a national federation, but are now flourishing as local organisations and publish a newspaper. Anti-militarist propaganda in the reserve and the militia, as well as agitation against the bourgeois military societies, are their chief tasks.

A few words must be added on the attitude taken by Belgian Social Democracy, as far as tactics are concerned, towards militarism.

On the question of war, and above all on the tactics to be adopted if a war breaks out, there is no unanimity of opinion. Only three facts can be mentioned here:

The Party Congress at Ghent in 1893 expressed its enthusiastic approval of a telegram from the *anciens soldats* (ex-soldiers) of Amsterdam which expressed the hope that the Congress would sanction the calling of a military strike in case of war, as the Dutch Socialists had suggested. The Louvain Congress of 1899 simply endorsed the proposal of De Winnes that to make propaganda for socialism was the best way of fighting the growth of military armament and of ensuring world peace. In 1905 the Socialist Federation of the Charleroi district resolved that in order to prevent war it was necessary:

> 1. To prevent troop mobilisation by calling a general strike of railwaymen;

> 2. To organise a general strike in the coal mines in order to deprive the belligerent powers of the fuel necessary for the navy and for troop transport;

3. To stop work in the docks, arsenals and munitions factories.

The history of the Young Guards also throws an interesting light on the subject. Their congress in 1897 decided among other things to induce the Socialist parties of other countries to organise their young people on an international and anti-militarist basis in order to make war impossible. The proceedings of the Brussels Congress of 1903 were also important. Two sharply opposed views were more or less equally represented. One view strongly defended, especially by de Man, used Hervé's arguments to propose the declaration of a military strike (collective refusal to serve), a general strike and revolutionary agitation in case of war. The other view was put by Troclet and Fischer, who simply endorsed the resolutions of the international congresses. The Troclet-Fischer resolution was passed by 17 votes to 15, with two abstentions.[156]

At the Ghent Congress of January 1906 a sharp departure was made from anarchist tactics, and individual refusal to serve was repudiated. A motion put by de Man suggests that to snatch the means of power in the form of the army from the ruling classes it is necessary to awaken proletarian class consciousness among the soldiers. Another of de Man's motions describes the army in its role against the enemy at home. The soldiers are advised to conduct themselves as properly as possible in the interests of anti-militarist agitation. The anarchistic dross was thus eliminated and things cleared up considerably.

France

In France anti-militarist propaganda began long ago and is very vigorous but not so well organised as in Belgium, nor does it follow the same tendency.

In 1894 the 12th Congress of the Socialist Revolutionary Labour Party (POSR) at Dijon passed a specially noteworthy resolution against militarism in its two forms, emphasising the harm done by militarism and the general danger it presented to the proletariat. The end of the resolution says: "In peacetime the standing army serves a police role, acting as a shooting machine. It drowns in blood the struggles of the miners and factory workers for their rights, the proletarian soldier in absurd anger raising his hand against his brother on strike".

Not only Social Democratic anti-militarism but also the anarchist form developed in France, together with the specifically French tendency of anti-patriotic Socialist anti-militarism (which however later left its mark in Italy and even in Switzerland).

Anarchist and semi-anarchist anti-militarism was supported chiefly by the weekly journal *Les Temps Nouveaux* (Modern Times) and its numerous and often clever publications. These, like the paper itself, are for the most part based on a proletarian standpoint. They contain valuable material contributed not only by men like Kropotkin but by syndicalists, especially Paul Delesalle. There are also the publications of the individualist paper *Libertaire*. French anarchists were also responsible for the foundation in 1902 of

---
156. On the debate, in which Vandervelde's intervention was decisive, see *Mouvement Socialiste* for August 15, 1903, pp.594ff., and *La Jeunesse Socialiste* for August 1903.

the International Anti-militarist Federation, and rather earlier of the Ligue Internationale pour la Défense du Soldat (International Soldiers' Defence League) with headquarters in Paris. The leading thinkers of this league – which seems to have disappeared – were the anarchists Janvion, Malato, then Georges Lhermite, editor of the radical paper *L'Aurore*, and Urbain Gohier. Their program aimed at the abolition of standing armies, the abolition of the system of military justice and material improvements and guarantees for the soldiers. But their activity went far beyond this program. The postcards, pamphlets and posters, often powerfully illustrated, which were published by the League continuously repeat the slogan "*A bas la justice militaire!*" (Down with military justice!) and the calls "Down with war!", "Down with militarism!", "Long live peace between nations!" But its influence could not extend beyond the borders of France.

The agitation for individual and collective refusal to serve and for desertion forms a large part of this propaganda, which of course is quite uneven. According to Kropotkin the military strike to be called against war is not to be merely passive but to go hand in hand with the social revolution and the defence of the revolution against the enemy abroad.[157] This is to refute the chief objection to anti-patriotism, or as the *Temps Nouveaux* calls it, anti-nationalism. It is well-known that Emile Henry, the anarchist and terrorist, threw his famous bomb at Carmaux in August 1892 as a warning in order to try to prevent a repetition in the miners' strike of the Fourmies massacre which had taken place the year before.[158]

The anti-patriotic Socialist current of anti-militarism, which displays many anarchist traits,[159] is supported on the one hand by the Yonne Federation of the United Socialist Labour Party (the Yonne being an almost completely agricultural department)[160] and on the other by a strong current within the anti-parliamentary trade unions. Anti-patriotism of course does not play such an important role in the trade unions, which are faced with the struggle against militarism on the home front, the most cruel and powerful enemy of workers on strike.

Since 1901 the Jeunesses Socialistes, the youth organisations of the Yonne, have published, in accordance with a resolution passed in 1900, a newspaper called *Pioupiou de l'Yonne*.[161] Originally it appeared bi-annually, then quarterly, and it is designed, as stated at the head of the first numbers, "for those called up to join their regiments". All the reactionary forces at the state's disposal were let loose against the *Pioupiou*, which was distributed free to all the conscripts of the department. Legal prosecutions literally rained from the sky,[162] though they generally ended in acquittal. This in spite of the fact that the call to disobey if ordered to use arms against strikers was explicitly made. *Pioupiou*, still published by Moneret in 1905, was strongly influenced by Hervé, who, with Yvetot, was

---
157. *Les Temps Nouveaux*, October 28, 1905.
158. In this connection see the pamphlet *Le patriotisme*, Libertaire Publications, Paris.
159. *Les Temps Nouveaux* takes a very friendly attitude towards it.
160. *Leur Patrie*, p.246. This is the explanation of the objection frequently made against Hervé that his support in the Yonne is to be explained by the old and deeply-rooted dislike of the peasants for military service.
161. Pioupiou – a popular expression for "recruit", with a certain affectionate and familiar connotation.
162. See *La Pioupiou en cour d'Assises* (The Recruit before the Jury), Auxerre 1904.

and is the leading figure and organiser of anti-patriotic anti-militarism. His work *Leur Patrie* (Their Fatherland) contains a detailed and clever exposition and formulation of his ideas, and since the middle of December 1906 he has been publishing in Paris a weekly paper, *La Guerre Sociale* (The Social War), which renders vigorous aid to anti-militarism. To any war, however it might have started, he knows only one solution: *plutôt l'insurrection que la guerre* (rather insurrection than war), and he fiercely attacks the attitude of the leaders of German Social Democracy to aggressive wars.[163] He is very far from supporting individual refusal to serve. In his case the struggle against militarism at home is relegated somewhat to the background. We shall deal elsewhere with Hervéism, which carries on its struggle with noteworthy tenacity and readiness for sacrifice.

As far as the form of Hervé's propaganda is concerned, the events of September 30, 1906 are characteristic. Hervé and a band of his supporters went to a fête at the Trocadero given by the Republican Youth of the 3rd *arrondissement* and by the French Educational League in honour of those called up to serve in the army. They made a demonstration against the patriotic-military event, came into collision with the police and were arrested.

As far as the anti-patriotic anti-militarism of the trade unions is concerned, the report laid before the Dublin Conference of trade union secretaries by the Confédération Générale du Travail gives a good idea of its character. In striking contrast to Hervéism, it unilaterally underrates the significance of "militarism abroad".

In this report the methods of anti-militarist educational work are divided into:

1. Solidarity work:

a. The "soldier's penny" (*"Sou du soldat"*);

b. Reception and care of soldiers as guests in the *bourses de travail* (trade union homes);

c. Solidarity with those comrades who evade military service or who are victimised for rebellion against discipline.

2. Propaganda work: public meetings, social evenings, send-offs for recruits, demonstrations, posters, manifestoes, pamphlets, leaflets, the special annual illustrated number of the paper *La Voix du Peuple* (Voice of the People), the widely-circulated organ of the French Trade Union Federation, and finally the new soldiers' handbook (*Nouveau Manuel du Soldat*), which had already been circulated in 100,000 copies in 1903. It led as everyone knows – and with the approval of the ex-Socialist Millerand – to the vigorous intervention of the administrative and judicial authorities.

The *Nouveau Manuel du Soldat* was published in accordance with the decision of the trade union congress held at Algiers on September 15, 1902, by the Federation of Trade Union Houses. A second edition appeared in the same year, and a third in 1905. It ends with an appeal to the soldiers either to desert or to make anti-militarist agitation in the barracks, and to those on active service not to fire, even when ordered, on the so-called

---

163. On Hervé's anti-parliamentarism, see *La Vie Socialiste*, pp.97ff. In *Mouvement Socialiste*, June 1, 1905, Fages says that the so-called *campagne antipatriotique* is in reality a *campagne anticapitaliste*.

"enemy at home", their brother workers.

The former organ of the Socialist Revolutionary Labour Party, *La Lutte Sociale* (The Social Struggle) ought to be mentioned here. It was published, probably for the first time in 1904, for the Union Fédérative du Centre by Allemane and Hervé, and was devoted to anti-militarist propaganda.

In 1905 the Socialists and syndicalists together[164] published the red poster which appealed to the soldiers not to turn their weapons against the proletariat, and if ordered to do so to turn them instead against their commanding officers rather than their class comrades.

Finally, anti-militarist propaganda is one of the main tasks of the French Young Socialist organisations. Until 1903 each of the three French parties had its own special organisation (Jeunesse Socialiste). Since 1902 the Jeunesses Syndicalistes, supported by the revolutionary trade unions, have appeared on the scene. At the moment they are in a rather chaotic situation.

The activity of the Young Socialist organisation of the Yonne has already been mentioned. Since 1900 *Le Conscrit*, still going in 1906, has appeared as the organ of the Revolutionary Young Socialists, and the paper *La Feuille du Soldat* (The Soldier's Paper) as the organ of the Union Fédérative des Jeunesses Socialistes du Parti Ouvrier (Federative Union of the Young Socialists of the Labour Party). Both call on proletarians in soldier's uniform to fulfil their duty to their class comrades. *La Feuille du Soldat* calls on them plainly to refuse to obey if ordered to turn their weapons against the working class, and to take part in the general strike when it is proclaimed. *Le Conscrit* emphatically rejects individual revolt as useless.

At the Congress of French Trade Unions in Amiens in October 1906 Delesalle was able to point out quite correctly that earlier trade union congresses had declared themselves for anti-militarist and anti-patriotic propaganda, and he announced that this position had been unanimously endorsed by the Committee. At the same congress a resolution moved by Yvetot was adopted, though opposed it is true by a large minority, calling for an intensification of anti-militarist and anti-patriotic propaganda. It was obvious that the minority was not opposed to anti-militarism or to an increase in anti-militarist propaganda but simply to the stress laid on anti-patriotic propaganda. The same thing was evident at the Congress of the French United Socialist Party held at Limoges in November 1906. The Hervé resolution, put forward by the Yonne Federation, got only a few votes. It formulated the anti-patriotic point of view, and appealed to the comrades to reply to every declaration of war, from whichever side it might come, by a military strike and an insurrection. But the resolution put forward by Guesde, emphasising the organically capitalist character of militarism and which considers that anti-militarism can only be furthered in the context of general Social Democratic propaganda, was also voted down, though the minority was three times larger. It demanded in the short term a reduction in the length of service, the refusal to vote military credits and the

---

164. With the co-operation of the Association Internationale Antimilitariste.

introduction of a citizen army. Vaillant's resolution, moved by the Seine Federation, was adopted. After stating the principles adopted by the international congresses it demands international action against war and makes it a duty to use every kind of action, from parliamentary intervention and public agitation and demonstrations to the general strike and insurrection, according to the needs of the situation. At the beginning of 1906 Vaillant, as we know, published in *Le Socialiste* his famous proclamation on the occasion of the outbreak of the Morocco conflict, which ended with the cry: *plutôt l'insurrection que la guerre*.

No decision was reached regarding militarism at home, but many other indications are available which make the attitude of French Social Democracy quite clear. The watchword is an appeal to the soldiers not to obey when they are used against strikes and against the working class. The *Manuel du Soldat* addresses the following words to the soldiers: "If they try to make you into murderers it is your duty to disobey! If you are sent against strikes, you will not shoot!" The famous words "*Vous ne tirerez pas!*" – used by comrade Meslier in the great trial of anti-militarists in December 1905 are therefore only an echo of the general cry of the class-conscious Socialists or syndicalists.

The appeal to conscripts issued jointly by Socialists and syndicalists in 1905 and mentioned above contains a drastic and fearless solution of the problem, calling on soldiers not to use their weapons against the working class, but rather to turn them against the officers who gave them that order. When this appeal was discussed in the Chamber, Sembat, in the name of the Socialists, declared: "I am asked what my opinion is regarding the advice to fire on officers. My answer is that when an officer has given the order to fire on strikers, I approve of this advice". And Lafargue has repeatedly endorsed this standpoint in *L'Humanité* in short, sharp terms.

The numerous trials of anti-militarists in France, which until recently almost always ended in acquittal, were a considerable help to propaganda. The *Pioupiou* trials have been dealt with above. Yvetot, having been acquitted ten times, was eventually convicted by a jury of the lower Loire in 1904 in connection with an anti-militarist speech and sentenced to – a fine of 100 francs. But later he too became acquainted with prison life. In 1905 two anarchists were arrested in Aix. One of them was condemned to three months' imprisonment for an anti-militarist manifesto which had been posted up on the walls of Marseilles. Morel and Frimat were also imprisoned, and prison sentences were also passed in Brest, Armentières and Limoges.[165] In the spring of 1906 convictions followed in Toulon and Rheims. The special number of the *Voix du Peuple* printed for recruits has been repeatedly seized. In October 1906 the editor, Vignaud, was arrested. Above all we should note the great anti-militarist trial in Paris in December 1905, at which Hervé and 25 others were sentenced to prison terms totalling 36 years, together with fines amounting to 2,500 francs. But these severe sentences were not fully enforced.

Anti-militarist propaganda has a massive pamphlet literature at its disposal. Apart

---

165. See *Les Temps Nouveaux*, No.12, 1905. On the prosecutions against Loquier and Lemaire at Epinal and Amiens, see ibid., No.26, 1905.

from the *Temps Nouveaux*, there are the *Librairie & Propagande Socialiste*, the *Société nouvelle de Librairie et d'Edition* (Georges Bellais), the *Librairie die Parti Socialiste* (SFIO) and the Stock publishing house which have made a specially important contribution to the publication of such pamphlets.

The successes of anti-militarist propaganda in France are considerable. In this connection we must not overestimate the significance of the fact that here and there an officer openly expresses anti-militarist opinions and takes the consequences in a spirit of great selflessness.[166] Such individual acts are not of great interest in connection with a purely proletarian class movement such as we take anti-militarism to be in France (as opposed to Russia). More important is the fact that the number of cases of desertion, of soldiers who refuse to serve or obey orders and who make anti-militarist demonstrations is on the increase. Very harsh sentences are sometimes passed in these cases,[167] on other occasions sentences which, from the standpoint of German conditions, are amazingly mild. Thus two marines were sentenced in October 1906 to 15 and 60 days' imprisonment respectively by a court martial in Cherbourg for having exclaimed in front of a patriotic monument: "Down with the army, down with the officers, we don't need an army!"

We will give only a few details here. On May 3, 1905, 61 men of the 10th Company of the 32nd Infantry Regiment simply left the barracks for a place nearby because of bad food and ill-treatment. In September 1906 the soldiers arranged a demonstration in connection with the suicide of a reservist in the Compiègne garrison, sang the *Internationale* and insulted the officers. At the beginning of August 1906 the *Eclair* published a circular of the War Minister Etienne addressed to the corps commanders. He informs them that the NCOs leaving the infantry school at Saint-Maixent had expressed anti-militarist ideas and explained that they were remaining in the army in order to win over adherents to their ideas. Above all we must draw attention to a number of strikes – for example at Dunkirk, Le Creusot, Longwy (Merrheim!) and Montceau-les-Mines – when the soldiers called in to intervene declared their solidarity with the strikers. It is no wonder that the *Nouvelliste de Rouen* treats the effect of Social Democracy on the army as "a very dangerous wound on the body of France which requires the most drastic treatment".[168]

In comparison with German conditions the war minister Etienne used very moderate terms in the above mentioned circular when speaking of the danger of anti-militarism and the methods of fighting it. And it cannot be denied that in France great scope has been given to anti-militarism with regard to the constitutional right of free expression of opinion. The reports of the trials of anti-militarists are very instructive in this connection. We remember how a few years ago the Socialist Fournière was permitted to lecture on social politics to the Polytechnic officers' school. And quite recently the lectures for

---

166. The case of Merrheim deserves special mention. At a strike at Longwy he made a direct appeal to his infantrymen to use no violence against the strikers even if they should provoke or attack the soldiers.
167. Especially in Algiers the death penalty is imposed for the slightest offence! See the Besançon affair, *L'Humanité*, December 11, 1906.
168. See von Zeppelin in the *Kreuz-Zeitung*, December 23, 1906.

officers at the School for Social Studies in Paris, in which Captain Demonge spoke quite openly and even in revolutionary terms against militarism, caused the flesh of our strict and narrow-minded militarists to creep. If we add the impending limitation of the scope of military justice and of the *biribi*, together with the government bill concerning the shortening of the term of service for the reserve and the militia (though it is true that this was rejected), and finally Picart's plan for the democratisation of the officer corps by the realisation of an *unité d'origine* (common origin) of officers and non-commissioned officers[169] – then France might appear to be an El Dorado of militarism. The position of Clemenceau towards anti-militarism – he is the president of a ministry in which sit two "Socialists", once *amor et deliciae* of all social optimists – shows that it is not a question of a fundamental change in militarism, but simply of a change in form, due for the most part to anti-clericalism.

Italy

The Italian labour movement in its different tendencies bears some resemblance to the French movement. Here too, together with the normal political party movement, we find anarchist offshoots and an anti-patriotic syndicalist movement which is anti-parliamentary and closely related to anarchism. The anti-militarist movement is also divided according to the same criteria. It goes back some time, but has only recently been systematically taken in hand by the Party. We must first mention the Young Socialist organisations and above all the Federazione Nazionale Giovanile Socialista, with headquarters in Rome, and to which a number of provincial federations are affiliated.[170] It published the *Gioventù Socialista* (Socialist Youth), edited by Paolo Orano, and has been active from the outset in the field of anti-militarism, like the Belgian Young Guards.[171]

In 1905 the Leghe delle Futture Conscritti (League of Future Conscripts) was founded as a special anti-militarist organisation, subsidiary to the National Federation with which it is closely connected. Both organisations are recognised by the Party.

At a session of the Party executive in Rome in October 1905 the following resolution moved by Ferri was passed, with only one vote against:

> The Party executive protests against police prosecution of Socialists and of their press in connection with the recent anti-militarist demonstrations. It notes with satisfaction the enthusiasm with which the Young Socialist organisations have carried on the anti-militarist agitation called for by the Party, and resolves that the whole Party, with the help of the executive, is to take part in this agitation. The aim is not merely to enlighten public opinion on the fact that huge amounts of state money are being wasted on the military administration, but above all to persuade the recruits and soldiers that, without ignoring their duty to defend

---

169. They want first of all to put the military schools on the same basis. There will be only one school for each branch of the army, to be attended by both officers and NCOs. This of course brings horror to our reactionaries (*Deutsche Tageszeitung*, December 22, 1906).
170. At the Milan Congress in September 1906 five provincial organisations and 24 sections from northern Italy were represented, comprising 2,400 members.
171. In this connection see the proceedings of the Milan Congress.

the country, they should not co-operate in the murder of workers. These murders, in their frequency and cruelty, are an insult to our land.

Apart from this, the Rome Party Congress of October 1906 gave an idea of the general way in which anti-militarist propaganda is carried on in Italy. Anti-militarism was a special item on the agenda. Two motions were presented. That of the syndicalist Bianchi read: "The ninth Congress of the Socialist Party, in the discussion on militarism, approves the activity and propaganda methods used by the Italian Young Socialist organisations". The other motion was presented by Romualdi, editor of *Avanti*, and states:

> Congress endorses the Party's anti-militarist traditions, and considers it necessary – in view of the refusal of the bourgeoisie to recognise that the army must stand on a position of genuine neutrality in the struggle between labour and capital – that, in order to prevent the murder of workers and the breaking of strikes, an agitational movement should be started with the aim of dissuading the young workers from taking up their arms in such situations and becoming strike-breakers. At the same time Congress considers it necessary to make propaganda among the workers for the idea that they should not use violence against the troops, both in order to avoid a reaction on the part of the soldiers and to prove that a common bond of brotherhood unites the striking workers and the soldiers.

Anti-patriotic as well as anarchist anti-militarism was represented in the discussion, but the strictly Social Democratic variety was dominant, while anti-militarist agitation among the soldiers was only opposed by a few delegates using arguments similar to those heard at the 1904 Bremen Congress of the German Social Democratic Party. The representatives of the Young Socialist organisation explained that their comrades did not carry on anti-militarist propaganda according to Hervé's method, but in order to reduce the army bill and to awaken a sense of solidarity between soldiers and workers. Finally it was decided not to put the motion of Ferri and Turati to the vote, but to remit the question to the Party executive for consideration. At the same time it is very important to note that Ferri's integralist resolution, which was adopted at the Congress by an overwhelming majority, contains the following passage:

> The Party is developing political activity whose object is: to intensify anti-clerical and anti-monarchical propaganda in view of the present situation and of the growing clericalism of the government; *to intensify anti-militarist agitation, whose aim is the education of Italian youth in socialism, in order to neutralise the tendency of the ruling classes to use the army as an instrument of coercion against the proletariat.*

In Italy too anti-militarist agitation has made the army unreliable as a weapon against the so-called enemy at home. But in Italy also class justice has been used, in the form of numerous trials and the infliction of severe punishments, to attack anti-militarists both inside and outside of the army. The Turin events of 1905 are well known.

Switzerland

Anti-militarism has made great strides in Switzerland, together with the ever more frequent use of soldiers in strikes.

At the Conference of the Swiss Social Democratic Party held at Olten in October 1903, a resolution was drafted which takes up the standard position towards war and demands a military constitution which "clearly determines the rights and duties of the state and of its citizens", and declares that the use of the army in strikes cannot be tolerated.

Dissatisfaction with this resolution led in April 1904 to the convocation of the Lucerne Congress, which set out, among others, the following demands:

> A considerable reduction in military expenditure, the people to decide on questions of expenditure above a total of one million francs, an improvement in the military and economic position of the soldier, abolition of military justice, prohibition of the use of troops in strikes.

The conference described it as the duty of the Party to use every means available to attain these goals, but without any more definite indication of those means.

The intervention of the military in strikes at La Chaux-de-Fonds and the Ricken made greater activity necessary, as well as the adoption of a clearer slogan. Heated discussions took place in meetings. The Federal Committee of the Trade Union Federation published a leaflet on September 15, 1904 which contained the sentences:

> In all cases we must try to persuade the soldiers not to fire on their fellow workers, not to use their weapons against them, and not only to refuse to obey on these occasions but also to attempt with every means to prevent such murder. Only then will they be acting in the spirit of our Federal Constitution, which states that the soldier in uniform is first of all a citizen.

The Party Conference which took place soon after at Zurich passed the following resolution:

> The Social Democratic Party calls upon the soldiers, when they are mobilised against strikes, to bear in mind their solidarity with the workers and not allow themselves to be used in actions which would vitiate the right of their class comrades to strike and hold meetings.

The following Party Conference at Geneva instructed the Party executive to draft a resolution on the military question for the next conference.

In the meantime anti-militarist agitation was being organised and systematised. In 1905 a Swiss Anti-militarist League was established, whose object is:

> 1. To enlighten the workers to the fact that in bourgeois society the army acts as a hindrance to the liberation of the working class;
>
> 2. To use all means suitable in rendering the army harmless as far as its use as a means of power by the capitalists is concerned.

The first congress was held in October 1905 and the League has grown rapidly since then. It issues leaflets to the workers' organisations and pamphlets addressed to agricultural and industrial workers, and displays considerable activity. Among the pamphlets we must make special mention of the widely circulated and almost classic text, *The Watchdog of Capitalism*.

In accordance with the decision of the Lucerne Congress of January 1906 preparations were put in hand for a central library, as well as for a translation of Hervé's *Leur Patrie*. The League also publishes the *Vorposten*, which is devoted, and with great skill, to anti-militarist agitation. As far as the question of militarism abroad is concerned, the League takes up the standpoint which has been much argued over: that although only the victory of socialism can abolish war, something must be done while this victory is not achieved to prevent the "mutual slaughter of and by those without property at the command of those who possess it", and that the only thing that is of use in this connection is the "withdrawal of military labour power", that is, the military strike. As far as the question of militarism at home is concerned, they of course make the appeal: "*Vous ne tirerez pas!*" (Don't shoot!)[172] The second proposal is naturally much more disagreeable to capitalism, especially in Switzerland, than the first. But it is still a fact that a favourite manoeuvre of the bourgeoisie is to try to work its mill of counter-agitation with "patriotic" wind, which it endeavours to raise by stamping this tendency as "unpatriotic", "treacherous" and resulting in the "disarming of the nation in the face of the enemy abroad".[173]

The Party Conference at Aarau, held in February 1906, was the occasion of a very interesting anti-militarist debate. It came to light that in Switzerland too the idea of the military strike and of a refusal to take part in army service against other countries has its supporters. The following important resolution was passed.

> 1. The Social Democratic Party strives together with the Social Democratic Parties of other countries to eliminate all possibilities of war among the civilised peoples as well as all instruments of war. It demands that international conflicts be settled by arbitration.
>
> 2. As long as this state of affairs has not been established among the peoples of central Europe, the Party recognises only a citizen army whose sole purpose is to protect the country from external attack.
>
> 3. The Party protests against the use of soldiers in strikes. Since this misuse has in fact taken place in recent years, it demands guarantees against its repetition. As long as these guarantees are not forthcoming, the Party advises the soldiers to refuse to obey when ordered to attack workers on strike or to draw weapons against them. The Social Democratic Party will in such cases attempt as far as possible to aid the individual concerned and his family with regard to the financial consequences, and for this purpose will get in touch with the trade union organisations. The Party considers that the best guarantee against the use of troops in cases of strikes lies in the strengthening of its political power at commune and state level.
>
> 4. The Party demands an army organisation which is based upon general military service, which is in harmony with democratic institutions and does not come into contradiction with

---
172. See *Vorposten*, "The Draft Resolution of the Party Committee".
173. See the *Leipziger Volkszeitung*, January 30, 1906, "A Split in Swedish Social Democracy?"

the principle that all have equal rights under the constitution. It demands the reduction of military expenditure and opposes all expenditure not absolutely necessary for national defence.

As a consequence of this resolution it was decided to establish a fund for the support of army resisters.

The first, second and fourth paragraphs of this resolution practically cover the draft resolution submitted by the Party executive.[174] The Party Conference however inserted paragraph 3 in the draft resolution, the passage which calls on soldiers to disobey orders in the event of intervention in strikes. The conference also made the wording of the resolution sharper and more definite, in accordance with the demand made in the *Vorposten*.

The Social Democrats of the Grütli, as is known, take up for the most part a thoroughly petty-bourgeois attitude to militarism. They condemn for example the refusal to vote for the budget! It will not be surprising if on the military question they are found to be so light in weight that they will be blown out of the Party like chaff. The new Party split which was rumoured to be going to take place at the Aarau conference has so far been avoided, in spite of the vigorous anti-militarist position taken up by the conference.

The publications of the study group of the workers' circle of Saint-Imier are also noteworthy. Among them one can find the useful pamphlet *The Army and Strikes*. The Young Socialist organisations, which probably only exist in French Switzerland, also play a certain role. The journal *La Jeunesse Socialiste* has been published in Lausanne since 1903 by a number of these organisations, but recently it has lost the character of a Young Socialist paper. We must also mention the Youth Society founded and directed in Zurich by the comrade and pastor Pflüger.

It is evident that in Switzerland too anarchism directs its attention to anti-militarism. There is an anarchist anti-militarist group in Geneva, apparently the only group in the whole of Switzerland which is affiliated to the International Anti-militarist Association, which we shall speak of later. The anarchist paper *Weckruf* (Wake-up call), which is published in Zurich and has been appearing since 1902, considers anti-militarist agitation – in the anarchist sense, of course – as one of its main tasks. We should not overlook the fact that it is at least a kind of proletarian anarchism which is being put forward here – or rather, that the anti-militarist arguments put forward by *Weckruf* have a largely proletarian character. The successes of Swiss anti-militarism, shown especially by the Geneva and Zurich strikes, have already been mentioned, together with the subsequent memorable action of the system of justice. In addition let us note the fact that many proletarian members of the militia refused to march against the masons' strike at La Chaux-de-Fonds. In spite of the "sympathy" of so-called public opinion, severe sentences were passed on six of the militiamen by military justice.[175]

---

174. On the struggles in the Party Committee over the drafting of the proposed resolution, see the *Leipziger Volkszeitung*, December 28, 1905.
175. See also Leo Tolstoy's *An die Soldaten und jungen Leute* (To Soldiers and Young People), Berlin-Charlottenburg 1906, pp.15–16 (cases of individual refusal to serve), and *Les Temps Nouveaux*, No.26, 1905 (four months' imprisonment without deduction of time spent in custody, and two years' loss of civil rights).

Austria

A specifically anti-militarist movement in Austria can only be said to have existed since the Young Socialist movement came into being. This movement was apparently founded in Vienna at the beginning of 1894 with the establishment of a Society of Young Assistant Workers. This society directed its agitation against the national Youth Societies and the Catholic Youth Associations and was soon copied in other places, so that since October 15, 1902 it has been possible to publish the paper *Der jugendliche Arbeiter* (The Young Worker), first as a bi-monthly, later monthly but bigger, as the organ representing the interests of the young workers of Austria. At Easter 1903 the Imperial Union of the Young Workers of Austria was founded, embracing all the local societies. Since April 1, 1903 *Der jugendliche Arbeiter* has been the official organ of this Imperial Union. A glance at the volumes of this cleverly edited paper shows that it understands how best to wage the struggle against militarism among young people.

We must further draw attention to the popular agitational pamphlet mentioned above and entitled *Lustig ist's Soldatenleben* (Merry is the Soldier's Life), which was published in Vienna as early as 1896. It contains an excellent description of the sins of militarism in their special Austrian version and exposes them in merciless fashion. We must also mention the collection *Lichtstrahlen* (Rays of light) issued by the same publisher, especially two pamphlets: *200 Millions for New Guns? Who is responsible and who will have to pay?* and *The Murderous and Ruinous Course of Austrian Militarism*. In this context we must also note the mass distribution of copies of Daszynski's speech to the Reichsrat on September 25, 1903, under the title *Down with Dualism and Militarism!*

Czech anti-militarism deserves special mention. Here too the Young Socialist movement plays an essential role. A youth paper, *Sbornik Mládeze*, has been appearing since May 1, 1900. The Czech Young Socialist organisations have explicitly named anti-militarism as one of their tasks. The Social Democratic Party Congress held in Budweis in 1900 refused, it is true, to permit the formation of special organisations of young workers. But this was aimed only at organisations outside the Party and led to a strengthening of ties between the Young Socialists and the general Party movement. The systematic organisation of young people is making progress. In many places committees were formed with the special task of carrying on agitation among the young workers. From May 15, 1901 the paper *Sbornik Mládeze* appeared monthly; since January 1, 1905 it has been appearing bi-monthly. The Prague Conference of the Social Democratic Party held in 1902 came out once more in favour of the principle of carrying on special agitation among young people and for organising them within the Party.

In 1903 a Union of Workers' Athletic Clubs was founded, and this too concerns itself especially with young people. A permanent committee for agitation was founded in Prague in December 1904, and other towns followed suit.

On April 29 the first conference of the Czech Social Democratic Youth was held in

Prague; 22 Young Socialist committees were represented by 127 delegates. Agitational work followed, carried on in numerous private and public meetings. In *Sbornik Mládeze a* special column is devoted to the question of militarism, and this has frequently been the cause of its confiscation.[176] In Prague a Workers' Academy has been established which is well attended. Conflicts between nationalism and militarism (the language question and the victimisation of individual soldiers) intensify the anti-militarist tendencies. Here we will single out for special mention the case of the soldier called Nemrava who refused to bear arms and was accordingly punished. Processions of recruits dressed in mourning who drove through the towns in red-trimmed wagons accompanied by funeral music became a regular occurrence.

The events which have taken place during the election campaigns of recent years prove that the army can no longer be regarded as completely reliable in its support of reaction and of the ruling classes.

Hungary

In Hungary, where the Party and the trade unions are one and the same thing, or rather, where the Party only exists in the form of the trade unions, a youth movement was founded in Budapest in 1894 in the form of unattached branches of apprentices' organisations. It was under the direction of adults and its primary aim was education, but it collapsed in 1897 as a consequence of the terrible persecution of Socialists carried out under Bänffy, the "saviour of the bourgeoisie". In 1899, after Bänffy's fall, branches of the Workers' Educational Association were started for young workers. They too of course devoted themselves to the education of their members, and they too were destroyed after brutal persecution by the police and courts in the winter of 1901–2. The young people were scattered among the general workers' educational and training organisations.

The powerful economic boom of 1904, during which the number of workers organised in trade unions increased five-fold (from 10,000 to 52,410 members), carried the youth movement with the tide. The movement, which is still on the increase, also acquired a socio-political character. The outward form was that of educational societies or of independent organisations (in the provinces), or (in some places, for example in Pressburg) of athletic clubs. In spite of all chicanery, brutality, surprise attacks, legal convictions and confiscations, the organisations flourished. A paper, *Az Ifjú Munkás* (The Young Worker), was founded with the assistance of adult workers. It represents the cornerstone of the movement, which is everywhere being helped out by the Party, and appears at present in a circulation of around 1,500. The Union of Young Workers was founded in April 1906, but at this moment – December 1906 – is still awaiting the ministerial sanction for which it has applied. These organisations stand openly for socialism, but it has unfortunately not been possible to establish whether they carry on specifically anti-militarist propaganda, and if so what form it takes.

---
176. See *Die Junge Garde*, Mannheim, June 1, 1906.

Holland

Here militarism has not yet – apart from the attempt to break the great railway strike of 1903 – taken on a specially oppressive form. Thus the Dutch Young Socialist Union, De Zaaier, Bond voor Jonge Arbeiders en Arbeidsters in Nederland (The Sower, Union of Young Working Men and Women of the Netherlands), which was founded in 1900 (temporarily suspended in 1903 and reorganised in 1906), has relegated anti-militarist activity to a somewhat subsidiary position.

In its paper *De Zaaier*,[177] founded in 1906 and excellently edited by Roland-Holst, the struggle against militarism nevertheless takes up a considerable space.

In the winter of 1902–3, Holland's "red winter", a great number of anti-militarist meetings were held by De Zaaier, especially in Amsterdam with comrade Roland-Holst. At the De Zaaier Congress of April 8, 1906, held in Utrecht, a resolution which described the class character of militarism was unanimously passed. The Congress appealed to the Union to educate young workers in regard to this characteristic by means of meetings, courses of lectures, especially in the recruiting period, and by leaflets and manifestoes, and as far as possible to act together with the Social Democratic Party in this propaganda work. Meetings against militarism are held every year in October when the recruits are called up. At the beginning of 1906 a meeting was held in Amsterdam by De Zaaier at which, after a speech by Mendels, a sharp demarcation line was drawn in regard to anarchist anti-militarism.

Both the Party Congresses and those of the trade unions have occupied themselves to a considerable degree with the question of anti-militarism, and especially with that of propaganda directed to the soldiers.[178]

The Socialistische Jongelieden Bond (Socialist Youth League) has existed for a long time in Holland. It publishes (or at least used to publish) the paper *De Jonge Werker*, edited by the Communist-anarchist Wink. It is under general anarchist influence, but does not openly endorse anarchism. Its membership is very small, and it seems always to be in the process of re-organisation. The typically anarchist form of anti-militarism also exists, conspicuously in the person of Nieuwenhuis.

There also exists a Bond van Miliciens en Oud-Miliciens (Union of Militia and Former Militia), which since 1903 has been publishing the monthly paper *De Milicien*. This League is a kind of politically neutral training organisation with a program directed towards the elimination of military abuses.[179] It has a naval counterpart in the form of the Matrozenbond (Sailors' Union), whose journal *Het Anker* (The Anchor) is edited by comrade Meyer and is published at Helder. This organisation has done a great deal of good in the way of improving the life of the sailors, and has even inspired strike

---

177. The Party Executive refused to support it for formal reasons. Previously the Union had made use of the Belgian-Flemish *De Zaaier* as its official organ.
178. See for example the Party Congress at Enschede in 1903 and the Trade Union Congress in May of the same year.
179. See the programmatic article in the *Milicien*, No.8, 1904. One of the main objects of its struggle is the so-called "third drill practice".

movements. At times it has come up against sharp attacks by the state authorities – the leaders being punished and the sale of the *Anker* on board ship prohibited. It has often occupied the discussion of the Chamber.

Sweden

The Social Democratic youth movement made its appearance in Sweden in the mid-'90s. The Socialist Youth Clubs amalgamated to form the Young Socialist Union, whose organ was *Brand* (Fire) and whose headquarters were situated in Landskrona. The Party did not look on this Union very favourably, and it gradually moved into anarchist channels. This is evident from its position on national defence and militarism abroad. An opposition movement was founded at Malmö in 1903, the excellent Social Democratic Youth Association. Since January 1, 1906 it has published the paper *Fram* (Forward), a very full and solid monthly which costs only 10 öre. But it finds almost no support in the Party. From 1903 to 1906 it grew from seven clubs with around 450 members to 300–400 clubs with between 14,000 and 15,000 members. By the end of 1906 it numbered some 25,000, with a large number of local organisations. *Fram* has a circulation of between 35,000 and 40,000 copies. The Socialist Union has about 10,000 members, and *Brand* (which is much smaller than *Fram* and inferior from the point of view of its contents) has a circulation of 10,000–12,000 copies.

Both organisations, in accordance with their statutes, have inscribed anti-militarism on their banners. To this end they use for the most part the printed word. The Social Democratic Youth issues numerous pamphlets under the name of the Malmö Socialdemokratiska Ungdoms förbundets Förlag, including *Ned med Vapnen* (Down with Weapons) by Z. Höglund and *Socialdemokratie och Anarchism* by Kate Dalström. According to *Fram* of March 1906, military expenditure was attacked on the grounds that the money thus wasted could be used for the benefit of "the small agricultural concerns, for the education of the people and for insuring the workers"! During the crisis of the Swedish-Norwegian Union, the first Congress of the Social Democratic Youth, held in 1905 in Stockholm, was the occasion of an excellent discussion on (among other things) the military question.[180] It issued the well-known appeal *Down with arms!*, which called on the proletariat to refuse to serve in the army in case of a war with Norway – for which comrade Z. Höglund was to suffer nine months' imprisonment.

The Liberal ministry, headed by the "half-Socialist" Staaff (like the "Socialist" Millerand in France and recently the Clemenceau-Briand-Viviani ministry) immediately reacted and thus acknowledged the importance of the movement. In May 1906 the infamous anarchist, or "muzzling", law was passed, which we shall speak of elsewhere, and severe sentences soon rained down. On September 27, 1906, Sundström was condemned by the Norrköping municipal court to one year's imprisonment with hard labour for

---

[180]. In this connection see the account of the activity of the organisation published in Malmö in 1905 and covering the period from March 1903 to May 1905.

having published a carefully written leaflet addressed to young men liable for military service. This sentence was the occasion, not only of anti-militarist demonstrations among soldiers, but also of an impressive protest demonstration in Norrköping. The police dispersed it with force. But the sentence also produced another, very funny effect, which confirmed the truth of the proverb: "He from whom God takes away an office is given back his senses". Staaff's ministerial glory did not last long. The cold winds of the winter following his fall brought him to his senses. The fire of class justice which, as minister, he had fondly kindled, he now as a plain citizen tried to extinguish with fire-buckets full of lawyer's eloquence. In December 1906 he undertook the defence of comrade Sundström when his appeal was heard before the higher court of Jönköping, trying to prove to the court that the law had not been properly interpreted. And the sentence was indeed reduced to six months! In the summer of 1906 there followed the conviction of comrade Olsson, who was sentenced to six months' imprisonment by the Jönköping municipal court for having written an anti-militarist leaflet. At the end of September the Young Socialists arranged anti-militarist demonstrations in Helsingborg and Bjuf in order to give a reception to the men who had been discharged and transferred to the reserve. Armed police intervened. Many of the participants in the Helsingborg demonstration of September 29 were sentenced by the municipal court at the end of October to between 13 months' and three years' imprisonment. These events are very promising beginnings which however can only influence the form and not the nature and success of anti-militarist propaganda in Sweden.

On October 14, 1906 interesting negotiations were carried on between the two organisations, especially with regard to the anti-militarist question, with a view to unification.[181]

Norway

Local Young Socialist organisations have existed in Norway for years, for instance at Christiania, Drammen, Larvik and Trondhjem. Since June 1901 the Kristiania Socialdemokratiske Ungdomslag has been publishing the excellent anti-militarist monthly (later quarterly) *Det Tyvende Aarhundrede* (The Twentieth Century).[182] A Federation of Young Socialist organisations (the Norges Socialdemokratiske Ungdomsforbund), with headquarters at Christiania, was founded at the Drammen Congress in June 1903. It is said to have about 2,000 members, including many girls. It publishes a monthly called the *Jung-Socialist*, edited by Solberg. Its aim is the furtherance of general, social and political education, and in particular the fight against militarism. Its position on militarism is that of the Social Democratic Party. At its Whitsun 1905 Congress a motion which explicitly stated that the anti-militarist struggle in every form should figure among its goals was rejected.

In connection with the specific anti-militarist activity of the Federation we should

---
181. See *Redogörelse för förhandlingarna*, etc., Landskrona 1906.
182. The present editor is Jacob Vidnes; it is apparently once again being published as a monthly. For the rest see *Fram*, March 1906.

mention the pamphlet of the Norwegian lieutenant Michael Puntervold, which was widely circulated in the garrison towns. The following recent event should also be related.

On October 10, 1906, an anti-militarist meeting was called at Christiania by the local Social Democratic youth association. It was announced by means of leaflets distributed in all the barracks and headed: "Orders for the mobilisation of all officers and men". In spite of a prohibition on the part of the military authorities the meeting was well attended. Sundström and Lieutenant Puntervold (who is in fact one of the editors of the *Social-demokraten*) were among the speakers, which itself was characteristic, though Puntervold had by this time already handed in his resignation from the army. Einar Li, another editor of the paper, who had refused to join the army and was being prosecuted in this connection, also spoke.

Denmark

In Denmark too the Young Socialist organisations are the main agents of anti-militarist propaganda. They developed in opposition to the reactionary youth movements, and especially to the Christian Youth Associations which had a great number of members.

The first Young Socialist organisation was founded in Jutland in 1893 or 1894, but it did not come into prominence until the end of the decade. Around the turn of the century a number of Social Democratic Fremskridtsklebber (Progress clubs)sprang up in the smaller communities of Jutland, and these worked in close liaison.

In 1900 an Ungdomsforening (Young People's Society) was founded at Copenhagen. In the spring of 1904 the local organisations in Copenhagen founded the Socialistik Ungdomsforbund i Danmark, which publishes a monthly paper called *Ny Tid* (New Times). This federation was originally incorporated in the Party and connected with the Swedish and Norwegian organisations. At the time when it was founded it counted 19 local groups. It divided the country into three districts for purposes of agitation, and devoted special attention to anti-militarist propaganda. Of its appeals – which had to be printed in Sweden, since no printer in Denmark would take on the task – 15 were seized one after another, but soon released again. Since militarist quarters were urging the foundation of a militaristic youth organisation, anti-militarist agitation on a large scale was launched in April 1906. Apart from meetings, 50,000 copies of *Ny Tid* were distributed over the whole country, especially to soldiers returning from leave. Complications and arrests of course followed.

The Socialist Union gradually ran into anarchist channels, in an even more marked manner than in Sweden. The Congress of April 20–21, 1905, at which seven clubs with about 500 members were represented, took up an attitude sharply antagonistic to the Social Democratic Party. This attitude probably does not correspond to the position of the individual clubs, though it was the cause of the foundation in Copenhagen of a specifically Social Democratic Youth Club, whose aim is above all the education and instruction of young workers and the fight against capitalism and anarchism. It is linked organisationally with the Party. The Party Congress held at Easter 1906 demanded the foundation of similar organisations throughout the country, and guaranteed moral and material support.[183]

America

The following facts are to be reported from the United States of America:

The program of the Social Democratic Party of North America, founded in 1874, does not contain any specific mention of militarism, which had not yet made itself conspicuous. In 1879, after the strike battle referred to earlier had been fought, a number of workers' military societies were founded by the Chicago and Cincinnati Socialists, under the influence of the ideas of Bakunin. They were called "Education and Defence Societies", and were vigorously opposed by the Party.

In the following period a large number of different ideas were expressed as to how to deal with the army and militia. The trade unions especially tried to keep aloof from all members of the standing army because of the frequent intervention of the army in strikes. Others expressed the opinion that it was precisely through close contacts with the members of the army that these dangers could be minimised.[184]

The Socialist Party of the United States considers both anti-militarism and anti-clericalism to be secondary tasks as far as the labour movement is concerned. Militarism is treated not as an unimportant but simply as a subsidiary question, and the Party is decided that it will not become a simple anti-militarist organisation. Lee remarks that although up to 1905 not a great deal of socialist propaganda had been done among the soldiers and militiamen, the Party had at least made a start on agitation.

In the 1904 Chicago platform of the Socialist Party the following demand is characteristically made in the minimum program under paragraph 5: "Prevention of the use of the army against workers on strike". Emphasis is also laid on the international solidarity of the workers.[185]

Spain

Here too there is not much to report. In anti-militarist agitation, as in the Young Socialist organisations generally, the characteristic features of the situation are a lack of clarity, splits and confusion – and anarchism. This is a consequence of the generally muddled situation in the Party. There is, however, one youth organisation which is recognised by the Social Democratic Party, the Federación Nacional de Iuventudes Socialistas, whose central committee is based in the industrial town of Bilbao. According

---

183. *Fram*, April and June 1906.
184. Lee, *La Vie Socialiste*, No.18, p.80.
185. During the Dutch anarchist anti-militarist congress at Zwolle in 1904 a letter was received from New York, and an expression of sympathy from the National Trade Union and Labor Congress in Canada. See *Ontwaking*, 4th year, December 1904.

to the statutes issued in 1906 its aims are education of young people in accordance with socialist principles and the use of those so trained in the Party.

Finland

In the spring of 1906 a club for young workers, a branch of the local Swedish Workers' Association, was founded in Helsingfors, which immediately attracted 40 members. On March 10, 1906, the club – which had meanwhile grown to 70 members – discussed the proposal put forward by *Fram* concerning affiliation with the Swedish association. The proposal was sympathetically received but rejected for technical reasons.[186] The club published the agitational paper *Kamrat*. It supported the foundation of other clubs in the country, and of a union which would unite all the Finnish organisations. The first Congress of Finnish Young Socialist Organisations was held at Tammerfors on December 9, 1906. The affiliation of the Union of Young Workers of Finnish Nationality to the Labour Party was decided on, and the requirement to carry on the "struggle against militarism in all its forms" was added to the statutes.

Russia

Russia is a special case and cannot be dealt with in detail here. A few general remarks have already been made. Let us simply repeat that the position of the officers *vis-à-vis* the Russian revolution is quite different from their position *vis-à-vis* the labour movement. Thus, the position taken up by Plekhanov in the *Diary of a Social Democrat*, No.7, on agitation among the officers is consistent in itself. The significance of the anti-militarist movement in Russia is very considerable, and the movement itself forms part of the boundless great revolution.

The international anti-militarist movement

It was apparently the French anarchists who first suggested the holding of an international anti-militarist congress, with a view to founding an international association. The motive was first of all the desire to establish on a more solid basis the maintenance of deserters abroad who, as a consequence of anarchist propaganda, had crossed the frontiers in rather large numbers. Most of the supporters of the idea of such a congress belonged to the Ligue Internationale pour la Défense du Soldat discussed above. This represented an unsuccessful attempt to constitute an international anti-militarist organisation which failed because of the narrowness of its program. It is said in any case that the idea of the anarchists found support in England and in other countries, and a committee was formed, to all appearances under the guiding influence of Nieuwenhuis.[187]

---
186. See *Fram*, April and May 1906.
187. See *De Vrije Socialist*, January 24, 1903.

The slogan under which the congress was called was as "expressive" as anyone could wish: "Not a man nor a penny for militarism".[188]

The propaganda for the congress, which originally was to have been held in March or April 1903 in London, was in the meanwhile bearing little fruit, in spite of the fact for example that the committee had approached even the Social Democratic organisations (without success, of course), the Belgian Young Guards[189] and every kind of religious and humanitarian anti-militarist tendency to take part. Finally, after the congress bad been arranged for September 1903 in Amsterdam and had then once again been indefinitely postponed, a special organ called *L'Ennemi du Peuple*[190] was founded in Paris in order to agitate for the congress. The first number appeared in August 1903, and was edited by the anarchist Janvion in a spirit of the most strict Stirnerism. At last, in June 1904, thanks above all to the great efforts of Nieuwenhuis, it was possible to hold the congress in Amsterdam with a considerable attendance. It was of course a queer mixture that was assembled there – anarchists of all shades from Holland, France, Belgium, Bohemia (representatives of a small group of miners), a number of representatives of Spanish anarchist trade unions, Dutch Tolstoyans, the evangelical pastor Schermerhorn and other similar varieties of Dutch humanitarian anti-militarism, and finally a number of British trade unionists.[191]

The congress was only with difficulty prevented from turning itself into an explicitly anarchist congress for the foundation of an anarchist league. The proceedings began of course with the expulsion of the Anarchist Individualists[192] and showed that the competing elements were quite unable to unite in common action.

Thus the Tolstoyans and Humanitarians were expelled next. Those who remained passed a number of resolutions:

> 1. A resolution proposed by the Dutch delegates which, while drawing attention to the intervention of the army in strikes, lays it down as the duty of the trade unions to fight militarism on principle, to establish friendly relations with the soldiers and above all to keep in constant contact with trade union members who have been called up.
>
> 2. The resolution put forward by Girault (France) which proposes that the trade unions should found youth organisations for the purpose of anti-militarist propaganda;
>
> 3. The resolution proposed by Vohryzeck (Bohemia), which recommends the tactics of the French trade unions to the trade unions "of the whole world";[193]

---

188. See *Ontwaking*, August 1904, p.185.
189. Nieuwenhuis assured them that there would be room in the league even for Social Democratic organisations if they were not frightened off by the consequences of the struggle against militarism and would recognise the above slogan. At the Young Guards Congress in 1903 such participation was unanimously rejected without a discussion, because the congress did not consider the basis clear and firm enough, nor anyway did it consider an international association outside of the Socialist International to be necessary or likely to cause anything but confusion.
190. *The Enemy of the People*, after the Ibsen play.
191. According to *Ontwaking*, August 1904, p.186, they represented 116,000 English miners of Durham and Northumberland! The above-mentioned Spanish trade unionists were, according to the same source, delegated by the Spanish Trade Union Federation and represented "at least 100,000 workers"!
192. Who protested against resolutions being passed in any form, and of course did not submit to the resolution of the congress to pass resolutions.
193. The execution of this decision was to have been the task of the Oxford Congress.

4. A Dutch resolution which proclaims the general strike as the means of opposing war;

5. Another Dutch resolution which demands anti-militarist education of the young, especially through influencing the mothers;

6. A French resolution on the question of individual refusals to serve.

There was therefore no shortage of resolutions. Apart from these, a lengthy manifesto was also adopted, whose vague ideological character was criticised by Nieuwenhuis himself with laudable severity.

Nevertheless, the International Anti-militarist Association was founded, and indeed with that splendid slogan "Not a man or a penny for the army". Nieuwenhuis was appointed secretary. It was decided at the same time that a second congress would be held in Oxford in 1905. The Oxford congress, however, never took place, any more than the congress planned for Geneva in June 1906.

On the agenda for Geneva were, among others, the following items, to be found under paragraph 2:

a. What do we do to prevent war?

b. What do we do if war breaks out?

c. What do anti-militarists do if during a war the workers of one country refuse to take up arms while their brothers in the enemy state make an armed attack on their country?

d. The attitude of the workers of neutral countries in the case of war.

The problem of international disarmament and of Hervéism is presented here in its practical significance and with all the frankness one could wish for.

Paragraph 3 is entitled: "Anti-militarism, partial strikes and the social general strike for the establishment of a communist society".

Under the influence of Nieuwenhuis a Dutch national anti-militarist congress was held at Zwolle in October 1904. Nieuwenhuis made a very optimistic report on the position of the International Association, and stated among other things that, apart from *L'Ennemi du Peuple*, a paper called *L'Action Antimilitariste* had been founded in Marseilles. The congress resolved to found a Dutch national anti-militarist society as a section of the International Association.

The Association is said to have made advances in France. A national congress was held at Etienne in July 1905 at which, according to the report of the A.I.A. (the International Association), "numerous groups took part". A National Committee was set up, and it was decided to publish a national organ. This, however, did not appear until October 1, 1906, and has since been published as a monthly under the title *L'A.I.A.* (the initials of the name of the organisation) as its bulletin. The congress also decided that in case of war the reservists should go on strike and the soldiers should refuse to obey orders and should mutiny. In the case of a general strike energetic support was to be given to the struggle of the labour organisations. Desertion was not among the actions recommended

MILITARISM AND ANTI-MILITARISM

by the Association, and indeed all material responsibility for such desertion (apart from exceptional cases) was repudiated.

The most important aspect of the congress was the decision not to bind the Association to any party "doctrine", whether anarchist or Socialist, but to preserve an independent, revolutionary character. Insurrection was however made a duty if it were decided on by the Association, and – here the anarchist tendency betrays itself – taking part in elections was forbidden. The Paris National Committee publishes in that city the bulletin *Publications of the A.I.A.*,[194] among which figures a pamphlet of 1906 concerning the aims, means and activity of the A.I.A.[195] The well-known leaflet entitled *Aux Conscrits* (To Conscripts), which suffered at the hands of the Paris courts on December 31, 1905, was signed by members of the National Committee. As far as one can gather from the bulletin there exists a considerable number of local groups ("sections"), but the bad financial position allows us to conclude that the membership is not very large. The pamphlet mentioned above concerning the goal, means and activity of the Association describes it in the following way:

> It is a fighting organisation. It demands of its members on given occasions a readiness for direct, violent and insurgent action. Its only concern and the only goal of its activity is to oppose militarism, to destroy it wherever possible, by the power of the will to revolt.

It is therefore anarchism and putschism after all. This is also shown by the strange discussion concerning the "reproach" made against the Association that it is *an organisation*.[196]

There also exist sections of the A.I.A. in Switzerland.

Apart from all that, there is the fact that during the sessions of the Socialist International Congresses held in Paris in 1900 and Amsterdam in 1904, international conferences of the Young Socialists were also held. On each occasion they asked the National Council of the Belgian Young Guards to establish an international link, but this was never done.

An international connection between the Young Socialist organisations has thus so far been attempted in vain. But it is probably not far away.

---

194. Among others, the paper *La Rue*, devoted to the struggle against tsarism, a leaflet addressed to mothers and entitled *A l'honneur militaire*, and the pamphlets *Lettre à un Conscrit* by Méric and *La Vache à Lait, Lettre à un Saint-Cyrien* (a pupil of the Officers' School at Saint-Cyr) by Georges Yvetot.
195. *L'A.I.A., son But, ses Moyens, son Action.*
196. *L'A.I.A.*, pp.15–16.

CHAPTER THREE
Threats to anti-militarism

On the question of militarism, reaction and capitalism are especially sensitive. They have quite clearly realised that in militarism they are defending their most important position of power against democracy and the working class. They stand in closed ranks against anti-militarism of both kinds – whether it concerns foreign or home affairs. The golden days when anti-militarism was treated in a half-hearted, often harmless and even merciful manner by the courts, spellbound by the use of traditional revolutionary phraseology, must be coming to an end in Belgium and even in France as anti-militarism becomes a serious threat to the anti-proletarian powers. As far as Germany is concerned, let us recall the decree of January 1894 issued by the war minister von Gossler (and published in the *Reichsanzeiger*) intended to muzzle the soldiers, to render them deaf and dumb. The non-commissioned officers and privates (not the officers, whose way of thinking can be relied on thanks to their birth and social position) are officially forbidden to engage in any recognisable activity of a revolutionary or Social Democratic character, or to possess or distribute revolutionary and Social Democratic publications. They are also forbidden (in order that all evasion or involuntary temptation shall be made impossible) to take part in any meetings, gatherings, festivities or collections of money without previous official sanction. Apart from that – and this is particularly characteristic of the ruthlessness with which militarism pursues its ends and its lack of concern for any feeling of honour and decency among the "fellows" – there is a rule that all members of the army on active service must make an official report if it comes to their notice that revolutionary or Social Democratic publications are to be found in the barracks or on other military premises. German militarism has thus created for itself a means of protection of an especially criminal kind against the penetration of Social Democratic or general anti-militarist poison into the active army, even if the actions involved are in themselves quite lawful and in no way constitute an incitement to disobedience, etc. This means of protection in fact goes even beyond the famous

Swedish muzzling law. That one person should inform on another, which is everywhere considered a rather nasty practice, is here elevated to an official duty. The soldier who is not an informer is put in prison for disobeying official orders!

The last straw however is that it is explicitly set down in the decree in question that these prohibitions and commands apply also to persons called up for purposes of training or inspection. This of course takes things too far. It is simply impossible to control such persons, to enforce for example that they sever their connections with the trade unions and other so-called revolutionary organisations for the duration of their training or even on the day of the inspection, or that they should for the period in question suspend their subscriptions to the labour papers (a technical impossibility), or even that they should for this period cease to read the forbidden revolutionary literature and banish it from their homes. Nevertheless, a case is known to the author in which a Potsdam court-martial in 1905 sentenced a worker to a long prison term because on the evening of inspection day he had taken part in a trade union meeting. On the other hand another prosecution of a worker in 1904 by the Potsdam criminal court failed. This man had sent to a non-commissioned officer whom he knew a Social Democratic paper dealing with the bad material situation of such ranks, and in the event he was acquitted.

The vigour with which von Gossler's decree is being applied to the men on active service is proved among other things by reports of soldiers who – in answer to an official inquiry or even as witnesses under oath – had stated their Social Democratic opinions, with the careful reservation "in civil life", being condemned by court martial. This is obviously quite illegal and immoral.

We might also recall the case of Colonel Gädke, which is important in many respects. As an officer in the reserve he was deprived of the right of wearing his uniform because, in a discussion on the Serbian royal murder he had said, quite generally, that in certain cases an officer's duty to his country may come before his duty to his king.

We should note the criminal and police prosecution of the Königsberg Society of Apprentices and Young Workers which took place in the summer of 1906. And, last but not least, there is the secret decree of the Prussian war minister published in the press at the beginning of October 1906 which is concerned with determining the means and methods as well as the extent of Social Democratic propaganda against militarism – a decree which at one and the same time of course reflects the fear and the bad conscience of our ruling classes. The anti-Social Democratic instructions of General von Eichhorn also belong to this category.

This sensitiveness towards anti-militarism is of course as international as capitalism and militarism themselves, and the reaction against anti-militarist activity is everywhere harsh and brutal, as we have already seen in another context.

The Swedish muzzling law against anti-militarist agitation, carried through by the "half-Socialist" Staaff in May 1906, deserves to be more thoroughly described. It was passed without a debate by the first Chamber, but by the second Chamber only after lively discussion, though by an overwhelming majority. It is probably typical, in its form, of the way in which anti-militarism will be "legally" fought in the future. This law considerably increased the normal penalties for serious infringements of public order (for example, for incitement by spoken or written word to criminal actions), raising the maximum penalty from two to four years' penal servitude! Moreover, it makes the public "approval" in the press of illegal actions and of incitement to break the law or disobey the legal authorities into a crime in itself, and makes it a duty of the military authorities to seize publications whose explicit aim is to undermine the soldiers' sense of duty and obedience, and to hand them over to the appointed authorities. Finally it gives the commanders of troops the right to forbid the soldiers to attend meetings whenever it can be assumed that statements might be made there which would constitute a threat to discipline. The fruits of this law have already been described.

Meslier[197] is quite right: everywhere reaction declares that the barracks is sacrosanct and inviolable territory, and treats anti-militarism as treason. But what he says of France also applies to Germany even in the present day (though with the reservation implied by our special form of monarchic-bureaucratic-agrarian capitalism): the most violent denunciations of anti-militarism come from the ranks of international capital, which raises its voice in hypocritical defence of "the interest of the fatherland".

A most interesting proof of this sensitiveness towards anti-militarism – and at the same time of the extent to which militarism abroad has taken second place to militarism at home – is furnished by the remarks of the German Kaiser. His speeches of January 26, 1895, and of March 22, 1901, called for a struggle against the attempts of Socialists to instruct the young. And in 1906, in an interview with the French journalist Gaston Menier, he described anti-militarism as an "international scourge" – especially French anti-militarism, the very anti-militarism which is claimed to be on the point of impairing the capacity for action and attack of the French army, the army of our "hereditary enemy"! Not much more is needed before we see the foundation of an International Anti-anti-militarist League!

---

197. See "Un côté de la question sociale" (One Aspect of the Social Question). Moltke moreover said in the Reichstag on March 19, 1869: "Let us be happy that we in Germany have an army that obeys. If we look at other lands we see that, instead of being a means of defence against the revolution, the army actually helps to bring it about. I advise you in the strongest terms never to be a party to the army changing its form in our country".

CHAPTER FOUR
Anti-militarist tactics

In itself anti-militarism is not necessarily proletarian or revolutionary, just as militarism is not specifically bourgeois or capitalist. We need only recall from the past, for example, the Russian Decembrists and Ernst Moritz Arndt's bourgeois-nationalist *Catechism for Soldiers* of September 1812 – it called upon the soldiers to rise up openly against the treacherous princes. In recent times we find decisive proof in the Russian revolution. But we must confine ourselves here to anti-militarism in the capitalist states.

1. Tactics against militarism abroad[198]

The final goal of anti-militarism is the abolition of militarism – that is to say, the abolition of the army in every form, together with all the other manifestations of militarism identified above, which at root represent nothing but secondary effects of the existence of the army. When the trappings disappear, the institution soon follows.

The proletariat could only achieve this goal directly if we presuppose an international situation which excludes the need to *use the army in the interest of the proletariat*, so that the interests of the proletariat need in no way contradict the national interest.

If we consider the question simply from a logical point of view, the need for an army organisation could also be eliminated as far as capitalism is concerned by removing the possibilities of conflict or by a process of international disarmament equally paced between the nations.

The removal of the possibilities of conflict would mean above all the renunciation of the policy of expansion which, as has been mentioned above, may find its natural conclusion in the globe coming under a single trust managed by the Great Powers. It would also mean what in the end comes to the same thing: the creation of a federal world state.

This however is for the moment a romantic dream of the future; the probabilities

---
198. See in this connection the inquiry in *La Vie Socialiste*, I, Nos.15–18; *Mouvement Socialiste*, 1905, and *Vorwärts* of September 17, 1905; also the protocols of the international congresses.

indicate that world politics will not attain this "state of permanence" before the proletariat realises its final aim and replaces capitalist world politics with its own.

Things are even worse as regards international disarmament. This would mean not only the abandonment of military competition by all the military states but also the renunciation of the chances of gain which one or other of the mightiest states, which might be most influential in bringing about disarmament, has or thinks it has (from this arises the proposal for arbitration to establish contingents in proportion to the size of each of the armies!). Disarmament means moreover neither more nor less than the abandonment of those international interests might cause the ruling classes, capitalism, to appeal to the *ultima ratio regum* (the last resort of kings), that is to say, to just those interests which are regarded by capitalism as most important, indeed vital for its life, especially the policy of expansion. The belief that all this can be carried out under the domination of capitalism before this natural state of permanence in world politics has been attained is simply blind faith. Certainly the influence exerted by the proletariat on foreign policy, directed against the world policy of expansion and in favour of a world federation, is growing ever stronger even in backward countries and may lead to the reduction of the danger of war and the pacification of world politics. But the increase in the influence of the proletariat also increases the danger of Bonapartist tricks, so that it is doubtful whether the sum total of the possibilities of war can be reduced. There can be no question of eliminating them.

Anti-militarism can also be a force in bringing about balanced international disarmament if it succeeds in rendering the existing armies incapable of action, or at least in crippling their activity. Hervé demands – this is the essence of his idea – that we should work at any price towards this aim of crippling the armies. A good number of more or less sound arguments have been raised against the feasibility of this plan. The most serious – though it does not apply to the proposal for a combination of disarmament and *revolution* – is that it is *impossible* to bring about *complete* international disarmament. Even in the most progressive countries there are always plenty of strike-breakers to be found! Precisely the more civilised nations would, relatively speaking, be weakened and thus become prey to the lower cultures.

But Hervé's idea is also acceptable in principle only if we assume that the proletariat under no circumstances and in no case has an interest in the defence of the nation. And the main dispute centres around this point. In this connection Kautsky's *Realpolitik*, which rightly is not satisfied with the superficial and confusing distinction between offensive and defensive wars, is preferable to the exaggerated anti-patriotism of the Yonne Federation, which fails to recognise the practical position. Until the economic and social state of permanence for which Social Democracy strives and the abolition of the class character of society have been realised all over the world, there exist possibilities of war which even Social Democracy – in fact precisely Social Democracy – cannot eliminate.

It is of course obvious, as we have pointed out above, that the normal causes of war under capitalism are so constituted that the proletariat has nothing to do with them – indeed, it must oppose them with all its strength. It is nevertheless incorrect to think that all wars are actions directed against the proletariat. This might be possible in a Bonapartist sense, and it may well be that a little Bonapartism is "always present". But the essential point as far as the causes of war are concerned is the fight for spoils, for profit between the capitalist classes of the world powers. It may of course be that as a result of such wars and during their course uprisings and revolutions will take place, and each of the belligerent powers may be forced to turn its weapons against its own proletariat. Thus a solidarity of interests of the ruling classes of these powers against the proletarian classes is brought into effect, but this would normally produce a tendency for the war to be terminated. And it is just as natural that every successful war based on capitalist motives, whether or not there is any intention in that direction, produces Bonapartist consequences, whereas if the course of the war is unsuccessful the chance that capitalist reaction may collapse balances the fact of the damage which civilisation is sure to suffer. The proletariat therefore has an especially strong reason to take action against war, and it is easy to see how things can get out of hand in this struggle – and easy too almost to approve such excesses. As a stimulant to thought Hervéism has a valuable mission to fulfil, and fulfils it.

We must first sort out the different kinds of war. The point is to be clear about these differences! Then we shall be able to tell in what cases disarmament can be pursued as a matter of principle. Of course the question of what basic position to take on the problem of war is of the greatest practical importance and in no way simply theoretical speculation. Nor does the question automatically decide itself when we are faced with a concrete case. On the contrary, it is precisely such a concrete case which, because of the excitement of the situation, easily introduces a tendency to blur a clear insight into what is happening. The events which took place in the German party at the time of the outbreak of the Franco-Prussian war and of the Herero rebellion warn us to be on our guard and to begin to sort out the question of principle.

It is moreover necessary to examine in each case, apart from the question of what is desirable in principle, the further question of what can be achieved in practical terms. And in this connection too Hervé cherishes dangerous illusions. The time is not yet ripe for a general strike and a military strike against every war harmful to the proletariat. Hervé exclaims: "With enough energetic anti-patriotic agitation, the mountain will come to Mohammed!" Here he shows his anarchist colours. We must point out that the greater part of the proletariat is not yet class-conscious and not yet enlightened from the Social Democratic point of view; even less can it be won for anti-patriotic action in a case which demands not only a certain coldblooded willingness for self-sacrifice but also presence of mind in the excitement of a passionate chauvinistic upsurge. It is impossible to attain complete success. The measure of success, of disarmament, will be directly proportionate to the measure of education and training which is enjoyed by the working class in each country: the most backward nation is the easiest to defend. An action of this kind would be a premium on cultural backwardness so long as the education and readiness for struggle of the great mass of the proletariat in the countries concerned in the war is not more or less simultaneously raised to the highest point. Organisation and the general revolutionary education of labour are the preconditions for a successful general and military strike in the case of war. To use straightforward anti-militarist propaganda for this purpose would be absurd.

Things are normally like this: when the proletariat has got so far as to be able to carry out such actions, it has got far enough to seize political power, for there are no more unfavourable conditions for the display of proletarian power than those normally present at the outbreak of a war.

And as far as Hervé's plan is concerned of combining a military strike with an insurrection – that is, the attempt to capture political power and give the revolution the means to defend itself – it would of course not itself be a premium on cultural backwardness. But it is necessary to ask whether such a plan can ever be realised – in so far as it is ever possible in a social revolution – on a national scale, leaving aside the feasibility of realising such a plan, like that of the military or general strike, on an international level. As far as the national level is concerned, the chances of success are in direct proportion to the development of the proletariat and the degree of the political, social and economic pressure under which it lives. And this pressure will constitute either a hindrance or a help in accordance with its intensity and its relation to the economic and ideological-political development of the proletariat. In countries where this pressure is moderate, therefore, in spite of the development of the proletariat – England, for example – not much more would be attained than in countries where the intensity is high but the proletariat little developed – for example in the agricultural and overwhelmingly Catholic industrial centres of Germany. What may be practicable for France, Belgium and Switzerland is by no means practicable for Germany. And anti-militarist propaganda on its own cannot supply what is lacking, even if it is perfectly suited to the task of awakening class consciousness. There is a further objection. Even insurrections *cannot be fabricated*. If we consider the question in a reasonable and level-headed way we cannot assume that *every* war – or even every war which is condemned by the proletariat and harmful to its interests, and even given energetic agitation – would immediately raise even the most receptive audience of the people, let alone all the peoples exploited by capitalism, to the revolutionary fever heat necessary for a successful revolt. War is a factor which does not appear with anything like the same regularity as the conflict with militarism at home. The masses generally look on it as a rather remote and theoretical danger. They do not see it as a pure manifestation of the class struggle, and the fact that it depends on the actions of foreign states makes it difficult to know just what is going on, not only with regard to the war itself but also with regard to the actions taken against it.

Here too Hervé underestimates the great driving forces which would have to be put into effect by such anti-war action if it were not to disintegrate in a ludicrous and dangerous manner like a bomb exploding in the pocket of someone about to throw it.

Again the point is to make the necessary distinctions! Don't measure everything by the same criterion! There are of course cases of wars which release revolutionary forces, which create a state of great social and political tension inside individual states and bring things to a head. This would be true for example of an intervention in Russia, though the likelihood of this is not very great. The outbreak of such a war would be the sign for the peoples of western Europe to declare a ruthless class war, it would be a force, a whiplash whose effect could only be an uprising against reaction at home; against the worshippers of the knout, against the ignominious hangmen of an unhappy people thirsting for freedom. In fact, Vaillant's slogan – *plutôt l'insurrection que la guerre!* – would find an enthusiastic echo among the peoples of all civilised lands.

Other cases are now imaginable in which such altruistic solidarity would surely spring up – a war between Sweden and Norway, for example. But this is not the normal development on which we can base the principles of our tactics. It is possible that in the foreseeable future a situation of this kind would be created by a war between France and Germany. It is the task of the Social Democratic movement in the two countries to promote this situation by revolutionary propaganda work. Much of course depends on the cause of the war in question. It cannot be denied that, for example, in spite of all efforts to drum up an atmosphere favourable to imperialist politics, colonial motives for war bring little grist to the mill of the warmongers.

If, for the time being, we can set complete disarmament as our object only in exceptional cases, there are no reasons of principle nor any practical reasons against the reduction of arms, which simply reduces the capacity of an army to *attack*. The abolition of the standing army and its substitution by a citizen army, a militia, together with a corresponding reduction in military expenditure – which goes hand in hand with the other measures, as Gaston Moch has expertly shown – and the weakening of all other dangerous military influences:[199] these are the demands which the class-conscious proletariat has quite logically inscribed everywhere on its banner.

There are therefore good reasons why the decisions of the international congresses (which contain the minimum anti-militarist program of the majority of the organisations whose principles are those of the modern labour movement) are only able to make certain general points on the question of "militarism abroad". Nor is it any less reasonable that the tactical programs of the individual parties in each country do not go into details on the question, or that the struggle against militarism normally takes place in the domain of general politics. That is to say, these parties try to make some progress towards their object by the influence they exert on the whole social order rather than by specialised propaganda. The resolution moved by Vaillant at the French Party Conference at Limoges, which is to be put before the Stuttgart Conference in 1907, is

---

199. See Moch, *Die Armee der Demokratie*; also Bebel, *Nicht stehendes Heer, sondern Volkswehr*, pp.44ff. He cites Berner, *Der männermordende völkerverderbende Militarismus in Österreich*, pp.52ff. Also *Handbuch für sozialdemokratische Wähler*, Berlin 1903, pp.20ff.

essentially a good one and a useful contribution.

The attacks of the anarchists, especially those of Nieuwenhuis, against this attitude of the Social Democratic movement are doomed to failure. The resolution in question may be a little fatalistic, but it is not empty words. And empty words and fantastic schemes are all we get from those whose attempts to solve the tactical problems of our day – which in any case can never be completely solved – consist in the announcement of quite unrealisable schemes.

2. Tactics against militarism at home

The problem of the struggle against militarism at home is much simpler and far more promising. Its obvious goal is disarmament, the unconditional and effective disarmament of the state power, and its method – which depends on political conditions in each country – lies between the slow, calm and thorough work of education and the French style: "*Soldats, vous ne tirerez pas!*"

This struggle, and the need to make it more concrete, is being forced upon the proletariat every day – especially in those countries where it is now normal to use the army against workers on strike or on political demonstrations. Everywhere – in France, Belgium, Italy, Switzerland and Austria – one can see clearly how the specialised forms of anti-militarist propaganda take on their own character and become a reality under the pressure of military intervention in the class struggle. This applies to France too, in spite of Hervéism, whose considerable support in the syndicalist movement can only be partly explained by its anti-patriotic tendencies. It also applies to America, as Lee shows.[200] And if in Germany we find that this kind of anti-militarist activity comes up against widespread apathy, this is not a little due to the fact that here bloodshed as a consequence of armed military intervention in strikes has largely been avoided. Must it be the fate of all progressive movements that they cover the well only when the child has fallen in? Will Social Democracy itself ignore the Cassandra calls, in spite of its optimistic and unambiguous program for the future?

3. Anarchist and Social Democratic anti-militarism

The goal of Social Democracy is determined by an economic and historical analysis; *only in this framework* does it find its justification. It is therefore far removed from all utopianism. The goal of anarchism is ideologically determined without any historical basis. This indicates the relation, the contradiction between the two movements.

The Social Democratic conception is historically organic, the anarchist conception arbitrary and mechanical. Anarchists of course regard men as the bearers of historical development as they understand it, and the will of these men as the agent, and so they

---

200. See *La Vie Socialiste*, No.18, p.80.

try to influence this will. Social Democracy too considers it necessary to influence the will of the working class.

But between the two ideas there exist fundamental differences.

For anarchism this process of influencing the will is the only essential precondition of success. For Social Democracy it is of subsidiary importance by the side of the stage of objective economic developments, none of which – with the best will in the world as far as the masses and a given class is concerned – can be skipped.

The anarchists consider that such an influence is always possible if energy be exerted. Social Democracy considers that, as a mass class manifestation, it is only possible when certain economic conditions have been fulfilled. The struggle of the two tendencies turns around these conditions, while differences within Social Democracy normally arise from a dispute as to whether such conditions are fulfilled in a given case. This is of course a difficult question to decide, and it is therefore difficult to determine to what degree one should attempt to influence the will, and especially what degree of predisposition is necessary in a given case. Personal optimism or pessimism play an important role here which cannot be eliminated. This is how the differences within the Social Democratic movement arise. Those who assume that influence can play a great role and demand only a small degree of predisposition tend towards the anarchist position – they are the anarchist-Socialists. In spite of the contrast – which is not contradictory – between anarchism and socialism, we therefore find all possible gradations between the tendencies, like colours in a spectrum.

The degree to which the will can be influenced depends on the degree of predisposition and upon the instability of the mental balance of the people or class in question. In times of excitement this instability is much greater than in times of calm. There exists therefore a potential which can at times be confusing or even dangerous, but is for the most part extremely useful. In times of excitement, then, more can be achieved than in quiet times. But this surplus normally vanishes as soon as calm is restored, together with the surplus of energy which it helped to produce. The history of revolutions is living proof of this fact.

The basic differences between the two fundamental conceptions is also shown by the fact that anarchism considers it possible for a handful of determined men to accomplish anything – of course by making use of the will of the masses, whether this remains active or passive. Socialism too considers that a well qualified and determined minority with a clear aim can carry the masses with it at decisive moments and exert an important influence. But the difference is this: while the goal of socialism in exerting such influence and its estimate of its feasibility lies in the possibility of awakening and carrying out the will of the masses (which the masses will be ready and able, given the situation, to display as their social will), the goal of anarchism is defined in terms of a true enlightened despotism, in the sense that a determined handful of usurpers carry out their own will and make use of the masses as a tool to that end.

Anarchism wants to spring, on an untamed horse, over the difficulties of the economic and social situation, or – depending on the circumstances – to bridle the horse by its tail. The *leit-motiv* is: in the beginning was the deed. Of course a time may come in the development of the class struggle when the action now proposed by anarchism will be feasible and correct. But the mistake of anarchism lies not in the absolute impracticability of its proposed methods, but in the relative impracticability which arises from the fact that it is incapable of reading the social relation of power at a given time, which in turn is due to a lack of historical and social insight. And if the proposals of anarchism can be realised and approved of at *later* stages of development, this represents no justification but rather a condemnation of anarchist tactics. It ought to be added however in justice that these tactics do often stimulate thought.

Anarchist and semi-anarchist anti-militarism is related to the anarchist and semi-anarchist conception of the general strike. The relation can be demonstrated by the fact that for this kind of anti-militarism the military strike is the schematic culmination. To grasp the essence of this anti-militarist tendency and its differences with Social Democratic anti-militarism, the following questions must be distinguished: the basis of anti-militarism, the methods of propaganda for anti-militarism, the final aim and object to be attained, and the means by which this object is to be gained.

The fundamental principle of the anti-militarist movement is the same for anarchism as for socialism in so far as both see in militarism an especially violent and mechanical barrier to the realisation of their social plans. But for the rest the principle of the one is as different from that of the other as the anarchist world outlook is from the Social Democratic. It is not possible here to go further into the question of how little anarchism understands the organically capitalist character of militarism and the laws of economic and social development which as a consequence have to be applied to it. Here lies the root of all the other essential differences between the socialist and anarchist forms of anti-militarism. They can be summed up as follows. Social Democratic anti-militarism in its struggle against militarism considers this system as a function of capitalism, recognising and applying to it the laws of economic and social development. Anarchism regards militarism more as something independent, arbitrarily and accidentally created by the ruling classes, and carries on the struggle against it, just as it carries on the struggle against capitalism in general, from a fantastic ideological standpoint, which ignores the laws of social and economic development. In restricting itself to surface phenomena, it attempts to knock militarism off the saddle by appealing out of thin air to individual determination; in short, it tries to achieve its goal in an individualist manner. Anarchism in fact is individualist not only in its social goal – in different degrees, according to the variety of anarchism, but also in its historical, social and political conception and in its methods.

The final goals of the anarchist and Social Democratic forms of anti-militarism, if we are satisfied with a slogan, are the same: the abolition of militarism, abroad as well as at home. But Social Democracy, in accordance with its conception of the essence of militarism, regards the complete abolition of militarism alone as impossible: militarism can only fall together with capitalism, the last class system of society. Capitalism of course is not something fixed, but a constantly evolving system which can be influenced and weakened to a considerable degree by contrary tendencies contained within it, and above all by proletarian tendencies. In the same way militarism, the manifestation of capitalism, is not incapable of being weakened, as is shown by the different forms it takes in different countries. Its connection with capitalism can also be loosened.

But the same thing holds to a greater or lesser degree of the other manifestations of capitalism, and it changes nothing of the organically capitalist[201] character of militarism, and nothing of the fact that the goal of Social Democracy's anti-militarist propaganda is not to fight the system as an isolated phenomenon, nor is its final aim the abolition of militarism alone. Anarchist anti-militarist propaganda, on the other hand, regards the simple abolition of militarism as its ultimate goal. Of course we cannot deny that anarchists too wage the struggle against capitalism (understood in the non-organic anarchist sense), but they wage it in parallel, and not together with the anti-militarist struggle. But even the anarchists, in their truly zig-zag theoretical course, quite often show glimpses of a more profound social insight.[202]

It is in the methods of struggle that the fundamentally different historical modes of interpretation are most apparent. Here we have to distinguish between the method of promoting an anti-militarist movement and the method of using such a movement against militarism. As far as the first method is concerned, anarchism works first of all with moral enthusiasm, with moral stimuli, with humanitarian arguments, with arguments about justice – in short, with all kinds of appeals to the will which ignore the class character of anti-militarism and seek to stamp it as an abstract efflux of a universal imperative of universal validity. It therefore quite consistently turns its attention not only to the men but also to the officers.[203] Anarchist anti-militarist propaganda therefore resembles, and in a way which brings it no credit, the pathetic declamations of Tolstoyans and the impotent incantations against war of the so-called friends of world peace like Bertha von Suttner.

Social Democratic anti-militarism, on the other hand, is based on the class struggle, and is therefore directed in principle exclusively to those classes which are necessarily enemies of militarism in that struggle – though of course it is happy to see the bourgeois splinters which fall in its direction in the course of disintegration. It educates in order to persuade, but the subject which it teaches is not that of categorical imperatives, of humanitarian positions, of ethical postulates of freedom and justice, but that of the class struggle and of the interests of the proletariat in this struggle, of the role of militarism in the class struggle and the role which the proletariat plays and must play in the same struggle. It deduces the task of the proletariat in the struggle against militarism from the

---

201. More correctly: arising organically from the systems of class society.
202. See for example Nieuwenhuis in *Ontwaking*, August 1904, pp.196ff.
203. It has already been shown that in Russia even the officers can be reached by anti-militarist propaganda based on the standpoint of the class struggle.

interests of the proletariat in the class struggle. Of course, it also uses, to a degree which must satisfy anyone, arguments of a moral kind – the whole pathos of the categorical imperative and of the basic rights of man, the beautiful but never practised principles preached by the bourgeoisie since the time of its dawn, and even religious and especially Christian ideas and conceptions. But all these play a subsidiary role. They serve to facilitate the process of opening the eyes of unenlightened workers, so that the daylight of class consciousness can penetrate their minds. They also serve to raise enthusiasm for action.

The anarchist method of applying anti-militarism, of giving effect to anti-militarist sentiments, is again of a more individualistic and fantastic character. It lays great stress on individual refusal to serve in the army, individual refusal to resort to arms and individual protest. Anarchist literature triumphantly reports all such cases with care and exactitude. It has of course two aims in view: furthering the above-mentioned action against militarism and carrying out a kind of propaganda by deed on behalf of the anti-militarist movement. It starts out from the supposition that heroic examples of this kind are admired and imitated, producing support and enthusiasm for the movement which these "heroes" endorse.

Things are different with Social Democratic anti-militarism. It knows of course that individual acts can and will be signals for and symptoms of mass movements, but signals and symptoms only. And even signals they can only be when tension has reached its highest critical point, when the only thing necessary is to light the fuse leading to the powder barrel. To bring about a gradual organic disintegration and demoralisation of the military spirit – that is the goal with which Social Democracy fights militarism. Everything else serves this end, or plays a subsidiary role. In any case there is even in the anarchist movement a growing tendency critical of individual action, as is shown by the International Anti-militarist Association.

As far as the military strike is concerned, anarchist tactics are quite fantastic. They expect – given good will and a great deal of energy – to conjure it out of the sky, whereas Social Democracy considers such a strike, like any other mobilisation of the troops on the side of the revolution, as simply a logically and psychologically necessary consequence of the disintegration of the "militarist spirit". This disintegration can only come about parallel to and in consequence of class factors and of education.

Very characteristic of anarchist anti-militarism is the little pamphlet by Domela Nieuwenhuis entitled *Le militarisme*.[204] For him it is not the crowned kings who are lords of the land, but the bankers, financiers and capitalists (not capitalism as an organically necessary social system). For him wars depend on the decisions of these bankers. For him reaction is the party in authority, which extends "from the Pope to Karl Marx". Without examining the class position of the soldiers he simply accepts the opinion of Frederick (prompted by a bad conscience): "When my soldiers begin to think, not one of them will remain in the army". He borrows methods of anti-militarist propaganda suggested by Laveleye in his book *Des causes actuelles de guerre en Europe et de l'arbitrage*

---

204. *Publications des Temps Nouveaux*, Paris 1901, No.17.

(On the current causes of war in Europe and on arbitration):

1. The removal of all restrictions on international traffic;

2. Cheaper freight, postal and telegraph charges;

3. Introduction of a uniform international system of coinage, weights and measures, and of uniform international legislation;

4. The establishment of equal rights for foreigners as compared with native inhabitants;

5. Promotion of the knowledge of foreign languages and especially of foreign cultures;

6. Creation of an extensive literature of writings and works of art which cultivate a love of peace and hatred of war and all its accomplices;

7. Promotion of everything which gives strength and effectiveness to the representative system and can help deprive the executive authority of the right to decide questions of war and peace;

8. Support of all those industrial undertakings which apply the surplus wealth of the country to increasing the prosperity of other lands, so that capital takes on a cosmopolitan character and links the interests of international capitalists;

9. (This is the point to which Nieuwenhuis objects) – Work by the clergy to fill the minds of the faithful with a horror of war, after the Quaker fashion;

To these methods of anti-militarism Nieuwenhuis adds others which he considers more effective, namely:

10. Promotion of the international interests of the workers;

11. The abolition of kings, presidents, upper chambers and parliaments as social institutions inimical to peace;

12. Abolition of embassies;

13. The reform of history teaching, its transformation into the history of civilisations;

14. The abolition of standing armies;

15. An arbitration system to settle international disputes;

16. A federal United States of Europe, after the fashion of the United States of America;

17. The military strike in case of war, together with the general strike;

18. Passive resistance and individual refusal to serve in the army;

19. Promotion of general development and of the conditions which make for the well-being of all mankind.

At this point, Nieuwenhuis makes the characteristic remark: "If men have anything to lose through war, it is in their interest to see that peace is kept" – as if it were the proletariat which disturbed peace.

The careful critic will see here nothing but a muddle[205] – muddle in the basic social and historical conception, muddle in the arrangement, muddle in the detail. The main point is not even mentioned. The most important point which does find a place – that which relates to certain economic bases of militarism – is mentioned on the side, almost as if by accident. Points of subsidiary, second and third-rate importance appear in the foreground, and by their side quite utopian and fantastic remedies. The means of anti-militarist propaganda are lumped together with anti-militarist action itself. The superficiality of the fundamental conception and the inclination to put everything on the basis of personal initiative and good will become quite evident. The final sentence of Nieuwenhuis' pamphlet is a revelation of the depth of the confusion in the anarchist conception: "Daring, more and ever more daring – that is what we need in order to triumph".

---

205. What Nieuwenhuis says in *Ontwaking*, pp.196ff., in his criticism of the manifesto of the A.I.A. Congress, is much clearer and more profound.

CHAPTER FIVE

The need for special anti-militarist propaganda

It is certainly true that militarism bears within itself the germs of its own destruction, and that capitalist culture in its entirety contains many mutually contradictory and destructive elements, not least those tendencies whose basis is scientific, artistic and ethical education and which are responsible for a determined attack on militarism. The subversive effect for example of the *Simplicissimus* literature must not be underestimated.[206] The story of Cromwell, the story of the year 1789 in France and that of 1806 in Germany show us how a military system can disintegrate and rot to the point where it destroys itself. It is true that in all violent conflicts between the people and the state power a peculiar psychology of blood becomes active and powerful, a suggestion, a hypnotism of blood, or even – to use Andreyev's phrase – a blood logic, which may in the space of a moment decisively reverse the balance of forces. But all this has no bearing on the question of the necessity for propaganda, which itself is a part of the organic process of disintegration, and the same holds of all the other manifestations of capitalism and indeed also holds of capitalism itself. Its relevance is restricted to the question of the chances of a successful process of agitation.

The special danger which militarism presents has been explained above. It stands before the proletariat as a robber armed to the teeth, and its ultimatum is not "*La bourse ou la vie*" (your money *or* your life), but "*La bourse* et *la vie*" (your money *and* your life) – which goes further than the morality of robbers. Besides the fact that it is a great danger for the future, militarism is an ever present, ever real danger, even when it is not actually on the attack. Not only is it the Moloch of economic life, the vampire of cultural development, the chief agent of falsification in the class struggle, it is also the

---

206. Major-General von Zeppelin was concerned with this danger – see the *Kreuz-Zeitung*, December 23, 1906.
(*Simplicissimus* was a satirical German journal, founded in Munich in 1896. Hostile to militarism and clericalism, it ridiculed the ruling authorities, for which it suffered a number of legal trials.)

factor which, explicitly or implicitly, in the last instance regulates the form of the political and economic movement of the proletariat in the class struggle. This in all important respects is indeed determined by militarism in its role as the chief pillar of the brutal might of capitalism. Militarism is crippling our activity. In the disruptive peace before the storm our Party life is becoming sluggish, and parliamentary work overcome by languor and paralysis.

The weakening of militarism requires the investigation of the possibilities of a continuation of peaceful development, or at least of a limitation on the possibilities of violent clashes. It also means above all the restoration to health, the revival of political life and of the Party struggle. The ruthless and systematic struggle against militarism already in itself leads to the revolutionary development and strengthening of the Party, and is a source of the revolutionary spirit.

From all this there follows the necessity, not only of a struggle, but also of a special kind of struggle against militarism. Such a ramified and dangerous structure can only be dealt with by action which is equally ramified, which is energetic, wide-ranging and daring, and which tirelessly pursues militarism into all its hiding-places, always *en vedette*, on the alert. The dangers presented in the fight against militarism also force one to take action which is more flexible and adaptable than agitation of a general kind. However unpopular this conception was and is in Germany, a number of points must be made which may overcome the attitude of reluctance and dispel such doubts. First, we have a special form of propaganda for women and young people. We also carry out specialised agitation not only among agricultural workers but also in the trade unions for the different trades. Finally, we can point to the successful anti-militarist propaganda conducted in other countries. It is only a matter of time, and probably a very short time, before the fundamental idea expressed in the motion No.114, rejected at Mannheim, is generally recognised.

Such action has also been made into a duty of German Social Democracy by the well-known and unanimous decision of the International Congress of 1900.

The demand for such special propaganda has absolutely nothing to do with the ahistorical, anarchist conception of militarism. We are quite clearly conscious of the role which militarism plays within capitalism, and of course have not the remotest idea of setting it above or on a level with capitalism, since it is simply an aspect of capitalism – or more correctly, a specially pernicious and dangerous manifestation of capitalism. But our whole agitation against capitalism is directed against these manifestations, in which capitalism takes on a concrete form. We can to a certain extent designate the field of the anti-militarist struggle as a special one; alongside the general political struggle, alongside the trade union struggle, for that matter even alongside the co-operative and educational struggle. To sum up: we are anti-militarists in so far as we are anti-capitalists.

If, from a historical point of view, anti-militarism has everywhere been transformed – in conjunction with the use of troops in civil war, against the internal enemy – from a set of generalities of a rather theoretical nature into a practical movement adapted to contemporary reality, this is no reason to hinder the development of specifically anti-militarist propaganda in lands in which the army has not so far been used in this way, or not within living memory. It has always been the pride of the Social Democratic movement that it does not wait to be burned before it is wary of the fire, but learns from history, from social science and from the experiences of fraternal parties to take an attitude of foresight and to build on these experiences. They have a clear message to relate as far as anti-militarism is concerned. And the time is ripe.

CHAPTER SIX

Anti-militarism in Germany and German Social Democracy

The program of German Social Democracy, together with that of international socialism (at least of the Marxist school), sets as its object the "seizure of political power" – that is, the abolition of the social domination of the capitalist oligarchy over the proletariat and its temporary substitution by democratic-proletarian rule. This includes, as a major point, the abolition of capitalist militarism, the most important element of the power of the capitalist oligarchy.

The minimum program deals with the question of militarism in a special manner, and sets out the special tasks and goals to be worked for. It thus meets all *principled* objections to a special anti-militarist propaganda form. It demands: "Universal training in the use of arms. A citizen army in place of a standing army. The people to decide on questions of war and peace. Settlement of international disputes by arbitration". It thus repudiates for the present and foreseeable future the unmistakably utopian standpoint which is directed not simply against militarism but against every kind of preparation for war, not simply against capitalist and reactionary wars but on principle against participation in any war, which not only fights against war but tries quite unrealistically to deny the real possibilities of war and their consequences. German Social Democracy, like the overwhelming majority of the foreign parties, even the French Party, is not anti-patriotic (like Hervé) or anti-national (Kropotkin), but rather indifferent to patriotism in accordance with its class position.

As a party of the proletariat Social Democracy is of course without dispute the *unconditional* enemy, the enemy *sans phrase* of the violence shown by militarism at home. To destroy it root and branch is one of its most important tasks.

What has been done in Germany so far to carry out the decision of the Paris Congress of 1900?

MILITARISM AND ANTI-MILITARISM

The attempt to develop special anti-militarist propaganda in Germany has been resisted by influential leaders of the movement, who say that there is no Social Democratic Party in the whole world which fights militarism as hard as German Social Democracy. There is much truth in this. Ever since the German Reich has existed ruthless and tireless criticism has been levelled by the German Social Democrats in parliament and in the press against militarism, the whole of its content and its harmful effects. It has collected material to indict militarism, enough to build a gigantic funeral pyre, and has waged the struggle against militarism as part of its general agitation with great energy and tenacity. In this respect our Party needs neither defence nor praise. Its deeds speak for themselves. Nevertheless, there is more to be done.

We by no means deny that the struggle waged against militarism has met with great success and that the form of the struggle has been well adapted to the goal. Nor do we deny that this kind of struggle will remain useful, and even indispensable, in the future, and bring more successes. But that does not settle the question. It does not resolve the problem of the education of young people, which is the most important part of the fight against militarism.

It is of course true that our general agitation opens people's eyes, and every anti-capitalist and Social Democrat is *per se* an excellent and reliable anti-militarist. The anti-militarist side of our general educational work leaves no doubt on this point. But to whom is our general agitation directed? It is and was rightly and necessarily designed for the adult man and woman worker. But we want to win over not only the adult workers, but also the children of the proletariat, the working-class youth. For the working-class youth is the working class-to-be, he is the future of the proletariat. "He who has the youth, has the future."

At this point someone will retort: he who has the parents has the children of these parents, he has the youth! In any case it would be a wretched Social Democrat who did not try his best to fill his children with the Social Democratic spirit, and bring them up as Social Democrats. It may be that the influence of the parents – together with the influence of the economic, social and political conditions under which the working-class youth grows up, but which, though the most important and obvious means of agitation and enlightenment, cannot be influenced by Party activity and must therefore be disregarded here – can easily overcome all the cunning of the attempts of reaction and capitalism to capture the child's mind. But this fact clearly does not refute our point. One cannot settle things so easily. In fact it is precisely a careful examination of the above trend of thought which shows where the failing in our present agitation lies, a failing which is growing continually more serious and urgently demands a solution.

"Every Social Democrat brings up his children as Social Democrats." But only to the best of his ability. This is the basis of the first important failing. How many people have a general understanding of how to teach, even if they have the time and inclination, and how many Social Democratic workers, even if they have the best of intentions, have the necessary leisure and the necessary knowledge to educate their children? And in how many cases do the women and other politically backward members of the family rather unfortunately constitute a serious counterweight to whatever educational influence the class-conscious father may possess? If the Party wants to do its duty properly it must go into every nook and corner to help with home education. What is required is general educational and especially agitational work among young people, which must have an anti-militarist aspect.

But further: how many proletarians are really educated in Social Democracy, educated to the point where they themselves can educate others on the fundamental principles of the standpoint and goals of the movement? How many workers are there in time of peace so ready for sacrifice and so tireless that they are even willing to undertake, to the best of their ability, the tough, painful, continuous hourly and daily work of education? And apart from those who are a quarter or half-educated, and the lukewarm who form an enormous mass: what a huge number of workers are total strangers to Social Democracy! Here is a great field full of the best hopes of the working-class, almost incalculable in its potential, whose cultivation must not at any cost wait upon the conversion of the backward sections of the adult proletariat. It is of course easier to influence the children of politically educated parents, but this does not mean that it is not possible, indeed a duty, to set to work also on the more difficult section of the proletarian youth.

The need for agitation among young people is therefore beyond doubt. And since this agitation must operate with fundamentally different methods – in accordance with its object, that is, with the different conditions of life, the different level of understanding, the different interests and the different character of young people – it follows that it must be of a special character, that it must take a special place alongside the general work of agitation, and that it would be sensible to put it, at least to a certain degree, in the hands of special organisations. Our agitational work, with the growth in its volume and the increase in the Party's tasks, and at a time when the decisive struggles are drawing ever nearer, has become so extraordinarily extensive and complex that the need for it to be divided up becomes more pressing – a division of labour of whose relative, but only relative, difficulties we are not by any means ignorant.

And now we can go even further. Within the framework of agitational work among young people, anti-militarist agitation fills a quite special and peculiar role. It must appeal to circles which are often not accessible to the attempts of Social Democracy to educate young people; it must stretch out much further than the general attempts at education can normally do in order to take in those sections of working-class youth which do not attend the workers' educational schools, courses and lectures, or read the general literature for young people. It must also appeal to those young workers who, as they grow older, can no longer be reached by these general educational efforts. The proper domain of this agitation is in fact young people between the ages of 17 and 21! It will have a more agitational character than that of general education. Its forms will also be different, at least to some extent. It is also, because of its rather dangerous character, best not to couple it with these general attempts. On the one hand, it might make the general work more difficult than is necessary and even bring it into discredit. On the other hand the division will ensure that the dangers facing specifically anti-militarist agitation are reduced to the minimum since things will be directed by comrades who have been familiarised with all the pitfalls. And finally, the anti-militarist material (ill-treatment of soldiers, military justice, etc.) is so colossal and scattered that even here division of labour and specialisation are required if the best possible use is to be made of the available matter. And not only does this matter need to be put to us; but also collected, sifted and worked over.

The last argument shows quite clearly that anti-militarist agitation, even among adults, can gain a great deal through specialisation.

The opportunity for work is obviously there, for rewarding work in plenty!

What successes have so far been achieved by the old methods in the development of anti-militarism in Germany?

It is true that a large part of the German army is already "red". A mere glance at the party groupings within the German nation shows this to be the case. And it was this obvious fact which caused the famous chief of the Imperial League, Lieutenant-General von Liebert, to take up his pen and write the well-known and amusing book *The Development of Social Democracy and its Influence on the German Army* – a book now held in contempt because of its fatalism even by the Social Democratic renegade Max Lorenz who, in accordance with his job, is now out to burn what he previously lauded. The same developments induced General von Eichhorn to introduce anti-Social Democratic instruction in the army in the autumn of 1906.[207] It is true that in the 1903 Reichstag election nearly one-third of the German electorate (male German subjects over 25) voted for Social Democracy. It may also be true that, in general and at least for the time being, it has a stronger following among the young than among the old. But it is nevertheless debatable whether this proportion holds good for the age group from 20 to 22. We should be quite clear on these points: that these young people do not at all belong to the elements who are firm in their convictions, and that there is all the world of difference between voting for Social Democracy, being a Social Democrat, and being ready to face all the personal risks involved in anti-militarist activity in the army. The "psychological" factors, the "suggestion" and "blood logic" mentioned above may be powerful agents in the destruction of military discipline, but it cannot be seriously suggested that even a third of the army has reached such a position as far as ideas and morale are concerned, nor that military intervention by the right in the form of violent unconstitutional action – a *coup d'état* – directed against the so-called internal enemy, the labour movement, would be impossible or even difficult.

Matters are undoubtedly more difficult for militarism when it comes to mobilising the reserve and militia, especially for war. Indeed, a military correspondent of *Vorwärts*

---
207. See *Sozialdemokratische Partei-Correspondenz*, December 8, 1906.

pointed out in October 1906 that among the members of those bodies who would be called up in case of war – who would then make up some four-fifths of the army – at least one million could be considered as unreliable from the point of view of militarism. But even on this point we have to take up a critical attitude and not forget that mass suggestion on militarist lines or mass psychosis and the methods of suggestion employed by the military authorities are capable of knocking a big hole in the above calculation.

What has been achieved in these fields has been achieved by means of the general propaganda carried out in the labour movement. German Social Democracy has as yet hardly done any specialised work on conscripts. We know of nothing suitable which has been published in this line, apart from the well-known *Handbook for Conscripts* and the leaflet issued by the Party executive in the summer of 1906. And both these publications deal only with the legal position of those in the army. True though it is that history is on our side, it is not true that everything happens of its own accord. This kind of quietism and fatalism is a big mistake from the point of view of historical materialism and fatal as far as agitation is concerned, and can only be countered by agitational activity and by specifically anti-militarist activity in particular. Anti-militarist propaganda in Germany must be very quickly and energetically improved.

The South German Young Guards have courageously taken on the task of providing a political solution to the problem. This is of course only a beginning, but it will – it must – soon find powerful support, if only to nip in the bud the anarchist anti-militarism which is starting to take root in Germany.[208]

And we keep asking: is German Social Democracy, the German labour movement, the nucleus and elite (as it likes to be called) of the new International, going to avoid tackling this problem – whether out of prudence or of over-confidence – until it is too late? Will it delay until it is forced to act by a dozen German equivalents of the murder at Fourmies, will it remain unarmed until the time when its strength and tactics are stretched to the limit by a world war or an intervention in Russia,[209] for which it will then have to bear the responsibility?

And finally: have the German workers not been sufficiently alerted by the police massacres of their class comrades, which might also be said to come into the domain of anti-militarist propaganda?

However this may be, German Social Democracy can no longer ignore the fact that, as far as militarism is concerned, the watchword is: *si vis pacem, para bellum!* Begin as early as possible with anti-militarist propaganda, in order that the dangers which militarism holds for the working class can be reduced to a minimum in advance!

The specially difficult character of this propaganda in Germany should really be no reason for it to be postponed. On the contrary, it is a good reason for it to be speeded up.

The German proletariat is ready enough now, and the general political situation at home under which it groans makes it even more vital for us to act.

---

208. See the monthly supplement to the *Freier Arbeiter*, *Antimilitarismus*, which has been appearing for some time.
209. The improbability of such a thing is beyond doubt, but it has not become more improbable in consequence of Prince Bülow's speech in the German Reichstag on November 14, 1906.

CHAPTER SEVEN

The anti-militarist tasks of German Social Democracy

The anti-patriotic form of anti-militarism has not been and will not be able to take root in German conditions. But Social Democratic propaganda will have to be filled to a much greater degree with the spirit of international working-class solidarity and with the appeal for peace between nations as one of the goals of the proletarian struggle for liberation. The demands set out in the anti-militarist program mentioned above form a suitable and unobjectionable basis for this task.

From a general point of view militarism in its internal form, together with all its evil manifestations (more evident in normal times), will in the future find itself in a rather more difficult position, and its role in the class war will become more evident. Where the main attack is to be launched is something that will be determined at the time by the national and international situation.

Whatever forms and methods of propaganda we have to introduce or adapt in Germany, we can of course assume that we shall have to keep within legal limits. The question of carrying out propaganda inside the army is therefore ruled out in advance.

German Social Democracy has not even done enough work in collecting documentary evidence against militarism. Details are normally available only of the military budget and the growth in indirect military burdens and the peace-time strength of the army. But the connection between these military burdens and the customs and taxation policy awaits closer examination. What is notably lacking is information on the ill-treatment of soldiers, on the exploits of military justice, on cases of suicide among soldiers, on health conditions in the army, on injuries suffered on active service, on conditions of pay and pensions, together with an account of the use of soldiers to force down wages and of related army decrees and their use (with men on the point of being disbanded) to break strikes, of intervention by the army and armed police forces in strike situations, of the victims of such actions, of the system of military boycott, of military intervention in politics, of the use of the military societies in the social and political struggle, and of such exploits of militarism in other countries, especially in the economic and political struggle. A special account therefore has to be opened for militarism, naval militarism and colonial militarism. We have insufficient knowledge and material relating to the militarist youth societies of our opponents, as well as to the and-militarist movement and its struggles.

The regular collection, sifting and study of all this material must be systematically taken in hand. It cannot be treated as a task secondary to the general agitation.

This material would of course first have to be put to use in our general agitational work, in parliament, in the press and in general leaflets and meetings. But it must be directed to specific objectives, into specific channels, in order to penetrate and take effect among those strata of the population which are especially important to the anti-militarist movement. We have to consider first of all not only the young people liable for military service but also their parents, and especially their mothers, who can render especially valuable service in educating their children in anti-militarism. There are also the older workers, whose influence on their younger comrades and the apprentices has to be put to the best possible use. And finally we have to step up the struggle, in terms of energy and method, against the military societies.

The agitation must never directly or indirectly incite to military disobedience. It will have attained its goal if it shows up the essence of militarism and its role in the class struggle, if it raises indignation and disgust in response to its exposure of the real character of militarism, its function as an enemy of the people.

Wherever the law permits, the chief agent of this propaganda must be the youth organisations, which already by awakening class consciousness are tending to weaken militarism and the militarist spirit. These youth organisations must make use of the press, of pamphlets, of leaflets, of lecture courses and education in order to spread the anti-militarist word as widely as possible in the form most acceptable to young people. Festivals and cultural events must be used to the same end. The members of the associations must in turn be educated in order to become propagandists of anti-militarism. By personal contact between friends of the same class and age, together with the circulation of literature, by these means the family, relations and friends, the workshop and factory will be transformed through the work of the youth organisations into centres of recruitment for anti-militarism.

The youth organisation itself must not limit its agitation to its own members, but continually widen its audience. It must address the whole of the class of young workers. It must also, in the way described above, win over the older workers. It must make systematic use of the press, leaflets, pamphlets, public meetings, lectures, galas, festivals and so on, attractive to young and old. Meetings organised on the occasion of the departure of the recruits as well as demonstrations of all kinds must serve the same goal.

The Party too must take up in press and parliament and in a systematic way – as it has already done, but more energetically – the material and social interests of the soldiers and non-commissioned officers.[210] Thus, in a quite irreproachable way, it can ensure the sympathy of these groups.

The foundation of special associations of ex-soldiers, as in Belgium and Holland, with the special task of opposing the military societies, is not to be recommended in Germany – the general political and trade union organisations are sufficient.

If we examine what has been done in other countries, we get an idea of what remains to be done. And if we take a glance at the program set out above, we recognise that the Party, in spite of all that it has done in the field of anti-militarism, has only begun to fulfil its task. It is, so to speak, at the kindergarten stage as far as anti-militarist propaganda is concerned.

These multiple activities obviously cannot all be carried out by one central organisation, but they can and must be centrally directed and controlled. The necessity of the establishment of such a centre is already evident, because only thus can the most careful use be made of all the legal possibilities of action. Like a net cast into the distance, anti-militarist propaganda must reach out to the whole people. The proletarian youth must be systematically inflamed with class consciousness and hate against militarism. Youthful enthusiasm will take hold of the hearts of the young workers inspired by such agitation. These young workers belong to Social Democracy, to Social Democratic anti-militarism. If everyone carries out his task, they must and will be won. *He who has the young people has the army.*

---

210. Improvement in pay, food, clothing, housing, treatment, lightening of the service, suppression of ill-treatment, reform of the system of complaints, of discipline and of punishment, as well as of military justice, etc.

APPENDIX ONE

Rosa Luxemburg: Theses on the Tasks of International Social Democracy

A large number of comrades from different parts of Germany[1] have adopted the following theses, which constitute an application of the Erfurt program to the contemporary problems of international socialism.

1. The world war has annihilated the work of 40 years of European socialism: by destroying the revolutionary proletariat as a political force; by destroying the moral prestige of socialism; by scattering the workers' International; by setting its Sections one against the other in fratricidal massacre; and by tying the aspirations and hopes of the masses of the people of the main countries in which capitalism has developed to the destinies of imperialism.

2. By their vote for war credits and by their proclamation of national unity, the official leaderships of the socialist parties in Germany, France and England (with the exception of the Independent Labour Party) have reinforced imperialism, induced the masses of the people to suffer patiently the misery and horrors of the war, contributed to the unleashing, without restraint, of imperialist frenzy, to the prolongation of the massacre and the increase in the number of its victims, and assumed their share in the responsibility for the war itself and for its consequences.

3. This tactic of the official leaderships of the Parties in the belligerent countries, and in the first place in Germany, until recently at the head of the International, constitutes

---
[1] These SPD members subsequently (1 January 1916) formed the Spartacus League, which became the Communist Party of Germany in December 1918.

a betrayal of the elementary principles of international socialism, of the vital interests of the working class, and of all the democratic interests of the peoples. By this alone socialist policy is condemned to impotence even in those countries where the leaders have remained faithful to their principles: Russia, Serbia, Italy and – with hardly an exception – Bulgaria.

4. By this alone official Social Democracy in the principal countries has repudiated the class struggle in war time and adjourned it until after the war; it has guaranteed to the ruling classes of all countries a delay in which to strengthen, at the proletariat's expense, and in a monstrous fashion, their economic, political and moral positions.

5. The world war serves neither the national defence nor the economic nor the political interests of the masses of the people whatever they may be. It is but the product of the imperialistic rivalries between the capitalist classes of the different countries for world hegemony and for the monopoly in the exploitation and oppression of areas still not under the heel of capital. In the era of the unleashing of this imperialism, national wars are no longer possible. National interests serve only as the pretext for putting the labouring masses of the people under the domination of their mortal enemy, imperialism.

6. The policy of the imperialist states and the imperialist war cannot give to a single oppressed nation its liberty and its independence. The small nations, the ruling classes of which are the accomplices of their partners in the big states, constitute only the pawns on the imperialist chessboard of the great powers, and are used by them, just like their own working masses, in wartime, as instruments, to be sacrificed to capitalist interests after the war.

7. The present world war signifies, under these conditions, either in the case of "defeat" or of "victory", a defeat for socialism and democracy. It increases, whatever the outcome – excepting the revolutionary intervention of the international proletariat – and strengthens militarism, national antagonisms, and economic rivalries in the world market. It accentuates capitalist exploitation and reaction in the domain of internal policy, renders the influence of public opinion precarious and derisory, and reduces parliaments to tools more and more obedient to imperialism. The present world war carries within itself the seeds of new conflicts.

8. World peace cannot be assured by projects utopian or, at bottom, reactionary, such as tribunals of arbitration by capitalist diplomatists, diplomatic "disarmament" conventions, "the freedom of the seas", abolition of the right of maritime arrest, "the United States of Europe", a "customs union for central Europe", buffer states, and other illusions. Imperialism, militarism and war can never be abolished nor attenuated so

long as the capitalist class exercises, uncontested, its class hegemony. The sole means of successful resistance, and the only guarantee of the peace of the world, is the capacity for action and the revolutionary will of the international proletariat to hurl its full weight into the balance.

9. Imperialism, as the last phase in the life, and the highest point in the expansion, of the world hegemony of capital, is the mortal enemy of the proletariat of all countries. But under its rule, just as in the preceding stages of capitalism, the forces of its mortal enemy have increased in pace with its development. It accelerates the concentration of capital, the pauperisation of the middle classes, the numerical reinforcement of the proletariat; arouses more and more resistance from the masses; and leads thereby to an intensified sharpening of class antagonisms. In peace time as in war, the struggle of the proletariat as a class has to be concentrated first of all against imperialism. For the international proletariat, the struggle against imperialism is at the same time the struggle for power, the decisive settling of accounts between socialism and capitalism. The final goal of socialism will be realised by the international proletariat only if it opposes imperialism all along the line, and if it makes the issue: "war against war" the guiding line of its practical policy; and on condition that it deploys all its forces and shows itself ready, by its courage to the point of extreme sacrifice, to do this.

10. In this framework, socialism's principal mission today is to regroup the proletariat of all countries into a living revolutionary force; to make it, through a powerful international organisation which has only one conception of its tasks and interests, and only one universal tactic appropriate to political action in peace and war alike, the decisive factor in political life: so that it may fulfil its historic mission.

11. The war has smashed the Second International. Its inadequacy has been demonstrated by its incapacity to place an effective obstacle in the way of the segmentation of its forces behind national boundaries in time of war, and to carry through a common tactic and action by the proletariat in all countries.

12. In view of the betrayal, by the official representatives of the socialist parties in the principal countries, of the aims and interests of the working class; in view of their passage from the camp of the working-class International to the political camp of the imperialist bourgeoisie; it is vitally necessary for socialism to build a new workers' International, which will take into its own hands the leadership and co-ordination of the revolutionary class struggle against world imperialism.

To accomplish its historic mission, socialism must be guided by the following principles:

1. The class struggle against the ruling classes within the boundaries of the bourgeois states, and international solidarity of the workers of all countries, are the two rules of life, inherent in the working class in struggle and of world-historic importance to it for its emancipation. There is no socialism without international proletarian solidarity, and there is no socialism without class struggle. The renunciation by the socialist proletariat, in time of peace as in time of war, of the class struggle and of international solidarity, is equivalent to suicide.

2. The activity of the proletariat of all countries as a class, in peace time as in war time, must be geared to the fight against imperialism and war as its supreme goal. Parliamentary and trade union action, like every activity of the workers' movement, must be subordinated to this aim, so that the proletariat in each country is opposed in the sharpest fashion to its national bourgeoisie, so that the political and spiritual opposition between the two becomes at each moment the main issue, and international solidarity between the workers of all countries is underlined and practised.

3. The centre of gravity of the organisation of the proletariat as a class is the International. The International decides in time of peace the tactics to be adopted by the national Sections on the questions of militarism, colonial policy, commercial policy, the celebration of May Day and, finally, the collective tactic to be followed in the event of war.

4. The obligation to carry out the decisions of the International takes precedence over all else. National Sections which do not conform with this place themselves outside the International.

5. The setting in motion of the massed ranks of the proletariat of all countries is alone decisive in the course of struggles against imperialism and against war.
Thus the principal tactic of the national Sections aims to render the masses capable of political action and resolute initiative; to ensure the international cohesion of the masses in action; to build the political and trade union organisations in such a way that, through their mediation, prompt and effective collaboration of all the Sections is at all times guaranteed, and so that the will of the International materialises in action by the majority of the working-class masses all over the world.

6. The immediate mission of socialism is the spiritual liberation of the proletariat from the tutelage of the bourgeoisie, which expresses itself through the influence of nationalist ideology. The national Sections must agitate in the parliaments and the press, denouncing the empty wordiness of nationalism as an instrument of bourgeois domination. The sole defence of all real national independence is at present the revolutionary class struggle against imperialism. The workers' fatherland, to the defence of which all else must be subordinated, is the socialist International.

APPENDIX TWO

V.I. Lenin: The Tasks of Revolutionary Social Democracy in the European War

These theses on the war were drawn up by Lenin in September 1914. They were discussed and approved at a meeting of the Bolshevik group in Berne, circulated among Bolshevik groups abroad and were smuggled into Russia for discussion by the Russian section of the Central Committee, Party organisations and the Bolshevik Duma group.

The theses were submitted to the conference of Swiss and Italian Socialists held in Lugano on 27 September 1914. Many of the ideas contained in the theses were incorporated in the conference's resolution. Lenin used them as a basis for writing the manifesto of the RSDLP Central Committee, "The War and Russian Social Democracy", which follows.

Reports have reached us from most reliable sources, regarding a conference recently held by leaders of the Russian Social Democratic Labour Party, on the question of the European war. The conference was not of a wholly official nature, since the Central Committee of the RSDLP has as yet been unable to gather, as a result of the numerous arrests and unprecedented persecution by the tsarist government. We do, however, have precise information that the conference gave expression to views held by the most influential circles of the RSDLP.

The conference adopted the following resolution, whose full text we are quoting below as a document:

Resolution of a group of Social Democrats

1. The European and world war has the clearly defined character of a bourgeois, imperialist and dynastic war. A struggle for markets and for freedom to loot foreign countries,

a striving to suppress the revolutionary movement of the proletariat and democracy in the individual countries, a desire to deceive, disunite, and slaughter the proletarians of all countries by setting the wage slaves of one nation against those of another so as to benefit the bourgeoisie – these are the only real content and significance of the war.

2. The conduct of the leaders of the German Social Democratic Party, the strongest and the most influential in the Second International (1889–1914), a party which has voted for war credits and repeated the bourgeois-chauvinist phrases of the Prussian Junkers and the bourgeoisie, is sheer betrayal of socialism. Under no circumstances can the conduct of the leaders of the German Social Democratic Party be condoned, even if we assume that the party was absolutely weak and had temporarily to bow to the will of the bourgeois majority of the nation. This party has in fact adopted a national-liberal policy.

3. The conduct of the Belgian and French Social Democratic party leaders, who have betrayed socialism by entering bourgeois governments,[2] is just as reprehensible.

4. The betrayal of socialism by most leaders of the Second International signifies the ideological and political bankruptcy of the International. This collapse has been mainly caused by the actual prevalence in it of petty-bourgeois opportunism, the bourgeois nature and the danger of which have long been indicated by the finest representatives of the revolutionary proletariat of all countries. The opportunists had long been preparing to wreck the Second International by denying the socialist revolution and substituting bourgeois reformism in its stead, by rejecting the class struggle with its inevitable conversion at certain moments into civil war, and by preaching class collaboration; by preaching bourgeois chauvinism under the guise of patriotism and the defence of the fatherland, and ignoring or rejecting the fundamental truth of socialism, long ago set forth in the *Communist Manifesto*, that the workingmen have no country; by confining themselves, in the struggle against militarism, to a sentimental philistine point of view, instead of recognising the need for a revolutionary war by the proletarians of all countries, against the bourgeoisie of all countries; by making a fetish of the necessary utilisation of bourgeois parliamentarianism and bourgeois legality, and forgetting that illegal forms of organisation and agitation are imperative at times of crises. One of the organs of international opportunism, *Sozialistische Monatshefte*, which has long taken a national liberal stand, is very properly celebrating its victory over European socialism. The so-called Centre of the German and other Social Democratic parties has in actual fact faint-heartedly capitulated to the opportunists. It must be the task of the future International resolutely and irrevocably to rid itself of this bourgeois trend in socialism.

5. With reference to the bourgeois and chauvinist sophisms being used by the bourgeois parties and the governments of the two chief rival nations of the Continent – the German and the French – to fool the masses most effectively, and being copied by both the overt and covert socialist opportunists, who are slavishly following in the wake of the bourgeoisie, one must particularly note and brand the following:

---

2. Among those who joined the bourgeois government of Belgium was Vandervelde, and in France Jules Guesde, Marcel Sembat and Albert Thomas.

When the German bourgeois refer to the defence of the fatherland and to the struggle against tsarism, and insist on the freedom of cultural and national development, they are lying, because it has always been the policy of Prussian Junkerdom, headed by Wilhelm II, and the big bourgeoisie of Germany, to defend the tsarist monarchy; whatever the outcome of the war, they are sure to try to bolster it. They are lying because, in actual fact, the Austrian bourgeoisie have launched a robber campaign against Serbia, and the German bourgeoisie are oppressing Danes, Poles, and Frenchmen (in Alsace-Lorraine); they are waging a war of aggression against Belgium and France so as to loot the richer and freer countries; they have organised an offensive at a moment which seemed best for the use of the latest improvements in military matériel, and on the eve of the introduction of the so-called big military program in Russia.

Similarly, when the French bourgeois refer to the defence of the fatherland, etc., they are lying, because in actual fact they are defending countries that are backward in capitalist technology and are developing more slowly, and because they spend thousands of millions to hire Russian tsarism's Black Hundred[3] gangs for a war of aggression, i.e., the looting of Austrian and German lands.

Neither of the two belligerent groups of nations is second to the other in cruelty and atrocities in warfare.

6. It is the first and foremost task of Russian Social Democrats to wage a ruthless and all-out struggle against Great-Russian and tsarist-monarchist chauvinism, and against the sophisms used by the Russian liberals, Cadets, a section of the Narodniks, and other bourgeois parties, in defence of that chauvinism. From the viewpoint of the working class and the toiling masses of all the peoples of Russia, the defeat of the tsarist monarchy and its army, which oppress Poland, the Ukraine, and many other peoples of Russia, and foment hatred among the peoples so as to increase Great-Russian oppression of the other nationalities, and consolidate the reactionary and barbarous government of the tsar's monarchy, would be the lesser evil by far.

7. The following must now be the slogans of Social Democracy:

First, all-embracing propaganda, involving the army and the theatre of hostilities as well, for the socialist revolution and the need to use weapons, not against their brothers, the wage slaves in other countries, but against the reactionary and bourgeois governments and parties of all countries; the urgent necessity of organising illegal nuclei and groups in the armies of all nations, to conduct such propaganda. in all languages; a merciless struggle against the chauvinism and "patriotism" of the philistines and bourgeoisie of all countries without exception. In the struggle against the leaders of the present International, who have betrayed socialism, it is imperative to appeal to the revolutionary consciousness of the working masses, who bear the entire burden of the war and are in most cases hostile to opportunism and chauvinism.

Secondly, as an immediate slogan, propaganda for republics in (Germany, Poland,

---

3. Monarchist gangs formed by the tsarist police to fight the revolutionary movement. They murdered revolutionaries, assaulted progressive intellectuals and organised pogroms.

Russia and other countries, and for the transforming of all the separate states of Europe into a republican United States of Europe.

Thirdly and particularly, a struggle against the tsarist monarchy and Great-Russian, Pan-Slavist chauvinism, and advocacy of a revolution in Russia, as well as of the liberation of and self-determination for nationalities oppressed by Russia, coupled with the immediate slogans of a democratic republic, the confiscation of the landed estates, and an eight-hour working day.

APPENDIX THREE

V.I. Lenin: The War and Russian Social Democracy

The European war, which the governments and the bourgeois parties of all countries have been preparing for decades, has broken out. The growth of armaments, the extreme intensification of the struggle for markets in the latest – the imperialist – stage of capitalist development in the advanced countries, and the dynastic interests of the more backward East European monarchies were inevitably bound to bring about this war, and have done so. Seizure of territory and subjugation of other nations, the ruining of competing nations and the plunder of their wealth, distracting the attention of the working masses from the internal political crises in Russia, Germany, Britain and other countries, disuniting and nationalist stultification of the workers, and the extermination of their vanguard so as to weaken the revolutionary movement of the proletariat – these comprise the sole actual content, importance and significance of the present war.

It is primarily on Social Democracy that the duty rests of revealing the true meaning of the war, and of ruthlessly exposing the falsehood, sophistry and "patriotic" phrasemongering spread by the ruling classes, the landowners and the bourgeoisie, in defence of the war.

One group of belligerent nations is headed by the German bourgeoisie. It is hoodwinking the working class and the toiling masses by asserting that this is a war in defence of the fatherland, freedom and civilisation, for the liberation of the peoples oppressed by tsarism, and for the destruction of reactionary tsarism. In actual fact, however, this bourgeoisie, which servilely grovels to the Prussian Junkers, headed by Wilhelm II, has always been a most faithful ally of tsarism, and an enemy of the revolutionary movement of Russia's workers and peasants. In fact, whatever the outcome of the war, this bourgeoisie will together with the Junkers, exert every effort to support the tsarist monarchy against a revolution in Russia.

In fact, the German bourgeoisie has launched a robber campaign against Serbia, with the object of subjugating her and throttling the national revolution of the Southern Slavs, at the same time sending the bulk of its military forces against the freer countries, Belgium and France, so as to plunder richer competitors. In fact, the German bourgeoisie, which has been spreading the fable that it is waging a war of defence, chose the moment it thought most favourable for war, making use of its latest improvements in military *matériel* and forestalling the rearmament already planned and decided upon by Russia and France.

The other group of belligerent nations is headed by the British and the French bourgeoisie, who are hoodwinking the working class and the toiling masses by asserting that they are waging a war for the defence of their countries, for freedom and civilisation and against German militarism and despotism. In actual fact, this bourgeoisie has long been spending thousands of millions to hire the troops of Russian tsarism, the most reactionary and barbarous monarchy in Europe, and prepare them for an attack on Germany.

In fact, the struggle of the British and the French bourgeoisie is aimed at the seizure of the German colonies, and the ruining of a rival nation, whose economic development has been more rapid. In pursuit of this noble aim, the "advanced" "democratic" nations are helping the savage tsarist regime to still more throttle Poland, the Ukraine, etc., and more thoroughly crush the revolution in Russia.

Neither group of belligerents is inferior to the other in spoliation, atrocities and the boundless brutality of war; however, to hoodwink the proletariat and distract its attention from the only genuine war of liberation, namely, a civil war against the bourgeoisie both of its "own" and of "foreign" countries – to achieve so lofty an aim – the bourgeoisie of each country is trying, with the help of false phrases about patriotism, to extol the significance of its "own" national war, asserting that it is out to defeat the enemy, not for plunder and the seizure of territory, but for the "liberation" of all other peoples except its own.

But the harder the governments and the bourgeoisie of all countries try to disunite the workers and pit them against one another, and the more savagely they enforce, for this lofty aim, martial law and the military censorship (measures which even now, in wartime, are applied against the "internal" foe more harshly than against the external), the more pressingly is it the duty of the class-conscious proletariat to defend its class solidarity, its internationalism and its socialist convictions against the unbridled chauvinism of the "patriotic" bourgeois cliques in all countries. If class-conscious workers were to give up this aim, this would mean renunciation of their aspirations for freedom and democracy, to say nothing of their socialist aspirations.

It is with a feeling of the most bitter disappointment that we have to record that the socialist parties of the leading European countries have failed to discharge this duty, the behaviour of these parties' leaders, particularly in Germany, bordering on downright betrayal of the cause of socialism. At this time of supreme and historic importance, most of the leaders of the present Socialist International, the Second (1889–1914), are trying to substitute nationalism for socialism. As a result of their behaviour, the workers' parties of these countries did not oppose the governments' criminal conduct, but called upon the working class to identify its position with that of the imperialist governments. The leaders of the International committed an act of treachery against socialism by voting for war credits, by reiterating the chauvinist ("patriotic") slogans of the bourgeoisie of their "own" countries, by justifying and defending the war, by joining the bourgeois governments of the belligerent countries, and so on and so forth. The most influential socialist leaders and the most influential organs of the socialist press of present-day Europe hold views that are chauvinist, bourgeois and liberal, and in no way socialist. The responsibility for thus disgracing socialism falls primarily on the German Social Democrats, who were the strongest and most influential party in the Second International. But neither can one justify the French socialists, who have accepted ministerial posts in the government of that very bourgeoisie which betrayed its country and allied itself with Bismarck so as to crush the Commune.

The German and the Austrian Social Democrats are attempting to justify their support for the war by arguing that they are thereby fighting against Russian tsarism. We Russian Social Democrats declare that we consider such justification sheer sophistry. In our country the revolutionary movement against tsarism has again assumed tremendous proportions during the past few years. This movement has always been headed by the working class of Russia. The political strikes of the last few years, which have involved millions of workers, have had as their slogan the overthrow of tsarism and the establishment of a democratic republic. During his visit to Nicholas II on the very eve of the war, Poincaré, President of the French Republic, could see for himself, in the streets of St. Petersburg, barricades put up by Russian workers. The Russian proletariat has not flinched from any sacrifice to rid humanity of the disgrace of the tsarist monarchy. We must, however, say that if there is anything that, under certain conditions, can delay the downfall of tsarism, anything that can help tsarism in its struggle against the whole of Russia's democracy, then that is the present war, which has placed the purses of the British, the French and the Russian bourgeois at the disposal of tsarism, to further the latter's reactionary aims. If there is anything that can hinder the revolutionary struggle of the Russia's working class against tsarism, then that is the behaviour of the German and the Austrian Social Democratic leaders, which the chauvinist press of Russia is continually holding up to us as an example.

Even assuming that German Social Democracy was so weak that it was compelled to refrain from all revolutionary action, it should not have joined the chauvinist camp, or taken steps which gave the Italian socialists reason to say that the German Social Democratic leaders were dishonouring the banner of the proletarian International.

Our party, the Russian Social Democratic Labour Party, has made, and will continue to make great sacrifices in connection with the war. The whole of our working-class legal press has been suppressed. Most working-class associations have been disbanded, and a large number of our comrades have been arrested and exiled. Yet our parliamentary representatives – the Russian Social Democratic Labour group in the Duma – considered it their imperative socialist duty not to vote for the war credits, and even to walk out of the Duma, so as to express their protest the more energetically; they considered it their duty to brand the European governments' policy as imperialist. Though the tsar's government has increased its tyranny tenfold, the Social Democratic workers of Russia are already publishing their first illegal manifestos against the war, thus doing their duty to democracy and to the International.

While the collapse of the Second International has given rise to a sense of burning shame in revolutionary Social Democrats – as represented by the minority of German Social Democrats and the finest Social Democrats in the neutral countries; while socialists in both Britain and France have been speaking up against the chauvinism of most Social Democratic parties; while the opportunists, as represented, for instance, by the German *Sozialistische Monatshefte*, which have long held a national-liberal stand, are with good reason celebrating their victory over European socialism – the worst possible service is being rendered to the proletariat by those who vacillate between opportunism and revolutionary Social Democracy (like the "Centre" in the German Social Democratic Party), by those who are trying to hush up the collapse of the Second International or to disguise it with diplomatic phrases.

On the contrary, this collapse must be frankly recognised and its causes understood, so as to make it possible to build up a new and more lasting socialist unity of the workers of all countries.

The opportunists have wrecked the decisions of the Stuttgart, Copenhagen and Basel congresses,[4] which made it binding on socialists of all countries to combat chauvinism in all and any conditions, made it binding on socialists to reply to any war begun by the bourgeoisie and governments, with intensified propaganda of civil war and social revolution. The collapse of the Second International is the collapse of opportunism, which developed from the features of a now bygone (and so-called "peaceful") period of history, and in recent years has come practically to dominate the International. The opportunists have long been preparing the ground for this collapse by denying the socialist revolution and substituting bourgeois reformism in its stead; by rejecting the class

---

4. The Stuttgart Congress of the Second International was held on August 18–24, 1907. Committees were set up to draft resolutions for the plenary meetings. Lenin worked on the committee which drafted a resolution on "Militarism and International Conflicts". Lenin and Luxemburg introduced into Bebel's draft the historic amendment on the duty of the socialists to use the war-created crisis to arouse the masses for the overthrow of capitalism. The amendment was adopted by the Congress.

The Copenhagen Congress was held between August 28 and September 3, 1910. The resolution "The Struggle Against Militarism and War" confirmed the Stuttgart Congress's resolution on "Militarism and International Conflicts" and listed the demands to be advanced by the socialist parliamentary deputies: (a) all conflicts between states to be unfailingly submitted for settlement by international courts of arbitration, (b) general disarmament; (c) abolition of secret diplomacy; (d) autonomy for all nations and their protection against military attacks and oppression.

The Basel Congress, held on November 24–25, 1912, was an extraordinary congress called in connection with the Balkan War and the imminent European war. The Congress adopted a manifesto emphasising the imperialist nature of the approaching world war, and called on the socialists of all countries to wage a vigorous struggle against war.

struggle with its inevitable conversion at certain moments into civil war, and by preaching class collaboration; by preaching bourgeois chauvinism under the guise of patriotism and the defence of the fatherland, and ignoring or rejecting the fundamental truth of socialism, long ago set forth in the *Communist Manifesto*, that the workingmen have no country; by confining themselves, in the struggle against militarism, to a sentimental, philistine point of view, instead of recognising the need for a revolutionary war by the proletarians of all countries, against the bourgeoisie of all countries; by making a fetish of the necessary utilisation of bourgeois parliamentarianism and bourgeois legality, and forgetting that illegal forms of organisation and propaganda are imperative at times of crises. The natural "appendage" to opportunism – one that is just as bourgeois and hostile to the proletarian, i.e., the Marxist, point of view – namely, the anarcho-syndicalist trend, has been marked by a no less shamefully smug reiteration of the slogans of chauvinism, during the present crisis.

The aims of socialism at the present time cannot be fulfilled, and real international unity of the workers cannot be achieved, without a decisive break with opportunism, and without explaining its inevitable fiasco to the masses.

It must be the primary task of Social Democrats in every country to combat that country's chauvinism. In Russia this chauvinism has overcome the bourgeois liberals (the "Constitutional-Democrats"), and part of the Narodniks – down to the Socialist-Revolutionaries and the "Right" Social Democrats. (In particular, the chauvinist utterances of E Smirnov, P Maslov and G Plekhanov, for example, should be branded; they have been taken up and widely used by the bourgeois "patriotic" press.)

In the present situation, it is impossible to determine, from the standpoint of the international proletariat, the defeat of which of the two groups of belligerent nations would be the lesser evil for socialism. But to us Russian Social Democrats there cannot be the slightest doubt that, from the standpoint of the working class and of the toiling masses of all the nations of Russia, the defeat of the tsarist monarchy, the most reactionary and barbarous of governments, which is oppressing the largest number of nations and the greatest mass of the population of Europe and Asia, would be the lesser evil.

The formation of a republican United States of Europe should be the immediate political slogan of Europe's Social Democrats. In contrast with the bourgeoisie, which is ready to "promise" anything in order to draw the proletariat into the mainstream of chauvinism, the Social Democrats will explain that this slogan is absolutely false and meaningless without the revolutionary overthrow of the German, the Austrian and the Russian monarchies.

Since Russia is most backward and has not yet completed its bourgeois revolution, it still remains the task of Social Democrats in that country to achieve the three fundamental conditions for consistent democratic reform, viz., a democratic republic (with complete equality and self-determination for all nations), confiscation of the landed estates, and an eight-hour working day. But in all the advanced countries the war has placed on the order of the day the slogan of socialist revolution, a slogan that is the more urgent, the more heavily the burden of war presses upon the shoulders of the proletariat, and the more active its future role must become in the re-creation of Europe, after the horrors of the present "patriotic" barbarism in conditions of the tremendous technological progress of large-scale capitalism. The bourgeoisie's use of wartime laws to gag the proletariat makes it imperative for the latter to create illegal forms of agitation and organisation. Let the opportunists "preserve" the legal organisations at the price of treachery to their convictions – revolutionary Social Democrats will utilise the organisational experience and links of the working class so as to create illegal forms of struggle for socialism, forms appropriate to a period of crisis, and to unite the workers, not with the chauvinist bourgeoisie of their respective countries, but with the workers of all countries. The proletarian International has not gone under and will not go under. Notwithstanding all obstacles, the masses of the workers will create a new International. Opportunism's present triumph will be short-lived. The greater the sacrifices imposed by the war the clearer will it become to the mass of the workers that the opportunists have betrayed the workers' cause and that the weapons must be turned against the government and the bourgeoisie of each country.

The conversion of the present imperialist war into a civil war is the only correct proletarian slogan, one that follows from the experience of the Commune, and outlined in the Basel resolution (1912); it bas been dictated by all the conditions of an imperialist war between highly developed bourgeois countries. However difficult that transformation may seem at any given moment, socialists will never relinquish systematic, persistent and undeviating preparatory work in this direction now that war has become a fact.

It is only along this path that the proletariat will be able to shake off its dependence on the chauvinist bourgeoisie, and, in one form or another and more or less rapidly, take decisive steps towards genuine freedom for the nations and towards socialism.

Long live the international fraternity of the workers against the chauvinism and patriotism of the bourgeoisie of all countries!

Long live a proletarian International, freed from opportunism!

*— **Central Committee of the Russian Social Democratic Labour Party***

APPENDIX FOUR

Manifesto of the International Socialist Conference at Zimmerwald (September 21, 1915)

The Zimmerwald conference, held in Zimmerwald, Switzerland on 5–8 September 1915, for the first time brought together the minority of anti-war socialist organisations in the Second International – about 40 delegates from 11 countries attended.

Despite their common opposition to militarism and war, there were significant political differences between the participants. The most left-wing positions were put forward by Lenin: opposition to war credits, a clear condemnation of the betrayal by the leadership of the Second International, and a call to revolutionary civil war. These did not appear in the final resolution, which represented a kind of "lowest common denominator" acceptable to all participants and was unanimously endorsed. The Bolsheviks and other left participants expressed their disagreements in an addendum; however, they decided to sign the Zimmerwald Manifesto, seeing it as a step forward in the struggle against the imperialist war.

Proletarians of Europe!

The war has lasted more than a year. Millions of corpses cover the battlefields. Millions of human beings have been crippled for the rest of their lives. *Europe is like a gigantic human slaughterhouse.* All civilisation, created by the labour of many generations, is doomed to destruction. The most savage barbarism is today celebrating its triumph over all that hitherto constituted the pride of humanity.

Irrespective of the truth as to the direct responsibility for the outbreak of the war, one thing is certain. *The war which has produced this chaos is the outcome of imperialism,* of the attempt on the part of the capitalist classes of each nation, to foster their greed for profit by the exploitation of human labour and of the natural treasures of the entire globe.

Economically backward or politically weak nations are thereby subjugated by the Great Powers who, in this war, are seeking to remake the world map with blood and iron in accord with their exploiting interests. Thus entire nations and countries, like Belgium, Poland, the Balkan states, and Armenia are threatened with the fate of being torn asunder, annexed as a whole or in part as booty in the game of compensations.

In the course of the war, its driving forces are revealed in all their vileness. Shred after shred falls from the veil with which the meaning of this world catastrophe was hidden from the consciousness of the peoples. The capitalists of all countries who are coining the red gold of war profits out of the blood shed by the people, assert that the war is for defence of the fatherland, for democracy, and the liberation of oppressed nations! They lie. *In actual reality, they are burying the freedom of their own people together with the independence of the other nations in the places of devastation.*

New fetters, new chains, new burdens are arising, and it is the proletariat of all countries, of the victorious as well as of the conquered countries, that will have to bear them. Improvement in welfare was proclaimed at the outbreak of the war – want and privation, unemployment and high prices, undernourishment and epidemics are the actual results. *The burdens of war will consume the best energies of the peoples for decades*, endanger the achievements of social reform, and hinder every step forward. Cultural devastation, economic decline, political reaction these are the blessings of this horrible conflict of nations. Thus the war reveals the naked figure of modern capitalism which has become irreconcilable, not only with the interests of the labouring masses, not only with the requirements of historical development, but also with the elementary conditions of human intercourse.

The ruling powers of capitalist society who held the fate of the nations in their hands, the monarchic as well as the republican governments, the secret diplomacy, the mighty business organisations, the bourgeois parties, the capitalist press, the Church – all these bear the full weight of responsibility for this war which arose out of the social order fostering them and protected by them, and which is being waged for their interests.

Workers!

Exploited, disfranchised, scorned, they called you brothers and comrades at the outbreak of the war when you were to be led to the slaughter, to death. And now that militarism has crippled you, mutilated you, degraded and annihilated you, the rulers demand that you surrender your interests, your aims, your ideals – in a word, *servile subordination to civil peace*. They rob you of the possibility of expressing your views, your feelings, your pains; they prohibit you from raising your demands and defending them. The press gagged, political rights and liberties trod upon – this is the way the *military dictatorship* rules today with an iron hand.

This situation which threatens the entire future of Europe and of humanity cannot and must not be confronted by us any longer without action. The socialist proletariat has waged a struggle against militarism for decades. With growing concern, its representatives at their national and international congresses occupied themselves with the ever more menacing danger of war growing out of imperialism. At *Stuttgart*, at *Copenhagen*, at *Basel*, the international socialist congresses have indicated the course which the proletariat must follow.

Since the beginning of the war, socialist parties and labour organisations of various countries that helped to determine this course have disregarded the obligations following from this. Their representatives have called upon the working class *to give up the class struggle*, the only possible and effective method of proletarian emancipation. They have granted credits to the ruling classes for waging the war; they have placed themselves at the disposal of the governments for the most diverse services; through their press and their messengers, they have tried to win the neutrals for the government policies of their countries; they have delivered up to their governments *Socialist Ministers* as hostages for the preservation of civil peace, and *thereby they have assumed the responsibility before the working class, before its present and its future, for this war, for its aims and its methods*. And just as the individual parties, so the highest of the appointed representative bodies of the socialists of all countries, the *International Socialist Bureau*, has failed them.

These facts are equally responsible for the fact that the international working class which did not succumb to the national panic of the first war period, or which freed itself from it, has still, in the second year of the slaughter of peoples, found no ways and means of taking up an energetic struggle for peace simultaneously in all countries.

In this unbearable situation, we, the representatives of the socialist parties, trade unions and their minorities, we Germans, French, Italians, Russians, Poles, Letts, Rumanians, Bulgarians, Swedes, Norwegians, Dutch and Swiss, we who stand, not on the ground of national solidarity with the exploiting class, but on the ground of the international solidarity of the proletariat and of the class struggle, have assembled to retie the torn threads of international relations and to call upon the working class to recover itself and to fight for peace.

This struggle is the struggle for freedom, for the *reconciliation* of peoples, for socialism. It is necessary to take up this struggle for peace, for a peace without annexations or war indemnities. *Such a peace, however, is only possible if every thought of violating the rights and liberties of nations is condemned.* Neither the occupation of entire countries nor of separate parts of countries must lead to their violent annexation. No annexation, whether open or concealed, and no forcible economic attachment made still more unbearable by political disfranchisement. *The right of self-determination of nations must be the indestructible principle in the system of national relationships of peoples.*

Proletarians!

Since the outbreak of the war, you have placed your energy, your courage, your endurance at the service of the ruling classes. Now you must stand up for your own cause, for the sacred aims of socialism, for the emancipation of the oppressed nations as well as of the enslaved classes, by means of the irreconcilable proletarian class struggle.

It is the task and the duty of the socialists of the belligerent countries to take up this struggle with full force; it is the task and the duty of the socialists of the neutral states to support their brothers in this struggle against bloody barbarism with every effective means. Never in world history was there a more urgent, a more sublime task, the fulfillment of which should be our common labour. No sacrifice is too great, no burden too heavy in order to achieve this goal: peace among the peoples.

Working men and working women! Mothers and fathers! Widows and orphans! Wounded and crippled! We call to all of you who are suffering from the war and because of the war: Beyond all borders, beyond the reeking battlefields, beyond the devastated cities and villages –

Proletarians of all countries, unite!

In the name of the International Socialist Conference:

For the German delegation: Georg Ledebour, Adolf Hoffmann.

For the French delegation: A Bourderon, A Merrheim.

For the Italian delegation: GE Modigliani, Constantino Lazzari.

For the Russian delegation: N Lenin, Paul Axelrod, M Bobrov.

For the Polish delegation: St Lapinski, A Warski, C Hanecki.

For the Inter-Balkan Socialist Federation: C Rakovsky (Rumanian delegation); Wassil Kolarov (Bulgarian delegation).

For the Swedish and Norwegian delegation: Z Hoglund, Ture Nerman.

For the Dutch delegation: Henriette Roland-Holst.

For the Swiss delegation: Robert Grimm, Charles Naine.

Glossary

Abdul Hamid II (1842–1918): last sultan of the Ottoman Empire to hold absolute power, from 1876 to 1909. Deposed and replaced by his half-brother, Sultan Mehmed V.

Adler, Victor (1852–1918): leader of the Social Democratic Party of Austria and an important figure in the Second International; publicly backed the Austrian government's decision to go to war.

Asquith, Herbert Henry (1852–1928): Liberal Party prime minister of Britain, 1908–16.

Auer, Ignaz (1846–1907): participant in the 1875 congress which founded the SPD, and later party secretary. A friend of Eduard Bernstein and on the right of the party.

Bakunin, Mikhail (1814–76): Russian anarchist who fought Marx and his followers for leadership of the First International.

Bebel, August (1840–1913): Founder and leader of the Social Democratic movement in Germany. A supporter of Marx, Bebel was the SPD's chief spokesman in parliament. Along with Wilhelm Liebknecht, he publicly opposed Prussia's war with France in 1870 and supported the Paris Commune; both were subsequently jailed for "preaching dangerous doctrines" and "plotting against the state".

Berchtold, Leopold (1863–1942): Austro-Hungarian politician who served as foreign minister at the outbreak of World War I.

Bernhardi, Friedrich von (1849–1930): Prussian general and military historian who saw war as a "divine business"; urged Germany to pursue an aggressive stance and ignore treaties.

Bernstein, Eduard (1850–1932): Leading member of the SPD, "revisionist" proponent of reformism, argued that socialism could be achieved by gradual democratisation of capitalist society.

Bethmann-Hollweg, Theobald von (1856–1921): Chancellor of Germany 1909–17; led Germany into World War I but was opposed by conservative military leaders and replaced as chancellor in July 1917.

Bismarck, Graf Otto von (1815–1898): Prussian aristocrat, key figure in the unification of Germany in 1871 and subsequently the first Chancellor of Germany. In 1878, he instituted a series of repressive Anti-Socialist Laws forbidding socialist organisations and meetings, outlawing trade unions, closing newspapers and banning the circulation of socialist literature.

Bülow, Prince Bernhard von (1849–1929): German Chancellor from 1900 to 1909; resigned in 1909 after pressure from Conservative and Centre Parties, replaced by Bethmann-Hollweg.

Caprivi, Graf Leo von (1831–99): Officer in the Prussian army, succeeded Bismarck as Chancellor of Germany, 1890–94.

Cavaignac, Louis-Eugène (1802–57): French general and politician, head of the executive power between June and December 1848; oversaw the suppression of the revolt by Parisian workers during the June Days uprising.

Clemenceau, Georges (1841–1929): French minister of the interior from 1906, known for his use of the army in social conflicts. Head of the French government, 1917–1920.

Delesalle, Paul (1870–1948): French anarchist and syndicalist prominent in the trade union movement.

Gneisenau, Graf August von (1760–1830): Prussian field marshal, Chief of Staff from 1813.

Gossler, Heinrich von (1841–1927): Prussian general, appointed as minister of war in 1896.

Grey, Sir Edward (1862–1933): Liberal Party politician, British foreign secretary 1905–16.

Guesde Jules (1845–1922): French socialist journalist and politician. Left opponent of Jaurès in the French Section of the Workers' International (SFIO), but moved to the right and served in the national unity government during WWI.

Habsburg: ruling dynasty of the Austro-Hungarian Empire.

Hervé, Gustave (1871–1944): French socialist, forced to leave his university post because of his anti-militarist views. Founded the paper *La Guerre sociale*. Later became an ardent nationalist, and left the Socialist Party in 1916; established the fascist National Socialist Party in 1927.

Hindenburg, Paul von (1847–1934): Field marshal who led the German army during World War I; President of Germany from 1925 until his death. Played a key role in the Nazi seizure of power, appointing Hitler as Chancellor of Germany in January 1933.

Hohenlohe-Schillingsfürst, Prince Chlodwig Karl von (1819–1901): Chancellor of Germany from 1894, introduced repressive social policies (law against subversion of 1894, Prussian anti-Socialist law of 1897).

Hohenzollen: ruling dynasty of Prussia, and subsequently of Germany.

Jaurès, Jean (1859–1914): Leader of the French Socialist Party and from 1905 of the French Section of the Workers' International (SFIO). Assassinated by a French nationalist on 31 July 1914.

Kautsky, Karl (1854–1938): Leading theorist of the SPD and the Second International. Advocated abstention on the Reichstag vote for war credits in 1914; left the SPD in 1917 and founded the Independent Social Democratic Party of Germany (USPD) with other socialists who had belatedly come to oppose the war.

Köpenick, Captain of: real name Friedrich Wilhelm Voigt (1849–1922) – fraudster who in 1906 became a folk hero by masquerading as a Prussian military officer and "confiscating" more than 4,000 marks from a municipal treasury.

Kropotkin, Pyotr Alexeyevich (1842–1921): Russian anarchist who welcomed the First World War, believing it would destroy the obsolete nation-state form. Hostile to the Bolshevik revolution.

Lieber, Ernst (1838–1902): leader of the reactionary Catholic Centre party in the Reichstag from 1891.

Liebknecht, Wilhelm (1826–1900): Founder, with Bebel, of German Social Democracy. Exiled in London from 1850 to 1862, where he became a member of the Communist League and developed a lifelong friendship with Marx. Jailed along with Bebel for opposing Prussia's war with France.

Lloyd George, David (1863–1945): Liberal Party prime minister of Britain, 1916–22.

Manteuffel, Edwin Freiherr von (1809–85): Prussian general, promoted to field marshal for his role in the Franco-Prussian War.

Millerand, Alexandre (1859–1943): French politician, formed the Independent Socialist Party in 1902 (in opposition to Jaurès' Socialist Party). Moved to the right and served as war minister during WWI, president 1920–24.

Miquel, Dr: Ex-republican who took part in the revolutionary movements of 1848, but became an extreme reactionary and a member of the National Liberal Party. Appointed Prussian finance minister in 1890.

Moltke, Graf Helmut von (1800–1891): Chief of the Prussian and German general staff. Directed operations in the Franco-Prussian War, 1870–71.

Nieuwenhuis, Ferdinand Domela (1846–1919): Dutch socialist and anti-militarist; became leader of the Dutch Social Democrats in 1879, later became an anarchist.

Pinkerton Agency: Private police force in the US, established around 1850. Hired by businesses to infiltrate unions, supply guards, keep strikers and suspected unionists out of factories, and recruit goon squads to intimidate workers.

Rohrbach Paul (1869–1956): German writer on foreign policy, racist supporter of German colonial expansion, exploitation of indigenous peoples and violent suppression of resistance.

Schädler, Franz-Xaver (1852–1913): Catholic priest, leading member of the Centre party in the Reichstag.

Scharnhorst, Gerhard von (1755–1813): Appointed head of the Army Reform Commission in 1807; collaborated with Gneisenau to introduce conscription.

Suttner, Bertha von (1843–1914): Austrian novelist and leading figure in the peace movement.

Thiers, Adolphe (1797–1877): French politician, president from 1871 to 1873. Most notorious for brutal suppression of the Paris Commune.

Vaillant, Édouard (1840 1915): French socialist politician, founding member of the French Section of the Workers' International (SFIO). Anti-war until WWI broke out, then supported the *Union Sacré*, the political truce in which the left agreed not to oppose the government or call any strikes (cf. the German SPD's *Burgfrieden*).

Wrangel, Graf Friedrich von (1784–1877): Prussian field marshal, responsible for suppressing the 1848 revolution in Germany.

This work was published by Red Flag Books, an Imprint of the revolutionary socialist organisation Socialist Alternative.

Red Flag Books offers hundreds of other titles covering Marxist politics, revolutionary history, and much more.

Browse our store at shop.redflag.org.au

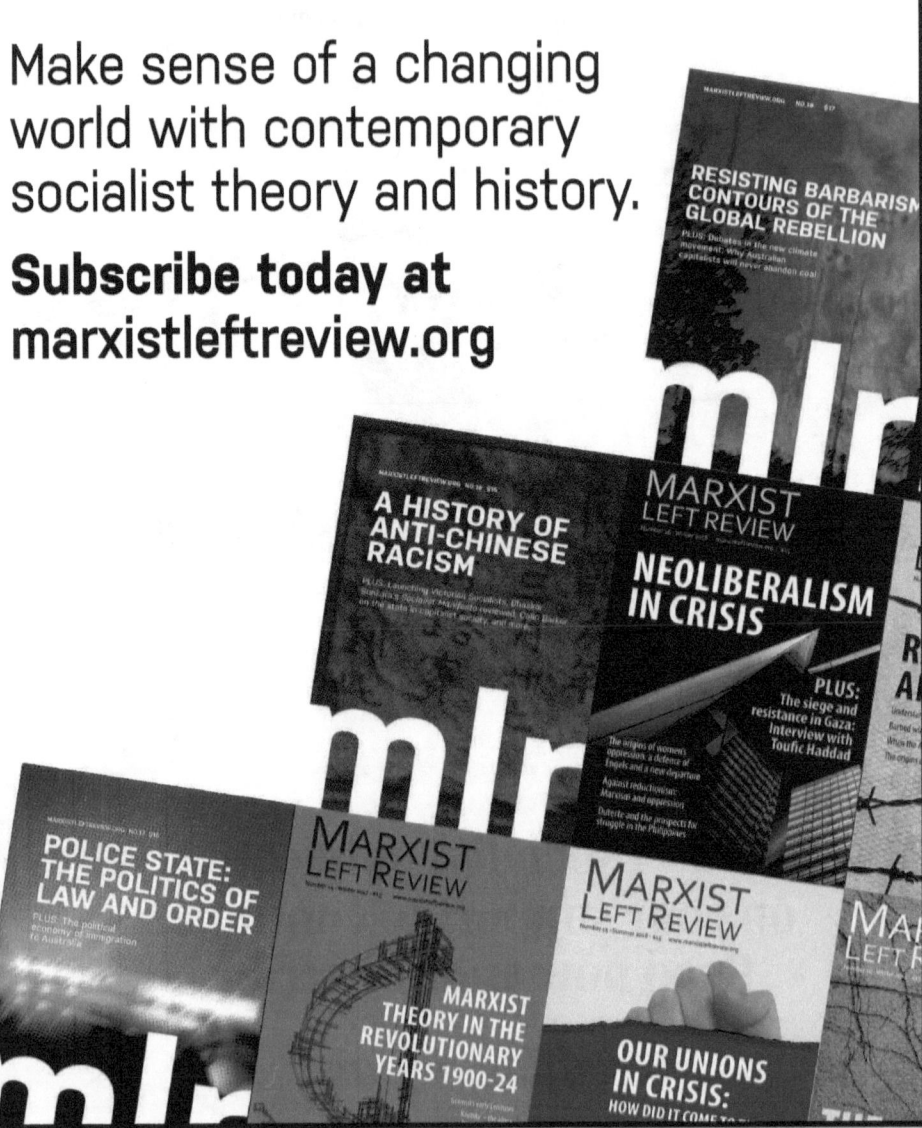